2 Peter & Jude
Preaching Verse-by-Verse

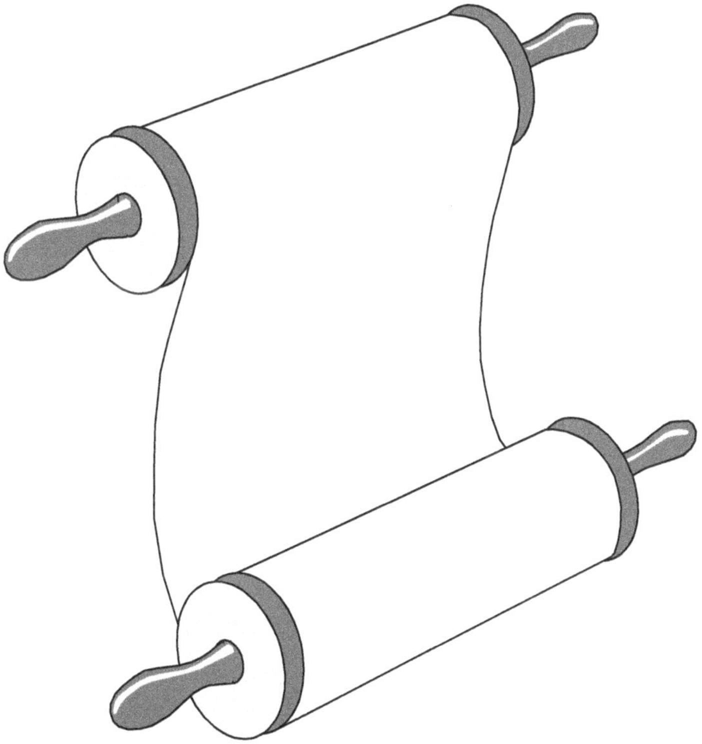

Pastor D. A. Waite, Th.D.,Ph.D.

Published by
THE BIBLE FOR TODAY PRESS
900 Park Avenue
Collingswood, New Jersey 08108 U.S.A.
Pastor D. A. Waite, Th.D., Ph.D.
Bible For Today Baptist Church
Church Phone: 856-854-4747
BFT Phone: 856-854-4452
Orders: 1-800-John 10:9
e-mail: BFT@BibleForToday.org
Website: www.BibleForToday.org
FAX: 856-854-2464

We Use and Defend
the King James Bible

Copyright, 2016
All Rights Reserved
May, 2016

BFT #4147

ISBN #978-1-56848-108-1

Acknowledgments

I wish to thank and to acknowledge the assistance of the following people:

- **The Congregation** of the **Bible For Today Baptist Church**—for whom these messages were prepared, to whom they were delivered, and by whom they were published. They listened attentively and encouraged their Pastor.
- **Yvonne Sanborn Waite**—my wife, who encouraged the publication of these sermons, read the manuscript, developed the various boxes, suggested sentences to underline, and gave other helpful suggestions and comments. The boxes help the reader to see some of the more important topics that are covered in the various chapters.
- **Patricia Canter**—a friend of Mrs. Waite who volunteered to take the cassette tapes of the verse-by-verse exposition of the book of 2Peter and Jude and put these words into digital format to be used for this book.
- **Tamara A. Waite**—one of our daughters-in-law, who attends our church services regularly, is a helper in many of our church projects, and has devoted many hours for her very-detailed verse verifications, and other detailed proofreading of the book before its publication.
- **Dr. Kirk DiVietro**—a friend for many years, one of our Dean Burgon Society faithful Vice Presidents, who is an expert on the use of computers. He has helped in various ways to make the computer work easier when performing the needed tasks.
- **Carl & Vicky Albert**—friends and attenders of our church by the Internet for many years who have assisted greatly in the proofreading of this book and in many other ways.
- **Bonlyn Walls**—one of our friends has also been an attender of our church through the Internet for many years. She has also helped with proofreading and comments on this book.

Foreword

- **The Beginning**. This book is the **twelfth** in a series of books based on my expository preaching from various books of the Bible. It is an attempt to bring to the minds of the readers two things: (1) the **meaning** of the words in the verses and (2) the practical **application** of those words to the lives of both saved and unsaved.
- **Preached Sermons.** These were messages that I preached to our **Bible For Today Baptist Church** in Collingswood, New Jersey. They were broadcast over the radio, and over the Internet by computer streaming around the world. I took half a chapter each Sunday as the messages were preached.
- **Other Verses.** In connection with both the **meaning** and **application** of the verses in this book, there are many verses from other places in the Bible that have been quoted for further elaboration on the teachings in this book. All the verses of Scripture that were used to illustrate further truth are written out in full for easy reference.
- **A Transcription.** This entire book was typed into computer format by Patricia Canter from the tape recordings of the messages as they were preached. In addition to the words used as I preached these sermons, I have added words for clarification as needed.
- **The Audience.** The intended audience for this book is the same as the audience that listened to the messages in the first place. These studies are not meant to be overly scholarly, though there are some references to various Greek Words used. My aim and burden is to try to help genuine Christians to understand the Words of God. It is also my hope that my children, grandchildren, great grandchildren, and many others might profit from this study of 2 Peter and Jude. There is a 27-page INDEX of words and topics.

Yours For God's Words,

D. A. Waite

Pastor D. A. Waite, ThD, PhD
Bible For Today Baptist Church

Table of Contents

Publisher's Data. i
Acknowledgments. ii
Foreword. iii
Table of Contents.. iv
2 Peter Chapter One. 1
2 Peter Chapter Two. 47
2 Peter Chapter Three.. 93
Jude Chapter One. 139
Index of Words and Phrases. 195
About the Author.. 223
Order Blank Pages.. 225
Defined King James Bible Orders. 231

2 Peter
Chapter One

The Background Of 2 Peter

The apostle Peter is the author of this second letter. It was written about 66 A.D. It was similar to 2 Timothy because 2 Timothy was written right before Paul's death in martyrdom. It appears that this book of 2 Peter was also written shortly before Peter's martyrdom.

Simon Peter was a servant, a bond slave, harkening to His Master and listening to His voice. He is an apostle of the Lord Jesus and "to them that have obtained like precious faith"-- just the same faith that Peter had, "through the righteousness of God and our Saviour Jesus Christ:"

Let's look at 19 different parts of Peter's life to form a background of the study of this book.

1. Peter's Call

PETER WAS CALLED BY THE LORD

The first thing about Peter is his call by the Lord Jesus Christ. Have you been called? Has the Lord Jesus called you—by other means or by listening here? Have you responded to that call by receiving the Lord Jesus Christ as your Saviour?

- **Matthew 4:18-20**

"And Jesus, walking by the sea of Galilee, saw two brethren, Simon called Peter, and Andrew his brother, casting a net into the sea: for they were fishers. And he saith unto them, Follow me, and I will make you fishers of men. And they straightway left *their* nets, and followed him."

Peter was called by the Lord Jesus Christ. He became a Christian; he responded to His call. Those that are outside of Christ today need to respond as well to His call for salvation.

2. Peter And The Other Apostles

The second thing about Peter's life is his place in the list of the original twelve apostles.

- **Matthew 10:1-2**

"And when he had called unto *him* his twelve disciples, he gave them power *against* unclean spirits, to cast them out, and to heal all manner of sickness and all manner of disease. Now the names of the twelve apostles are these; The first disciple was Simon, who was called Peter, and Andrew his brother; James *the son* of Zebedee, and John his brother;"

The Lord Jesus called his twelve apostles and gave them power over the spirits, and to heal all manner of diseases. Notice that Simon Peter was the first apostle listed in this list.

- **Matthew 10:5-6**

"These twelve Jesus sent forth, and commanded them, saying, Go not into the way of the Gentiles, and into *any* city of the Samaritans enter ye not: But go rather to the lost sheep of the house of Israel."

PETER'S FIRST CALL WAS TO THE JEWS

Peter and the other apostles were not, at first, to go to the Gentiles or to the Samaritans, but only to the lost sheep of Israel. Later, they went to the Gentiles, but not at first.

- **Matthew 10:8**

"Heal the sick, cleanse the lepers, raise the dead, cast out devils: freely ye have received, freely give."

Peter, as an apostle of the Lord Jesus Christ, was therefore able to perform these miracles.

3. Peter Walking On Water

The third thing about Peter's life was that he walked on water. When Peter saw the Lord Jesus on the sea, here's what he said:

- **Matthew 14:28**

"And Peter answered him and said, Lord, if it be thou, bid me come unto thee on the water."

PETER LOST HIS FAITH AND WAS SINKING

The Lord Jesus Christ asked Peter to walk to Him on the water, which he did. All of a sudden, Peter lost his faith and began to sink. He cried out: *"Lord, save me!"* This is the shortest prayer in the New Testament.

- **Matthew 14:30**

"But when he saw the wind boisterous, he was afraid; and beginning to sink, he cried, saying, Lord, save me."

This privilege of walking on water was a miraculous thing indeed.

4. Peter's Confession Of Faith

The fourth thing about Peter's life was his confession about the Lord Jesus Christ. May all genuine Christians take a similar stand like that of Peter. Here is the background and his confession.

- **Matthew 16:13-17**

"When Jesus came into the coasts of Caesarea Philippi, he asked his disciples, saying, Whom do men say that I the Son of man am? And they said, Some *say that thou art* John the Baptist: some, Elias; and others, Jeremias, or one of the prophets. He saith unto them, But whom say ye that I am? And Simon Peter answered and said, **Thou art the Christ, the Son of the living God**. And Jesus answered and said unto him, Blessed art thou, Simon Barjona: for flesh and blood hath not revealed *it* unto thee, but my Father which is in heaven."

This testimony by Peter was powerful. The Lord Jesus Christ commended him for it, saying it was revealed to him by God the Father.

5. Peter's Contradiction And Rebuke

The fifth thing about Peter was his contradiction and rebuke of the Lord Jesus Christ. I hope true Christians today never engage in this kind of activity. In effect, Peter made the Lord Jesus Christ to be a liar. Because of that, the Lord rebuked Peter.

- **Matthew 16:21-23**

"From that time forth began Jesus to shew unto his disciples, how that he must go unto Jerusalem, and suffer many things of the elders and chief priests and scribes, and be killed, and be raised again the third day. **Then Peter took him, and began to rebuke him, saying, Be it far from thee, Lord: this shall not be unto thee**. But he turned, and said unto Peter, Get thee behind me, Satan: thou art an offence unto me: for thou savourest not the things that be of God, but those that be of men."

He told him his future, but Simon didn't like that. In other words, Peter called the Lord Jesus a liar--not speaking the truth, but speaking falsely. What a horrible sin committed in these words! May genuine Christians never rebuke the Words of their Lord Jesus Christ as He has revealed them in the Bible. What He says in His Word, He means!

> **PETER WAS INFLUENCED BY THE SATAN**
> When the Lord Jesus Christ said, *"Get thee behind me, Satan,"* He did not mean that Satan indwelt Peter (as he did Judas Iscariot). He meant that Satan was influencing Peter and what he was saying on this occasion.

6. Peter On The Mount Of Transfiguration

The sixth thing about Peter is found in Matthew 17. He appeared with James and John on the Mount of Transfiguration.
- **Matthew 17:1-2**

"And after six days Jesus taketh Peter, James, and John his brother, and bringeth them up into an high mountain apart, And was transfigured before them: and his face did shine as the sun, and his raiment was white as the light."
- **Matthew 17:5**

"While he yet spake, behold, a bright cloud overshadowed them: and behold a voice out of the cloud, which said, This is my beloved Son, in whom I am well pleased; hear ye him."

Peter, James, and John had the great privilege of going to the Mount and seeing the glory of the Lord Jesus Christ Who was transfigured before them.

7. Peter And The Question Of Tribute

The seventh thing about Peter involved the discussion of the tribute money.
- **Matthew 17:24-27**

"And when they were come to Capernaum, they that received tribute *money* came to Peter, and said, Doth not your master pay tribute? He saith, Yes. And when he was come into the house, Jesus prevented him, saying, What thinkest thou, Simon? of whom do the kings of the earth take custom or tribute? of their own children, or of strangers? Peter saith unto him, Of strangers. Jesus saith unto him, Then are the children free. Notwithstanding, lest we should offend them, go thou to the sea, and cast an hook, and take up the fish that first cometh up; and when thou hast opened his mouth, thou shalt find a piece of money: that take, and give unto them for me and thee."

The Lord Jesus Christ said to Peter, in order not to offend people, go catch a fish. Open the mouth of the first fish that you find in the sea. In it you will find a piece of money. Take this money and give it to the tax collector for you and Me. Peter was involved in this miracle of this fish and the money in its mouth.

8. Peter And Forgiveness
The eighth thing about Peter's life is the teaching of forgiveness.
- Matthew 18:21-22

'Then came Peter to him, and said, Lord, how oft shall my brother sin against me, and I forgive him? till seven times? Jesus saith unto him, I say not unto thee, Until seven times: but, Until seventy times seven."

FORGIVING FOUR HUNDRED AND NINETY TIMES

Peter wondered how often he had to forgive these people that keep sinning and sinning. Then the Lord Jesus Christ told him to forgive, not seven times, but seventy times seven. That's four hundred and ninety times. If a person comes and says "I'm sorry and repents," then forgive him or her, regardless of how many times they might have sinned against you.

9. Peter And What Reward Do I Get?
The ninth thing about Peter's life, seems to be his wondering about what reward he might get for doing something. May we never follow Peter in this!
- Matthew 19:27-29

"Then answered Peter and said unto him, Behold, we have forsaken all, and followed thee; what shall we have therefore? And Jesus said unto them, Verily I say unto you, That ye which have followed me, in the regeneration when the Son of man shall sit in the throne of his glory, ye also shall sit upon twelve thrones, judging the twelve tribes of Israel. And every one that hath forsaken houses, or brethren, or sisters, or father, or mother, or wife, or children, or lands, for my name's sake, shall receive an hundredfold, and shall inherit everlasting life."

PETER LOOKED FOR A SELFISH REWARD

So Peter wondered what the disciples were going to receive. There is a reward for those who are faithful to the Lord Jesus Christ.

10. Peter's Lying Boast
The tenth thing about Peter is his lying boast. May none of us lie like Peter lied.
- Matthew 26:31-35

"Then saith Jesus unto them, All ye shall be offended because of me this night: for it is written, I will smite the shepherd, and the sheep of the flock shall be scattered abroad. But after I am risen again, I will go before you into Galilee. Peter answered and said unto him, Though all *men* shall be offended because of thee, *yet* will I never be offended. Jesus said unto him, Verily I say unto thee, That this night, before the cock crow, thou shalt deny me thrice. Peter said unto him, Though I should die with thee, yet will I not deny thee. Likewise also said all the disciples."

PETER CALLED JESUS A LIAR A SECOND TIME

The Lord Jesus Christ said all shall be offended. The Lord also predicted His crucifixion on the cross at Calvary. Peter didn't like what the Lord said. He didn't want to admit that he would be offended by Him. In effect, Peter called the Lord Jesus Christ a liar. May genuine Christians never deny their Lord and Saviour as Peter did three times.

11. Peter Falling Asleep During Prayer

An eleventh thing about Peter was his falling asleep in the garden of Gethsemane.

- **Matthew 26:37-41**

"And he took with him Peter and the two sons of Zebedee, and began to be sorrowful and very heavy. Then saith he unto them, My soul is exceeding sorrowful, even unto death: tarry ye here, and watch with me. And he went a little further, and fell on his face, and prayed, saying, O my Father, if it be possible, let this cup pass from me: nevertheless not as I will, but as thou *wilt*. And he cometh unto the disciples, and findeth them asleep, and saith unto Peter, What, could ye not watch with me one hour? Watch and pray, that ye enter not into temptation: the spirit indeed *is* willing, but the flesh *is* weak."

SLEEPING INSTEAD OF WATCHING

In other words, the Lord Jesus Christ told these apostles to "*watch*" with Him. For this, they had to stay awake. Peter and the other two apostles failed the Lord Jesus Christ by sleeping instead of watching. May no true Christians today be sleeping instead of watching and serving their Saviour.

12. Peter's Swordsmanship

The twelfth thing about Peter was his use of his sword.

- **John 18:10-11**

"Then Simon Peter having a sword drew it, and smote the high priest's servant, and cut off his right ear. The servant's name was Malchus. Then said Jesus unto Peter, "*Put up thy sword into the sheath: the cup which my Father hath given me, shall I not drink it?*"

PETER TOOK MATTERS INTO HIS OWN HANDS

The multitudes went out after Jesus in the garden of Gethsemane and wanted to take Him to Calvary and crucify Him. Peter took his sword and smote the high priest, cutting off his right ear. The Lord did not want Peter to defend him in this way. Peter was told to put his sword back into his sheath. The cross of Calvary was what God the Father gave to His Son as His important mission to atone for the sins of the entire world.

13. Peter Following Afar Off

The thirteenth thing about Peter is his following the Lord Jesus Christ afar off.
- Matthew 26:58

"But Peter followed him afar off unto the high priest's palace, and went in, and sat with the servants, to see the end."

FOLLOWING AFAR OFF FOR FEAR

Peter was a bystander who was ashamed of His Saviour. He wanted to see the end, but he was afar off. He didn't want to be too close for fear. Maybe he was afraid for his life. May genuine Christians never follow the Lord Jesus only afar off and be ashamed of Him.

14. Peter's Threefold Denial

The fourteenth thing was Peter's threefold denial of the Lord Jesus Christ.
- Matthew 26:69-70

"Now Peter sat without in the palace: and a damsel came unto him, saying, Thou also wast with Jesus of Galilee. But he denied before *them* all, saying, I know not what thou sayest."

This was Peter's first denial of the three.
- Matthew 26:72-75

"And again he denied with an oath, I do not know the man. And after a while came unto *him* they that stood by, and said to Peter, Surely thou also art *one* of them; for thy speech bewrayeth thee. Then began he to curse and to swear, *saying*, I know not the man. And immediately the cock crew. And Peter remembered the word of Jesus, which said unto him, Before the cock crow, thou shalt deny me thrice. And he went out, and wept bitterly."

PETER LIED THREE TIMES AT CHRIST'S TRIAL

Peter had a certain accent that made the man to know that Peter was from Galilee. Three different times Peter denied that he even knew the Lord Jesus Christ. Peter was a blasphemer. May we never follow Peter in that. *"And immediately the cock crew,"* just as the Lord predicted. Peter did repent about that. I hope we will weep bitterly if we should ever deny the Lord Jesus Christ as Peter did there.

15. Peter Going To The Tomb

The fifteenth thing about Peter was his going to the empty tomb of the Lord Jesus Christ.

- John 20:1-3

"The first *day* of the week cometh Mary Magdalene early, when it was yet dark, unto the sepulchre, and seeth the stone taken away from the sepulchre. Then she runneth, and cometh to Simon Peter, and to the other disciple, whom Jesus loved, and saith unto them, They have taken away the Lord out of the sepulchre, and we know not where they have laid him. Peter therefore went forth, and that other disciple, and came to the sepulchre."

JOHN WAS PATIENT AT CHRIST'S TOMB

The other disciple (probably the Apostle John) was younger and outran Peter. He got to the tomb first, but did not enter into it then. He just waited. Peter, though he arrived later than John, immediately went into the sepulchre. He saw the linen clothes lying, but the Lord Jesus Christ was not there.

- John 20:7-8

"And the napkin, that was about his head, not lying with the linen clothes, but wrapped together in a place by itself. Then went in also that other disciple, which came first to the sepulchre, and he saw, and believed."

CHRIST'S RESURRECTION WITNESSED CLEARLY
Peter saw clearly that the Lord Jesus Christ was bodily raised from the grave. John also saw the empty tomb and believed that the Saviour was resurrected bodily.

16. Peter's Return To Fishing
The sixteenth thing about Peter was his backsliding. The Lord Jesus Christ called him to be a fisher of men, but then Peter went back to his old occupation of fishing for fish.
- John 21:1-3

"After these things Jesus shewed himself again to the disciples at the sea of Tiberias; and on this wise shewed he *himself*. There were together Simon Peter, and Thomas called Didymus, and Nathanael of Cana in Galilee, and the *sons* of Zebedee, and two other of his disciples. Simon Peter saith unto them, I go a fishing. They say unto him, We also go with thee. They went forth, and entered into a ship immediately; and that night they caught nothing."

PETER FORSOOK HIS DIVINE CALLING
Peter went back to his old occupation. He had not given up his old job. **He forsook his Divine calling and began his backsliding.** In addition to this, he persuaded six of the other apostles to join him in this venture. This shows how a bad testimony can influence others to follow it.

17. Peter Throwing Himself Into The Water
The seventeenth thing about Peter was that he was eager to go from his boat to meet the Lord Jesus Christ on the shore.
- John 21:7

"Therefore that disciple whom Jesus loved saith unto Peter, It is the Lord. Now when Simon Peter heard that it was the Lord, he girt *his* fisher's coat *unto him*, (for he was naked,) and did cast himself into the sea."

PETER'S EAGER SWIM TO SHORE
Compulsive Peter dove into the water and swam to the shore to see the risen Lord Jesus Christ. He was eager to do that.

18. Peter's Restoration

The eighteenth thing about Peter was his restoration, and statements three times, that he loved the Lord Jesus Christ.
- John 21:15-17

"So when they had dined, Jesus saith to Simon Peter, Simon, *son* of Jonas, lovest thou me more than these? He saith unto him, Yea, Lord; thou knowest that I love thee. He saith unto him, Feed my lambs. He saith to him again the second time, Simon, *son* of Jonas, lovest thou me? He saith unto him, Yea, Lord; thou knowest that I love thee. He saith unto him, Feed my sheep. He saith unto him the third time, Simon, *son* of Jonas, lovest thou me? Peter was grieved because he said unto him the third time, Lovest thou me? And he said unto him, Lord, thou knowest all things; thou knowest that I love thee. Jesus saith unto him, Feed my sheep."

> **CHRIST QUESTIONED PETER'S TRUE LOVE**
>
> The Lord Jesus Christ questioned Peter three times. Let not true Christians be grieved when the Lord Jesus Christ might ask them some very important questions. We read about this in the Bible. After Peter's threefold denial of the Lord Jesus Christ around the enemy's fire, he was restored.

19. Peter's Sermon To The 120 Disciples

The nineteenth thing about Peter was his sermon to the 120 disciples in the upper room.
- Acts 1:13-15

"And when they were come in, they went up into an upper room, where abode both Peter, and James, and John, and Andrew, Philip, and Thomas, Bartholomew, and Matthew, James *the son* of Alphaeus, and Simon Zelotes, and Judas *the brother* of James. These all continued with one accord in prayer and supplication, with the women, and Mary the mother of Jesus, and with his brethren. And in those days Peter stood up in the midst of the disciples, and said, (the number of names together were about an hundred and twenty,)"

> **PETER RESTORED TO FELLOWSHIP WITH THE LORD**
>
> Peter preached this sermon to these 120 disciples after he was back in fellowship with the Lord Jesus Christ. May genuine Christians follow Simon Peter's good things, but stay away from any of the bad things.

2 Peter 1:1

"Simon Peter, a servant and an apostle of Jesus Christ, to them that have obtained like precious faith with us through the righteousness of God and our Saviour Jesus Christ:"

Peter identifies himself as both a servant and also an apostle of the Lord Jesus Christ. He is writing to those who have also obtained fellowship in the Lord Jesus Christ by precious faith. Let's look at numerous verses that discuss precious things.

Verses On "Precious" Things

- **1 Peter 1:7**

"That the trial of your faith, being much more precious than of gold that perisheth, though it be tried with fire, might be found unto praise and honour and glory at the appearing of Jesus Christ:"

Genuine saving faith in the Lord Jesus Christ is more precious than gold.

- **Psalms 49:8**

"(For the redemption of their soul *is* precious, and it ceaseth for ever:)"

The redemption of those who are lost in sin is precious in the sight of God.

- **Psalms 116:15**

"Precious in the sight of the LORD *is* the death of his saints."

> **FOR TRUE CHRISTIANS, DEATH IS PRECIOUS**
> It is precious in the sight of the Lord when those true Christians die. Many people look at death for genuine Christians and say it is horrible because of all the weeping and sorrow that goes with it. **But in the Lord's sight, those who are His saints (true Christians), death is precious.** For those who are not genuine Christians, it is a totally different and sad picture.

- **Psalms 126:6**

"He that goeth forth and weepeth, bearing precious seed, shall doubtless come again with rejoicing, bringing his sheaves *with him*."

Those who are seeking to win souls to the Lord Jesus Christ must bear precious seed which is the Words of God. It is important that the right Scriptures be used for the seed to be "*precious.*" In English, the proper seed is the King James Bible which has been accurately

translated from the proper and preserved Hebrew, Aramaic, and Greek Words.
- **Psalms 139:17**
"How precious also are thy thoughts unto me, O God! how great is the sum of them!"

The thoughts of God are also precious. Many of these thoughts have been revealed to us in the Words of God in the Bible.
- **Proverbs 20:15**
"There is gold, and a multitude of rubies: but the lips of knowledge *are* a precious jewel."

KNOWLEDGEABLE LIPS ARE PRECIOUS JEWELS
The lips of knowledge are considered by the Lord a precious jewel.

- **Isaiah 28:16**
"Therefore thus saith the Lord GOD, Behold, I lay in Zion for a foundation a stone, a tried stone, a precious corner *stone*, a sure foundation: he that believeth shall not make haste."

This refers to the Lord Jesus Christ Who was and is the Precious and Sure foundation of the true church.
- **Matthew 26:7**
"There came unto him a woman having an alabaster box of very precious ointment, and poured it on his head, as he sat *at meat*."

Judas thought the woman's anointing of the head of the Lord Jesus Christ with this precious ointment a waste of money. It was an anointing prior to His death on Calvary for the sins of the world.
- **1 Peter 1:7**
"That the trial of your faith, being much more precious than of gold that perisheth, though it be tried with fire, might be found unto praise and honour and glory at the appearing of Jesus Christ:"

"THE FAITH" REFERS TO THE DOCTRINES
The Greek Word for *"faith"* is preceded by the Greek article, HE. This therefore refers to the doctrines of the Bible. This *"faith"* is declared to be *"precious"* even though tried by fire.

- **1 Peter 1:18-19**

"Forasmuch as ye know that ye were not redeemed with corruptible things, *as* silver and gold, from your vain conversation *received* by tradition from your fathers; But with the precious blood of Christ, as of a lamb without blemish and without spot:"

CHRIST'S BLOOD IS PRECIOUS TO GOD THE FATHER

God declares in His Word here that the blood of the Lord Jesus Christ, His Son, is *"precious."*

John MacArthur's Heresy On The Blood

JOHN MACARTHUR–A HERETIC ON CHRIST'S BLOOD!

John MacArthur disagrees with God's Words here. He simply erases the literal word, *"blood"* and transforms it, by metonym, into the word *"death."* MacArthur, therefore, denies that the precious blood of the Lord Jesus Christ can save, can cleanse, can draw true Christians near to God and many more doctrines of the blood. I have explained, in a short tract, fourteen things which are accomplished by the blood of the Lord Jesus Christ. It is six pages in length (BFT #2548-T.)

- **1 Peter 2:4**

"To whom coming, *as unto* a living stone, disallowed indeed of men, but chosen of God, *and* precious,"

The Lord Jesus Christ, though rejected of men, was chosen by God and precious to God the Father and all genuine Christians, though hated and despised by many non-Christians.

- **1 Peter 2:6-7**

"Wherefore also it is contained in the scripture, Behold, I lay in Sion a chief corner stone, elect, precious: and he that believeth on him shall not be confounded. Unto you therefore which believe *he is* precious: but unto them which be disobedient, the stone which the builders disallowed, the same is made the head of the corner,"

THE PRECIOUSNESS OF CHRIST

In these verses, the Lord Jesus Christ is precious in two aspects:

(1) precious as the chief corner stone, and

(2) precious to those true Christians who have genuinely trusted in Him.

- **2 Peter 1:1**

  "Simon Peter, a servant and an apostle of Jesus Christ, to them that have obtained like precious faith with us through the righteousness of God and our Saviour Jesus Christ:"

Genuine faith in the Lord Jesus Christ is truly precious.

- **2 Peter 1:4**

  "Whereby are given unto us exceeding great and precious promises: that by these ye might be partakers of the divine nature, having escaped the corruption that is in the world through lust."

In this verse, we see that the promises of God, as revealed in the Bible, are great and precious to those who are true Christians.

Verses On Righteousness

- **Romans 3:22**

  "Even the righteousness of God *which is* by faith of Jesus Christ unto all and upon all them that believe: for there is no difference:"

RIGHTEOUSNESS ONLY BY GENUINE FAITH

For any person in the world to obtain righteousness with God, they must exercise genuine faith in the Lord Jesus Christ as the One Who died for their sins.

- **Romans 4:3**

  "For what saith the scripture? Abraham believed God, and it was counted unto him for righteousness."

We see, in this verse, Abraham's righteousness by his genuine faith apart from any of his works.

- **Romans 4:5**

  "But to him that worketh not, but believeth on him that justifieth the ungodly, his faith is counted for righteousness."

No one has any righteousness of their own. Salvation is not of works, but only by genuine faith in the Lord Jesus Christ.

- **Romans 10:10**

  "For with the heart man believeth unto righteousness; and with the mouth confession is made unto salvation."

Again, it is by true faith from the heart that people can believe on the Lord Jesus Christ and only then receive God's righteousness.

- **2 Corinthians 5:21**

  "For he hath made him *to be* sin for us, who knew no sin; that we might be made the righteousness of God in him."

CHRIST–THE SIN OFFERING FOR EVERY PERSON
God the Father made God the Son (Who was without any sin of any kind) to be a sin offering for every person who ever lived in this world. Only by true faith in the Lord Jesus Christ can people receive righteousness before God.

- Philippians 3:9

"And be found in him, not having mine own righteousness, which is of the law, but that which is through the faith of Christ, the righteousness which is of God by faith:"

Righteousness before God can be obtained only by genuine faith in the Lord Jesus Christ as Saviour.

2 Peter 1:2

"Grace and peace be multiplied unto you through the knowledge of God, and of Jesus our Lord,"

GOD'S GRACE AND PEACE
Peter's salutation is *"Grace and peace."* *"Grace"*(CHARIS) appeals to the Greek Gentiles. *"Peace"* (SHALOM) appeals to the Jews. Notice that the *"knowledge"* that Peter highlights is *"the knowledge of God, and of Jesus our Lord."* It is a limited type of knowledge. Not everybody has the knowledge of our Saviour.

Verses On Knowledge
There are various verses on the type of knowledge that Peter wanted his readers to have.

- Luke 1:77

"To give knowledge of salvation unto his people by the remission of their sins,"

Luke speaks about the knowledge regarding salvation. That's a very valuable knowledge. It's not the knowledge a person might get in colleges, seminaries, and universities.

- Romans 10:2

"For I bear them record that they have a zeal of God, but not according to knowledge."

The unsaved Jews had zeal, but not a knowledge of the things of the Lord Jesus Christ. True Christians should be zealous, but also knowledgeable about the teachings of the Bible.

- **Romans 15:14**
"And I myself also am persuaded of you, my brethren, that ye also are full of goodness, filled with all knowledge, able also to admonish one another."

The genuine Christians at Rome were filled with the knowledge of Bible truths and thus were able to admonish their fellow Christians. The Bible should be the foundation of all proper admonition.

- **1 Corinthians 1:5**
"That in every thing ye are enriched by him, in all utterance, and *in* all knowledge;"

This refers to the knowledge about God and His Words. This is important indeed.

- **2 Corinthians 4:6**
"For God, who commanded the light to shine out of darkness, hath shined in our hearts, to *give* the light of the knowledge of the glory of God in the face of Jesus Christ."

The knowledge of the glory of God can only be found by truly trusting in His Son, the Lord Jesus Christ.

- **2 Corinthians 8:7**
"Therefore, as ye abound in every *thing, in* faith, and utterance, and knowledge, and *in* all diligence, and *in* your love to us, *see* that ye abound in this grace also."

The genuine Christians in Corinth abounded in knowledge as well as in other things. This knowledge concerned the Words and will of their God and Saviour.

- **Ephesians 1:17**
"That the God of our Lord Jesus Christ, the Father of glory, may give unto you the spirit of wisdom and revelation in the knowledge of him:"

PAUL'S PRAYER FOR THE EPHESIAN CHRISTIANS
Paul's prayer for the true Christians at Ephesus was that they might be given a revelation in the knowledge of both the Father of glory and of the Lord Jesus Christ.

- **Ephesians 4:13**
"Till we all come in the unity of the faith, and of the knowledge of the Son of God, unto a perfect man, unto the measure of the stature of the fulness of Christ:"

There is not complete unity among churches, even in Bible-believing churches. One day, in God's own time, there will be a unity of the doctrines of the faith. That time seems a long way off for now.

- Philippians 1:9

"And this I pray, that your love may abound yet more and more in knowledge and *in* all judgment;"

> **LOVE WITH KNOWLEDGE AND DISCERNMENT**
>
> The love of one group of genuine Christians for another group should abound more and more in knowledge of God's Words as well as in judgment. <u>They must have judgment as well as knowledge.</u> This means discernment. They cannot be like a vacuum cleaner which has no discernment. It sucks up everything in its path whether it's dirt, or a hundred-dollar bill. Love must have both knowledge and discernment.

- Philippians 3:8

"Yea doubtless, and I count all things *but* loss for the excellency of the knowledge of Christ Jesus my Lord: for whom I have suffered the loss of all things, and do count them *but* dung, that I may win Christ."

<u>Paul had fame, fortune, position in life, and many other things prior to his salvation. But when he became a true Christian, he counted all these things as loss compared to the knowledge of the Lord Jesus Christ his Saviour.</u>

- Colossians 1:9

"For this cause we also, since the day we heard *it*, do not cease to pray for you, and to desire that ye might be filled with the knowledge of his will in all wisdom and spiritual understanding;"

> **GOD'S WILL FOUND IN GOD'S WORDS**
>
> Do genuine Christians want to know His will? Paul prayed that they might have a full knowledge of God's will in wisdom and spiritual understanding. That *"will"* is found in the Words of God in the Bible.

- Colossians 1:10

"That ye might walk worthy of the Lord unto all pleasing, being fruitful in every good work, and increasing in the knowledge of God;"

> **INCREASING IN THE KNOWLEDGE OF GOD**
>
> True Christians might ask how they can *"increase in the knowledge of God."* The answer is quite simple. They must do at least three things:

> (1) They must <u>read</u> God's Words;
> (2) They must <u>understand</u> God's Words; and
> (3) They must <u>practice</u> God's Words daily the rest of their lives. This will increase them in the personal knowledge of God.

- **2 Peter 3:18**

"But grow in grace, and *in* the knowledge of our Lord and Saviour Jesus Christ. To him *be* glory both now and for ever. Amen."

<u>Genuine Christians must not remain babes in Christ</u>. They should grow both in God's grace and the knowledge of their Lord and Saviour, Jesus Christ. This is found in careful study of God's Words in the Bible.

2 Peter 1:3

"According as his divine power hath given unto us all things that pertain unto life and godliness, through the knowledge of him that hath called us to glory and virtue:"

> **THINGS PERTAINING TO LIFE AND GODLINESS**
> Every true Christian by means of God's Divine power, has been given all things pertaining to life and godliness. This is all possible through the knowledge of the Lord Himself.

Verses On Power

<u>There are many things in Scripture that talk about power</u>.

- **Romans 1:16**

"For I am not ashamed of the gospel of Christ: for it is the power of God unto salvation to every one that believeth; to the Jew first, and also to the Greek."

<u>The clear gospel of Christ is God's power unto salvation to those who genuinely believe and receive it</u>.

- **1 Corinthians 1:18**

"For the preaching of the cross is to them that perish foolishness; but unto us which are saved it is the power of God."

<u>The preaching of the cross is God's power to those who are truly saved</u>.

- **2 Corinthians 4:7**
"But we have this treasure in earthen vessels, that the excellency of the power may be of God, and not of us."

God's power can shine out of the lives of true Christians.
- **2 Corinthians 12:9**
"And he said unto me, My grace is sufficient for thee: for my strength is made perfect in weakness. Most gladly therefore will I rather glory in my infirmities, that the power of Christ may rest upon me."

THE POWER OF CHRIST NEEDED

Paul said he wanted the power of Christ to rest upon him, even though his thorn in the flesh was not removed.

- **Ephesians 3:7**
"Whereof I was made a minister, according to the gift of the grace of God given unto me by the effectual working of his power."

Paul was transformed from being a hateful, Christ-despising Jew, into a victorious and genuine Christian by God's effective power in his life.
- **Ephesians 3:20**
"Now unto him that is able to do exceeding abundantly above all that we ask or think, according to the power that worketh in us,"

In the life of true Christians resides God the Holy Spirit. His power enables them to do above all that they ask or think.
- **Philippians 3:10**
"That I may know him, and the power of his resurrection, and the fellowship of his sufferings, being made conformable unto his death;"

The bodily resurrection of the Lord Jesus Christ was accomplished through the power of God. Paul wanted that same power in his life and ministry.
- **Colossians 1:11**
"Strengthened with all might, according to his glorious power, unto all patience and longsuffering with joyfulness;"

Genuine Christians can be strengthened with all might in the power of the Holy Spirit if they are walking in His power and light.
- **2 Timothy 3:5**
"Having a form of godliness, but denying the power thereof: from such turn away."

> **HAVING ONLY A <u>FORM</u> OF GODLINESS**
> In churches that do not believe or preach the Bible doctrines in all of their truth, the people have a form of godliness, but they deny the power of godliness by their unbelief in the Saviour.

2 Peter 1:4

"Whereby are given unto us exceeding great and precious promises: that by these ye might be partakers of the divine nature, having escaped the corruption that is in the world through lust."

<u>God gives true Christians many promises by which to escape the corruption of the world.</u> Here are five of these promises:

Five Promises Of God

1. The Promise of Everlasting Life.
- John 3:16

"For God so loved the world, that he gave his only begotten Son, that whosoever believeth in him should not perish, but have everlasting life."

2. The Promise of Redemption and Forgiveness.
- Ephesians 1:7

"In whom we have redemption through his blood, the forgiveness of sins, according to the riches of his grace;"

3. The Promise of Our Saviour's Presence With Us.
- Matthew 28:20

"Teaching them to observe all things whatsoever I have commanded you: and, lo, I am with you alway, *even* unto the end of the world. Amen."

- Hebrews 13:5

"*Let your* conversation *be* without covetousness; *and be* content with such things as ye have: for he hath said, I will never leave thee, nor forsake thee."

4. The Promise of The Indwelling Holy Spirit.
- 1 Corinthians 6:19

"What? know ye not that your body is the temple of the Holy Ghost *which is* in you, which ye have of God, and ye are not your own?"

5. The Promise of An Eternal Home In Heaven.
- **John 14:2**
"In my Father's house are many mansions: if *it were* not *so,* I would have told you. I go to prepare a place for you."
- **John 14:3**
"And if I go and prepare a place for you, I will come again, and receive you unto myself; that where I am, *there* ye may be also."
- **Philippians 1:23**
"For I am in a strait betwixt two, having a desire to depart, and to be with Christ; which is far better:"

These promises will help genuine Christians to escape the corruption that is in this wicked world through lust.

2 Peter 1:5

"And beside this, giving all diligence, add to your faith virtue; and to virtue knowledge;"

With the Greek article, "*faith*" refers in this verse to the doctrines and theology of the Bible. To this faith or doctrine, two other important features must be added. They must be added with diligence.

THE MEANING OF THE GREEK WORD, "ARETEN"

The Greek Word for "*virtue*" is ARETEN. Some of the meanings of that Greek Word are:

"*1) a virtuous course of thought, feeling and action; 1a) virtue, moral goodness; 2) any particular moral excellence, as modesty, purity*"

Then, in addition to "*virtue*" should be added the element of "*knowledge.*" The Greek Word for "*knowledge*" is GNOSIS.

Some of the meanings of this Greek Word are:
"*1) knowledge signifies in general intelligence, understanding; 1a) the general knowledge of Christian religion; 1b) the deeper more perfect and enlarged knowledge of this religion, such as belongs to the more advanced; 1c) esp. of things lawful and unlawful for Christians; 1d) moral wisdom, such as is seen in right living.*"

> **DON'T STAY BABES IN CHRIST, BUT MATURE**
> Genuine Christians should add, increase, and grow in the Lord. They should not stay babes in Christ. They should mature after they have been saved by true faith in the Lord Jesus Christ.

2 Peter 1:6

"And to knowledge temperance; and to temperance patience; and to patience godliness;"

> **THE MEANING OF THE GREEK WORD, "ENKRATEIA"**
> Then true Christians should add to their knowledge temperance. The Greek Word for *"temperance"* is ENKRATEIA. One of the meanings of this Greek Word is:
> > *"1) self-control (the virtue of one who masters his desires and passions, esp. his sensual appetites)"*

This must be added to faith and knowledge. To temperance must be added patience.

> **THE MEANING OF THE GREEK WORD, "HUPOMONE"**
> The Greek Word for *"patience"* is: HUPOMONE. Some of the meanings for this Greek Word are:
> > *"1) steadfastness, constancy, endurance; 1a) in the NT the characteristic of a man who is not swerved from his deliberate purpose and his loyalty to faith and piety by even the greatest trials and sufferings; 1b) patiently, and steadfastly; 2) a patient, steadfast waiting for; 3) a patient enduring, sustaining, perseverance."*

> **THE MEANING OF THE GREEK WORD, "EUSEBEIA"**
> The final quality to be added to patience is godliness. The Greek Word for *"godliness"* is EUSEBEIA. Some of the meanings of this Greek Word are:
> > *"1) reverence, respect; 2) piety towards God, godliness"*

> **THE SIXTH THING TO BE ADDED TO CHRISTIANS**
> Godliness is the sixth thing that should be added to the lives and ministries of genuine Christians.

2 Peter 1:7

"And to godliness brotherly kindness; and to brotherly kindness charity."

Here are the seventh and eighth elements that should be added.

> **THE MEANING OF THE GREEK WORD, "PHILADELPHIA"**
> The seventh is brotherly kindness. The Greek Word for "*brotherly kindness*" is PHILADELPHIA. Some of the meanings of this Greek Word are:
> > "*1) love of brothers or sisters, brotherly love 2) in the NT, the love which Christians cherish for each other as brethren*"

The eighth thing to be added is charity.

> **THE MEANING OF THE GREEK WORD, "AGAPE"**
> The Greek Word for "*charity*" is AGAPE. Some of the meanings of this Greek Word are:
> > "*1) brotherly love, affection, good will, love, benevolence; 2) love feasts*"

Brotherly kindness or love is mentioned by the Lord Jesus Christ in many verses. Here is one of them:
- John 13:35

"By this shall all *men* know that ye are my disciples, if ye have love one to another."

> **CHRISTIANS SHOULD LOVE DESPITE DIFFERENCES**
> Genuine Christians don't necessarily agree with everything that fellow genuine Christians believe, but they should love each other anyhow. That was the thing that I tried to instill in the group that assembled at Greenville, South Carolina on September 26th a few years ago. I talked for five hours--from 1:00 to 6:00. I talked about the beliefs of two of our brothers in Christ that differ with me on their views of the Greek and Hebrew original Words.

> **FALSE TEXTS & VERSIONS=356 DOCTRINAL ERRORS**
> For those who know the truth, there are a total of at least 356 false doctrinal passages found in the Gnostic Critical Greek Text. These passages are specified very clearly by Dr. Jack Moorman in his book, *Early Manuscripts, Church Fathers, and the Authorized Version* (BFT #3230 @ $20.00 + $8.00 S&H). All 356 of these doctrinal passages are found on pages 119 through 312.

The pastor of the local Baptist church in Greenville, South Carolina, invited two professors at Bob Jones University to debate this topic which was something like this: "Resolved that the Critical Greek Text And The Modern Versions Based Upon Them Do Not Change Bible Doctrines." The two professors from Bob Jones University were to take the affirmative on this question to defend their position, and I would take the negative. Both of these professors refused to accept the pastor's request to debate me on this question.

Since they refused to debate it, the debate went on in their absence. I quoted from the books and articles by both Dr. Samuel Schnaiter and Dr. Mark Minnick where both of them repeatedly stated that there were no doctrinal changes involved in either the Critical Greek Text or in the modern versions based upon them. It is clear why both these Bob Jones University professors refused to take the affirmative side of that debate question. If they had come and taken that side, they would have definitely lost the debate because of the gigantic amount of evidence against their position.

No matter how strongly I disagree with these men on this subject, I can still love them as brethren in Christ. I have said many times to our church and others that I only wish that they would love me back. I have never seen this in either of these professors. Love of the brethren is essential.

2 Peter 1:8

"For if these things be in you, and abound, they make you that ye shall neither be barren nor unfruitful in the knowledge of our Lord Jesus Christ."

> **EIGHT THINGS PREVENT UNFRUITFULNESS**
> When Peter speaks of "these things," I believe he is referring to the eight things that he has previously mentioned: (1) faith; (2) virtue; (3) knowledge; (4)

temperance; (5) patience; (6) godliness; (7) brotherly kindness; and (8) charity or love.

Peter wants these eight things to be possessed by his readers, but he also wants these virtues to abound in them.

THE MEANING OF THE GREEK WORD, "PLEONAZO"

The Greek Word for *"abound"* is PLEONAZO. Some of the meanings of this Word are:

"1) to superabound; 1a) of things; 1a1) to exist in abundance; 1a2) to increase; 1a3) be augmented; 2) to make to increase: one in a thing."

If in fact these virtues not only are in the readers but also abound in them, then two things will be true: (1) they will not be barren, and (2) they will not be unfruitful in the knowledge of the Lord Jesus Christ.

THE MEANING OF THE GREEK WORD, "ARGOS"

The Greek Word for barren is ARGOS. Some of the meanings of *"barren"* are:

"1) free from labour, at leisure; 2) lazy, shunning the labour which one ought to perform."

If these virtues are possessed by genuine Christians, they will not be lazy and unwilling to work for the Lord Jesus Christ.

THE MEANING OF THE GREEK WORD, "AKARPOS"

The Greek Word for unfruitful is AKARPOS. Some of the meanings of *"unfruitful"* are:

"1) metaph. without fruit, barren, not yielding what it ought to yield"

If these virtues are found in true Christians, they will not be without fruit and barren in that sense in the knowledge of the Lord Jesus Christ.

Verses About Barren

The word, *"barren"* is used 23 times in the King James Bible in one of the senses of that word. Here are a few of these verses.

- **Genesis 11:30**

"But Sarai was barren; she *had* no child."

At this point in Sarah's life, she had no children. God does not want genuine Christians to be spiritually barren.
- **Psalms 113:9**
"He maketh the barren woman to keep house, *and to be* a joyful mother of children. Praise ye the LORD."

God intercedes for barren women on occasion, and allows them to be mothers of children.
- **Joel 2:20**
"But I will remove far off from you the northern *army*, and will drive him into a land barren and desolate, with his face toward the east sea, and his hinder part toward the utmost sea, and his stink shall come up, and his ill savour shall come up, because he hath done great things."

This describes a land with no fruit. God does not want His true Christians to be barren. They will not be barren as long as these eight virtues are possessed and abound.
- **Matthew 13:22**
"He also that received seed among the thorns is he that heareth the word; and the care of this world, and the deceitfulness of riches, choke the word, and he becometh unfruitful."

Genuine Christians today must not be unfruitful in the knowledge of the Lord Jesus Christ.
- **Ephesians 5:11**
"And have no fellowship with the unfruitful works of darkness, but rather reprove *them*."

LEAVE & REPROVE DARK & UNFRUITFUL WORKS
The unfruitful works of darkness and wickedness contrary to the clear teachings of God's Words, the Bible, must be reproved and brought into the public view. That Greek Word for *"reprove"* is ELENCHO. It means bring something out into the open and shine the light upon it.

- **Titus 3:14**
"And let ours also learn to maintain good works for necessary uses, that they be not unfruitful."

Good works should follow a person's genuine acceptance of the Lord Jesus Christ as their Saviour. Not that people are saved by their good works, but once they are saved, the Holy Spirit of God can work in them and through them to bring forth fruitful and beneficial good works that are acceptable unto the Lord Jesus Christ.

2 Peter 1:9

"**But he that lacketh these things is blind, and cannot see afar off, and hath forgotten that he was purged from his old sins.**"

Once again, Peter is referring to the eight virtues. If they are lacking in the lives of any true Christians, three things are true:
(1) they are blind;
(2) they can't see afar off; and
(3) they have forgotten that they were purged from their old sins.

THE MEANING OF THE GREEK WORD, "MUOPAZO"

The Greek Word for blindness is MUOPAZO. Some of the meanings of "*blindness*" are:

"*1) to see dimly, see only what is near*"

It is the term where the word, "*myopia*" comes from. With this malady, distant objects appear blurred. I have myopia in one of my eyes where I can't see distant objects clearly.

Spiritually speaking, God wants all of his genuine Christians to be able to see things close at hand and also things in the more distant future. He does not want them "blind" in this sense.

Verses About Blindness

- John 9:39

"And Jesus said, For judgment I am come into this world, that they which see not might see; and that they which see might be made blind."

MULTITUDES TODAY ARE SPIRITUALLY BLIND

Those who thought they could see (like the self-righteous Pharisees) were spiritually blind. Those who realized they were spiritually blind (like the publicans and sinners) would be able to be made to see by trusting the Lord Jesus Christ as their Saviour.

- John 9:40

"And *some* of the Pharisees which were with him heard these words, and said unto him, Are we blind also?"

Yes, they were spiritually blind indeed. They got the point of the story.

- **John 9:41**

"Jesus said unto them, If ye were blind, ye should have no sin: but now ye say, We see; therefore your sin remaineth."

The Lord Jesus Christ gave vision to a man who was born blind. The Pharisees believed that they didn't need to be healed of spiritual blindness by the Lord Jesus Christ. They thought they could see spiritually so their sin remained on their shoulders.

- **Acts 13:11**

"And now, behold, the hand of the Lord *is* upon thee, and thou shalt be blind, not seeing the sun for a season. And immediately there fell on him a mist and a darkness; and he went about seeking some to lead him by the hand."

Paul caused Elymas the sorcerer to be blinded because he was interfering with the reception of the gospel by Sergius Paulus.

- **Acts 9:9**

"And he was three days without sight, and neither did eat nor drink."

Paul was blinded by the Lord for three days.

- **2 Corinthians 4:4**

"In whom the god of this world hath blinded the minds of them which believe not, lest the light of the glorious gospel of Christ, who is the image of God, should shine unto them."

Satan blinds the minds of those who do not believe in the Lord Jesus Christ as their Saviour.

- **Ephesians 4:18**

"Having the understanding darkened, being alienated from the life of God through the ignorance that is in them, because of the blindness of their heart:"

In this case, it is blindness of the heart rather than the eyes.

Verses On Purging

Peter reminds his readers that they have forgotten that they were once purged from their sins by truly trusting the Lord Jesus Christ as their Saviour.

- **Psalms 79:9**

"Help us, O God of our salvation, for the glory of thy name: and deliver us, and purge away our sins, for thy name's sake."

God alone can purge or cleanse away sins when people genuinely trust the Lord Jesus Christ as their Saviour. Purgatory can't do it. There is no such thing in the Bible. The work of the Lord Jesus Christ on the cross at Calvary is the only purgation or cleansing place for the sins of mankind.

- **1 Corinthians 5:7**
"Purge out therefore the old leaven, that ye may be a new lump, as ye are unleavened. For even Christ our passover is sacrificed for us:"

Once true Christians have formed a local church, they should purge out any leaven or poison among them to keep the church unleavened or pure.

- **Hebrews 9:22**
"And almost all things are by the law purged with blood; and without shedding of blood is no remission."

ONLY CHRIST'S SINLESS BLOOD CAN PURGE SINS
In the law of Moses, sins were purged by the blood of clean animals. In the New Testament, it is only the spotless blood of the Lord Jesus Christ, the Lamb of God, whereby sins can be purged, remitted, and forgiven.

2 Peter 1:10

"Wherefore the rather, brethren, give diligence to make your calling and election sure: for if ye do these things, ye shall never fall:"

It is important that everyone who professes to be saved should be diligent to be sure and certain of their salvation. The calling is the invitation for a person to come to the Lord Jesus Christ and to choose Him as their Saviour. This makes sure that the person has entered into this elect Body, the Church, which Body was formed in eternity past.

Once a person is genuinely saved and redeemed, they will never fall from that salvation, though they might fall out of fellowship with the Lord.

Verses On Calling

- **2 Timothy 1:9**
"Who hath saved us, and called *us* with an holy calling, not according to our works, but according to his own purpose and grace, which was given us in Christ Jesus before the world began,"

The calling of the Lord Jesus Christ to be saved is a holy calling.

- **Matthew 11:28**
"Come unto me, all *ye* that labour and are heavy laden, and I will give you rest."

This is the call by the Lord Jesus Christ to come unto Him in true faith. Before that call becomes effective, it must be accepted.

- **Hebrews 3:1**

"Wherefore, holy brethren, partakers of the heavenly calling, consider the Apostle and High Priest of our profession, Christ Jesus;"

> **A HEAVENLY CALLING IS A SUMMONS TO HEAVEN**
>
> The Heavenly calling is a calling to go to Heaven where God the Father and the Lord Jesus Christ are.

Verses On Falling

- **Romans 14:13**

"Let us not therefore judge one another any more: but judge this rather, that no man put a stumblingblock or an occasion to fall in *his* brother's way."

God wants genuine Christians to be careful not to cause another true Christian to fall.

- **1 Corinthians 10:12**

"Wherefore let him that thinketh he standeth take heed lest he fall."

True Christians should take heed not to be so arrogant that they think they couldn't fall into sin. They should be aware of the dangers of falling that surround them and be strong against such a fall.

- **Jude 1:24**

"Now unto him that is able to keep you from falling, and to present *you* faultless before the presence of his glory with exceeding joy,"

> **CHRIST CAN KEEP CHRISTIANS FROM FALLING**
>
> The Lord Jesus Christ is able to keep true Christians from falling. They must rely upon Him and on God the Holy Spirit Who indwells them every moment of every day to prevent any falling. One day, they will be presented faultless in Heaven with glory and exceeding joy.

2 Peter 1:11

"For so an entrance shall be ministered unto you abundantly into the everlasting kingdom of our Lord and Saviour Jesus Christ."

This verse eleven talks about the entrance of genuine Christians into the everlasting and Heavenly kingdom of their Saviour. While I was listening to a Roman Catholic Mass, a priest mentioned that everyone in their Catholic Church and everyone in the world would be in Heaven. That certainly is not the Heaven spoken of in the Bible. True faith in the Lord Jesus Christ as Saviour is the only way to the Bible's Heaven.

Verses About Heaven

- **Psalms 16:11**

"Thou wilt shew me the path of life: in thy presence *is* fulness of joy; at thy right hand *there are* pleasures for evermore."

Someone in God's presence would be in Heaven where there are "pleasures for evermore."

- **Psalms 116:15**

"Precious in the sight of the LORD *is* the death of his saints."

A CHRISTIAN'S DEATH IS PRECIOUS IN GOD'S SIGHT

When genuine Christians enter into Heaven at their physical death, this is *"precious"* in the LORD's sight, though it might not be so in the sight of the people who have lost their loved one.

- **John 14:2-3**

"In my Father's house are many mansions: if *it were* not *so*, I would have told you. I go to prepare a place for you. And if I go and prepare a place for you, I will come again, and receive you unto myself; that where I am, *there* ye may be also."

When the Lord Jesus Christ spoke of His "Father's house," He was speaking of Heaven.

- **John 17:24**

"Father, I will that they also, whom thou hast given me, be with me where I am; that they may behold my glory, which thou hast given me: for thou lovedst me before the foundation of the world."

Where the Lord Jesus Christ was going is Heaven where genuine Christians will behold His glory.

- **Philippians 1:23**

"For I am in a strait betwixt two, having a desire to depart, and to be with Christ; which is far better:"

Paul said he would be "*with Christ*," when he departed from this life. He meant that he would be in Heaven where the Lord Jesus Christ is.

- **2 Corinthians 5:8**

"We are confident, *I say*, and willing rather to be absent from the body, and to be present with the Lord."

> **AFTER DEATH A PERSON GOES TO HEAVEN OR HELL**
> This is a clear verse showing that there is no such thing after a person's death as an in-between place called purgatory. For Paul, and for all true Christians, being absent from the body in death would be an immediate presence with the Lord in Heaven.

- **2 Corinthians 12:3-5**

"And I knew such a man, (whether in the body, or out of the body, I cannot tell: God knoweth;) How that he was caught up into paradise, and heard unspeakable words, which it is not lawful for a man to utter. Of such an one will I glory: yet of myself I will not glory, but in mine infirmities."

> **PAUL WAS STONED TO DEATH AT LYSTRA**
> When comparing these verses to Acts 14:19-20, it would seem clear that Paul was speaking about himself here. In this Acts passage, when Paul was stoned at Lystra, he died and went to Heaven where he was given great personal revelations about that Place mentioned above. Then, God miraculously restored him to life again.

"And there came thither certain Jews from Antioch and Iconium, who persuaded the people, and, having stoned Paul, drew him out of the city, **_supposing he had been dead_**. Howbeit, as the disciples stood round about him, he rose up, and came into the city: and the next day he departed with Barnabas to Derbe." (Acts 14:19-20)

- **2 Timothy 4:6-7**

"For I am now ready to be offered, and the time of my departure is at hand. I have fought a good fight, I have finished *my* course, I have kept the faith:"

At this point, Paul's departure to Heaven was at hand. He was ready because the Lord Jesus Christ had saved his soul, and he faithfully served Him.

2 Peter 1:12

"Wherefore I will not be negligent to put you always in remembrance of these things, though ye know them, and be established in the present truth."

BIBLE'S VERBAL, PLENARY PRESERVATION NEEDED
  The Apostle Peter wanted his readers to remember the things he was writing about, though they knew them. This remembrance for you and me is made possible because God has preserved His Hebrew, Aramaic, and Greek Words down to this very day. Unlike most other Bible translations, these preserved Words were the foundation and source of the excellent and accurate King James Bible English translation. This enables genuine Christians not to forget things they once knew.

Verses on Remembrance
- Psalms 6:5

"For in death *there is* no remembrance of thee: in the grave who shall give thee thanks?"

For those who are not genuine Christians, there is no remembrance of the Lord after they have died.

- John 14:26

"But the Comforter, *which is* the Holy Ghost, whom the Father will send in my name, he shall teach you all things, and bring all things to your remembrance, whatsoever I have said unto you."

THE BIBLE'S VERBAL, PLENARY INSPIRATION
  In this verse, the Lord Jesus Christ is speaking about the method that would be used in the inspiration of the books of the New Testament. God the Holy Spirit would preserve and bring to remembrance those things the Lord Jesus Christ had said to them.

- 1 Corinthians 11:24

"And when he had given thanks, he brake *it*, and said, Take, eat: this is my body, which is broken for you: this do in remembrance of me."

THE BIBLICAL VIEW OF THE LORD'S SUPPER
  The Lord's Supper was to be an ordinance for Bible-believing churches to remember the sacrificial death of the Lord Jesus Christ at Calvary until He returns. The Lord's

> Supper is not the transubstantiation of Christ's body and blood as wrongly taught by the mass of the Roman Catholic Church. It is not the consubstantiation of Christ's body and blood as wrongly taught by Lutheran Churches. It is not the impartation of some special grace as wrongly taught by many of the Reformed and Presbyterian Churches. It is only to be practiced by genuine Christians in remembrance of what the Lord Jesus Christ did in His vicarious death on the cross.

- **1 Timothy 4:6**

"If thou put the brethren in remembrance of these things, thou shalt be a good minister of Jesus Christ, nourished up in the words of faith and of good doctrine, whereunto thou hast attained."

Paul told Pastor Timothy to bring the doctrines and teachings of the Bible to remembrance for those to whom he preached.

- **2 Timothy 2:14**

"Of these things put *them* in remembrance, charging *them* before the Lord that they strive not about words to no profit, *but* to the subverting of the hearers."

Pastor Timothy and all true Christian pastors today should put their people in remembrance of the teachings of the Words of God.

- **Jude 1:5**

"I will therefore put you in remembrance, though ye once knew this, how that the Lord, having saved the people out of the land of Egypt, afterward destroyed them that believed not."

> **GOD'S DELIVERANCE OF ISRAEL OUT OF EGYPT**
> Jude wanted his readers (1) to remember God's deliverance of Israel out of Egyptian bondage, as well as, (2) the destruction of the Egyptian armies that sought to return the Jews to bondage.

Verses On Being Established

God wants every genuine Christian to be fully established, strengthened, and made firm in His Words and doctrines.

2 Peter And Jude–Preaching Verse-by-Verse

THE MEANING OF THE GREEK WORD, "STERIZO"
The Greek Word for *"establish"* is STERIZO. Some of the meanings of that Greek Word are:
"1) to make stable, place firmly, set fast, fix; 2) to strengthen, make firm; 3) to render constant, confirm, one's mind"

- **Psalms 40:2**
"He brought me up also out of an horrible pit, out of the miry clay, and set my feet upon a rock, *and* established my goings."

Once the psalmist got right with the Lord, God established his works and ways.

- **Psalms 112:8**
"His heart *is* established, he shall not be afraid, until he see *his desire* upon his enemies."

Once true Christians are saved, their hearts must be established and made firm to serve the Lord Jesus Christ daily.

- **Psalms 119:90**
"Thy faithfulness *is* unto all generations: thou hast established the earth, and it abideth."

GEOCENTRICITY IS CLEARLY TAUGHT IN THE BIBLE
In this verse, we learn that our earth has been established. This verse, along with scores of others argues for geocentricity rather than heliocentricity which is believed by most people today–even genuine Christians. The earth does not move, but it is the center of the universe according to many Bible verses, regardless what our present-day scientists affirm.

- **Proverbs 4:26**
"Ponder the path of thy feet, and let all thy ways be established."

God wants all true Christians to have their ways established in His paths as taught in the Bible.

- **Acts 16:5**
"And so were the churches established in the faith, and increased in number daily."

Churches that are not established in the doctrines of the faith, waver and move from Bible truth. They must not drift from God's Words, but be *"established in the faith."*

- **Romans 1:11**
"For I long to see you, that I may impart unto you some spiritual gift, to the end ye may be established;"

> **TRUE BIBLE TEXTS & TRANSLATIONS NEEDED**
> Paul agrees with Peter and desired his readers from Rome to be established in the doctrines and teachings of the Bible. It would be impossible for genuine Christians to be established in Bible truth if that Bible had not been verbally and plenarily inspired by God, as well as, had been verbally and plenarily preserved by God in the original Hebrew, Aramaic, and Greek Words. For those who speak English, they should follow the King James Bible whose words are based on the proper original, inspired, and preserved Hebrew, Aramaic, and Greek Words. 99% of the other English Bibles (as well as foreign language Bibles) are based on spurious and false Hebrew, Aramaic, and Greek Words. They should not be used by true Christians anywhere in the world.

2 Peter 1:13

"Yea, I think it meet, as long as I am in this tabernacle, to stir you up by putting you in remembrance;"

Peter repeats his desire to put his listeners in "*remembrance*" as long as he was in his earthly tabernacle. The word, "tabernacle" refers to his body.

Verses On The Body As A Tabernacle

- **2 Corinthians 5:1**

"For we know that if our earthly house of *this* tabernacle were dissolved, we have a building of God, an house not made with hands, eternal in the heavens."

Paul likens his body to an "*earthly house*" like a "*tabernacle*" or temporary tent.

- **2 Corinthians 5:4**

"For we that are in *this* tabernacle do groan, being burdened: not for that we would be unclothed, but clothed upon, that mortality might be swallowed up of life."

Paul said that he often groaned in his earthly tabernacle. He wanted to be clothed upon from Heaven with some kind of intermediate body awaiting his glorified body.

Peter wrote that as long as he was here, he was going to "*stir up*" his readers. He wanted to stir them up for the good, not the bad.

Verses On Stir Up
- **Proverbs 15:1**

"A soft answer turneth away wrath: but grievous words stir up anger."

Genuine Christians should not want to use grievous words which would stir up anger.

- **2 Timothy 1:6**

"Wherefore I put thee in remembrance that thou stir up the gift of God, which is in thee by the putting on of my hands."

Paul wanted Pastor Timothy to stir up the special gift that God gave him when Timothy was ordained as a Pastor at Ephesus.

2 Peter 1:14

"Knowing that shortly I must put off this my tabernacle, even as our Lord Jesus Christ hath shewed me."

Peter knew that he would die very soon. He knew it would be his last letter before he went home to be with his Lord Jesus Christ.

THE UNCERTAINTY OF THE DAY OF OUR DEATH

Though most genuine Christians today do not know when the hour of their death will come, Paul and Peter knew that this event was near. Peter was even shown by the Lord Jesus Christ, the way he should die. The verse below explains this.

> *"Verily, verily, I say unto thee, When thou wast young, thou girdedst thyself, and walkedst whither thou wouldest: but when thou shalt be old, thou shalt stretch forth thy hands, and another shall gird thee, and carry thee whither thou wouldest not."* **(John 21:18)**

Tradition recounts that Peter died by crucifixion upside down, with his head toward the ground and his feet in the air. The verse above would seem to indicate a crucifixion.

2 Peter 1:15

"**Moreover I will endeavour that ye may be able after my decease to have these things always in remembrance.**"

> **PETER WANTED HIS WORDS REMEMBERED**
>
> Again, Peter spoke about his death. He wanted the things that he was writing to be remembered by others. This was made possible by God's verbal, plenary preservation of the Bible's original inspired Hebrew, Aramaic, and Greek Words. Because of this, we have Peter's two books available for us today to read, to study, and to follow. You can get our verse-by-verse book on 1 Peter by ordering BFT #2945 @ $12.00+ $7.00 S&H.

- Luke 9:30-31

"And, behold, there talked with him two men, which were Moses and Elias: Who appeared in glory, and spake of his decease which he should accomplish at Jerusalem."

In this verse, Moses and Elias talked about the decease and death of the Lord Jesus Christ and what He would accomplish at Jerusalem.

> **VERBAL, PLENARY PRESERVATION NEEDED**
>
> In Peter's case, he also talked about the death of the Lord Jesus Christ on the cross. Peter wanted, after he died, to have "*these things*" in remembrance. These things are today in remembrance because of God's miraculous verbal, plenary preservation of the original Words of the Bible.

Not everyone believes in the preservation of the Words of the Bible. But I believe the Bible clearly teaches that God has preserved forever the verbal, plenary, inspired, original Words of Hebrew, Aramaic, and Greek.

The Roman Catholic Church doesn't believe that. The modernist-liberal-apostate teachers and ministers don't believe that. The new-evangelical teachers and ministers don't believe that. Even many fundamentalist teachers and ministers don't believe that either.

Bible colleges and seminaries such as Bob Jones University, Calvary Baptist Seminary, Central Baptist Seminary, Pillsbury Baptist Bible College, and many other fundamentalist seminaries have never believed this doctrine.

All these so-called Bible-believing, fundamental schools have denied God's promise to preserve His original verbal, plenary inspired Words of Hebrew, Aramaic, and Greek. Men from these and other fundamental schools believe and teach that there are "*scribal errors*" in God's Hebrew, Aramaic, and Greek Words. They teach that the Words have not been preserved, but only the thoughts, ideas, and concepts have been preserved.

KING JAMES BIBLE FAITHFUL TO PETER'S WORDS

Peter says that he wants his readers to remember his words. I believe that the Hebrew, Aramaic, and Greek Words underlying our King James Bible have been preserved verbally and plenarily, and that the King James Bible is the only accurate translation in the English language of those original, inspired, and inerrant Words.

2 Peter 1:16

"For we have not followed cunningly devised fables, when we made known unto you the power and coming of our Lord Jesus Christ, but were eyewitnesses of his majesty."

THE MEANING OF THE GREEK WORD, "SOPHIZO"

The Greek Word for "*cunningly devised*" is SOPHIZO. Some of the meanings of this Greek Word are:

> "*1) to make wise, teach; 2) to become wise, to have understanding; 2a) to invent, play the sophist; 2b) to devise cleverly or cunningly*"

THE MEANING OF THE GREEK WORD, "MUTHOS"

The Greek Word for "*fables*" is MUTHOS. Some of the meanings of this Greek Word are:

> "*1) a speech, word, saying; 2) a narrative, story; 2a) a true narrative; 2b) a fiction, a fable; 2b1) an invention, a falsehood*"

Sad to say, many people today believe that the Bible is only a myth and a falsehood. The Apocrypha found today in the Roman Catholic Bibles and in other Bibles are fables and myths rather than God's truths. These should be avoided.

Verses On Fables

The word, *"fables,"* is used five times in the New Testament.
- **1 Timothy 1:4**

"Neither give heed to fables and endless genealogies, which minister questions, rather than godly edifying which is in faith: *so do*."

Paul is telling Pastor Timothy not to give any heed or listen to fairy tales and things that are false.
- **1 Timothy 4:7**

"But refuse profane and old wives' fables, and exercise thyself *rather* unto godliness."
- **2 Timothy 4:4**

"And they shall turn away *their* ears from the truth, and shall be turned unto fables."

TURNING AWAY FROM TRUTH LEADS TO LIES

Once a person turns their ears away from the truth of the Bible, they will then turn to fables, falsehoods, and lies.

- **Titus 1:14**

"Not giving heed to Jewish fables, and commandments of men, that turn from the truth."

FABLES TURN PEOPLE AWAY FROM TRUTH

In the days of Titus, there were many Jewish fables made up by men. These fables had the effect of turning people from the truths of the Bible.

The Mount Of Transfiguration

Peter reminded his readers that he, along with James and John, were *"eyewitnesses"* of the *"majesty"* of the Lord Jesus Christ on the Mount of Transfiguration.
- **Mark 9:1-8**

"And he said unto them, Verily I say unto you, That there be some of them that stand here, which shall not taste of death, till they have seen the kingdom of God come with power. And after six days Jesus taketh *with him* Peter, and James, and John, and leadeth them up into an high mountain apart by themselves: and he was transfigured before them. And his raiment became shining, exceeding white as snow; so as no fuller on earth can white them. And there appeared unto them Elias with Moses: and they were talking with Jesus. And Peter answered and said to Jesus, Master, it is good for us to be here: and let us make three tabernacles; one for thee, and one for Moses, and one for

Elias. For he wist not what to say; for they were sore afraid. And there was a cloud that overshadowed them: and a voice came out of the cloud, saying, This is my beloved Son: hear him. And suddenly, when they had looked round about, they saw no man any more, save Jesus only with themselves."

2 Peter 1:17

"For he received from God the Father honour and glory, when there came such a voice to him from the excellent glory, This is my beloved Son, in whom I am well pleased."

Peter recounts the honor and glory that the Lord Jesus Christ received from God the Father on this occasion. The Father was well pleased with His beloved Son.

God The Father's Being Well Pleased With His Son

> "And lo a voice from heaven, saying, This is my beloved Son, **in whom I am well pleased**." (Matthew 3:17)

> "While he yet spake, behold, a bright cloud overshadowed them: and behold a voice out of the cloud, which said, This is my beloved Son, **in whom I am well pleased**; hear ye him." (Matthew 17:5)

> "And there came a voice from heaven, saying, Thou art my beloved Son, **in whom I am well pleased**." (Mark 1:11)
>
> "And the Holy Ghost descended in a bodily shape like a dove upon him, and a voice came from heaven, which said, Thou art my beloved Son; **in thee I am well pleased**." (Luke 3:22)

GOD THE FATHER IS WELL-PLEASED WITH HIS SON

Everything about the Lord Jesus Christ pleased God the Father. It was of such importance that it was repeated twice in Matthew's Gospel and once each in the Gospel of Mark and the Gospel of Luke.

2 Peter 1:18

"**And this voice which came from heaven we heard, when we were with him in the holy mount.**"

Peter is referring once again to his being with James and John on the Mount of Transfiguration. They were all eyewitnesses of the glory of the Lord Jesus Christ. They heard God the Father's direct Words. Today, genuine Christians can hear His voice in the written Words of God. In English, be sure to read from the King James Bible which is an accurate translation from the proper, original, inspired, inerrant, and preserved Hebrew, Aramaic, and Greek Words.

2 Peter 1:19

"**We have also a more sure word of prophecy; whereunto ye do well that ye take heed, as unto a light that shineth in a dark place, until the day dawn, and the day star arise in your hearts:**"

ALL PROPHECY HAS BEEN PRESERVED BY GOD

Peter stated that "*we have.*" This is in the Greek present tense which means that even in Peter's day, they continued to have this sure and certain word of prophecy of both the Old and the New Testaments. Peter believed, as I do, in both the verbal, plenary inspiration of the Old and New Testaments, but also the verbal, plenary preservation of those Hebrew, Aramaic, and Greek Words. What he said about the Old Testament is true also in the New Testament.

Not only did Peter want true Christians to possess the Words of God, but he also wanted his readers (including us today) to take heed, follow, and obey these Words of God.

THE BIBLE SHINES AS A LIGHT IN DARK PLACES

His analogy of light shining in a dark place is also powerful. The Scriptures of both the Old and the New Testaments are like a light shining in dark places of the heart as well as dark places in the world all around us. The Words of the Bible will continue to shine and be preserved "*until the day dawn, and the day star arise in your hearts.*" God's Words will continue to shine until the heavens are opened and all genuine Christians go to their Heavenly Home.

2 Peter 1:20

"Knowing this first, that no prophecy of the scripture is of any private interpretation."

"*No prophecy of the scripture*" refers to that which has been written down in the original Hebrew, Aramaic and Greek Words, is of any "*private interpretation.*"

> **THE MEANING OF THE GREEK WORD, "IDIOS"**
>
> The Greek Word for "*private*" is IDIOS. Some of the meanings of "IDIOS" are:
>
> "*1) pertaining to one's self, one's own, belonging to one's self*"
>
> Whenever genuine Christians read their Bibles, they cannot take a particular verse or verses and interpret in isolation or in private. They must be interpreted in the light of the teachings of the entire Bible.

An illustration of the need for this comes to my mind. A pastor years ago was against women putting their hair in a knot on top of their heads. To prove he was right, he quoted the following verse:

"*Let him which is on the house **top not come down** to take any thing out of his house:*" (Matthew 24:17)

This is a humorous example of someone trying to make a "private" interpretation of the Bible which is not borne out in the entirety of the Words of God. In fact, it doesn't even make sense within the verse itself.

2 Peter 1:21

"For the prophecy came not in old time by the will of man: but holy men of God spake as they were moved by the Holy Ghost."

> **THE ORIGINATION OF THE BIBLE'S WORDS**
>
> The Scriptures were given by God the Holy Spirit and not by the will of men. The writers were called "*holy men of God.*" The method that God used to give us the Books of the Bible was by the writers being "*moved*" or directed by the Holy Spirit. In verse 19 above, concerning this "*prophecy,*" Peter says that "*we have*" it. This is the Greek present tense which means a continuation of possession. This speaks of the verbal plenary preservation of the Bible.

Verses On Bible Preservation

There are several other verses that speak clearly of God's promise to preserve His original Hebrew, Aramaic, and Greek Words.

- **Psalms 12:6-7**

"The words of the LORD *are* pure words: *as* silver tried in a furnace of earth, purified seven times. Thou shalt keep them, O LORD, thou shalt preserve them from this generation for ever."

These verses clearly teach that God's Words will be both kept and preserved by the Lord from David's generation, and forevermore in all generations—including ours.

BIBLE'S VERBAL, PLENARY PRESERVATION DENIED

It is sad that many of our otherwise "Fundamentalist" brethren reject the preservation of the original, inspired Hebrew, Aramaic, and Greek Words of the Bible. Teachers from Bob Jones University (and from many other schools) who are otherwise Fundamental in their doctrines, are heretical in this important Bible doctrine.

- **Matthew 5:17-18**

"Think not that I am come to destroy the law, or the prophets: I am not come to destroy, but to fulfil. For verily I say unto you, Till heaven and earth pass, one jot or one tittle shall in no wise pass from the law, till all be fulfilled."

VERBAL, PLENARY PRESERVATION TAUGHT HERE

These verses also teach the verbal, plenary preservation of every part of the Hebrew, Aramaic, and Greek Words. The law, the prophets, or any other part of the Old Testament will not pass, even to the extent of *"one jot or one tittle."* The *"jot"* is the Hebrew Word YODH which is like our comma. It is the smallest Hebrew letter. The *"tittle"* has been interpreted as one of the accents in the Hebrew language. It is similar to our "period." This being so, the Lord Jesus Christ extends the verbal, plenary preservation of the Old Testament (and, by extension, to the New Testament).

Though true Christians in our age of grace are not under any part of the law or the prophets, these parts of the Old Testament will not pass away from the Bible. Nothing will *"pass"* away *"Till heaven and earth pass."*

BIBLE'S ORIGINAL WORDS WILL NEVER PASS AWAY
It is important to note that the Greek Words behind the English words "*in no wise*" are OU ME. This Greek negative expression is the strongest negative in the entire Greek language. It means "*never, never, never.*"

It is very sad, to me, that teachers in the past at Bob Jones University, Calvary Baptist Theological Seminary, Central Baptist Theological Seminary, Pillsbury Baptist Bible College, and other so-called "Fundamental" schools have taken a heretical position on this particular and clear Biblical doctrine of the verbal, plenary preservation of the inspired and inerrant Hebrew, Aramaic, and Greek Words of the Bible.

- Matthew 24:35

"Heaven and earth shall pass away, but my words shall not pass away."

Once again, the Greek words for "*not*" are OU ME. As I mentioned before, this is the strongest negative in the Greek language. It means never, never, never. Though heaven and earth will pass away, the Lord Jesus Christ said that "*my words shall not pass away.*"

What did He mean by "*my words*"? Notice what the Lord Jesus Christ told His apostles:

> "I have yet many things to say unto you, but ye cannot bear them now. Howbeit when he, the Spirit of truth, is come, he will guide you into all truth: for *he shall not speak of himself*; but whatsoever he shall hear, that shall he speak: and he will shew you things to come. He shall glorify me: for *he shall receive of mine, and shall shew it unto you*. All things that the Father hath are mine: therefore said I, that *he shall take of mine, and shall shew it unto you*." (John 16:12-15)

THE METHOD OF THE BIBLE'S ORIGINATION
Here are a few things that should be noted from these verses which speak of the coming and inspiration of the New Testament [and by extension, what happened in the composition of the Old Testament as well, since the Lord Jesus Christ is the LOGOS ("*The Revelator*")]:

1. The Holy Spirit would not speak "*of*" or from Himself as to the source of the Words.
2. The Holy Spirit would receive the Words from the

Lord Jesus Christ and would show them unto the human writers.

3. In other words, the Lord Jesus Christ conveyed to the Holy Spirit His Words; then, the Holy Spirit conveyed Christ's Words to the "*holy men of God*" whom God used to write down those Words.

4. These Words of the Lord Jesus Christ will <u>never, never, never</u> pass away. This teaches clearly the verbal, plenary preservation of the Hebrew, Aramaic, and Greek Words given by the Lord Jesus Christ Himself.

- 1 Peter 1:24-25

"For all flesh *is* as grass, and all the glory of man as the flower of grass. The grass withereth, and the flower thereof falleth away: But the word of the Lord endureth for ever. And this is the word which by the gospel is preached unto you."

<u>In this verse, we are told that "*the Word of the Lord endureth for ever.*" This means the verbal plenary preservation of every one of the original verbal plenary inspired Hebrew, Aramaic, and Greek Words.</u>

THE KING JAMES BIBLE ACCURATELY TRANSLATES THE ORIGINAL HEBREW, ARAMAIC, & GREEK WORDS

The King James Bible is the only accurate English translation of those preserved Words. If we don't have God's Words preserved in the Hebrew, Aramaic, and Greek, and properly translated into the language of the people, how can the "*gospel*" be preached clearly and accurately? <u>Bible preservation is of the utmost importance for accurate, faithful, and true gospel preaching.</u>

2 Peter Chapter Two

2 Peter 2:1

"But there were false prophets also among the people, even as there shall be false teachers among you, who privily shall bring in damnable heresies, even denying the Lord that bought them, and bring upon themselves swift destruction."

FALSE TEACHERS HAVE BEEN PREDICTED

Not only were there false prophets in the Old Testament, but Peter predicted there would be false teachers in his day. These false teachers would bring in damnable heresies. This would include their denial of the Lord Jesus Christ whose death on Calvary *"bought them,"* though they did not receive nor accept Him as their Saviour. Swift destruction would be their punishment.

SPECIFIC HERESIES ABOUND TODAY WORLDWIDE

False prophets and false teachers were not reserved either to the Old Testament, or to the days of the Apostle Peter. Their heresies abound all around the world in our day as well. The Lord Jesus Christ is denied by the modernist liberals and other cults. They don't believe in His virgin birth, His deity, His bodily resurrection, the Biblical purpose of His death on the cross of Calvary, and many other parts of Bible Christology.

Not only are there theological modernists, liberals, and apostates who have forsaken the very fundamental doctrines of the Christian faith, but there are others who have compromised many of those same doctrines. There are not only apostate false teachers today, but there are groups who have some Biblical truths, yet have many other false doctrines. These false teachers will privately bring in damnable heresies which include denying the Lord Jesus Christ who bought them in His death on the cross.

> ### UNLIMITED ATONEMENT IS CLEARLY TAUGHT
> Notice the words in 2 Peter 2:1, *"denying the Lord that bought them."* This does not teach the universal salvation of everyone in the world, but it teaches the doctrine of unlimited atonement of the Lord Jesus Christ. He died for everyone in the world and bought them by the shedding of His blood on the cross. But this does not make them redeemed or saved. <u>They must each genuinely trust from their heart the Lord Jesus Christ as their Saviour Who died for them as John 3:16 clearly tells us:</u>
>> *"For God so loved the world, that he gave his only begotten Son, that <u>whosoever</u> believeth in him should not perish, but have everlasting life."*

Verses On False Prophets In The New Testament
- **Matthew 7:15**

"Beware of false prophets, which come to you in sheep's clothing, but inwardly they are ravening wolves."

<u>These false prophets deceive by appearing outwardly as sheep, but what they are inwardly is ravening wolves.</u> A *"ravening"* wolf is searching for prey, looking for an animal to kill and eat, leaving no survivors.

- **Matthew 24:11**

"And many false prophets shall rise, and shall deceive many."

<u>Their method is deception which deceives many.</u>

- **Matthew 24:24**

"For there shall arise false Christs, and false prophets, and shall shew great signs and wonders; insomuch that, if *it were* possible, they shall deceive the very elect."

<u>The signs and wonders used by these false prophets will deceive almost everyone on earth, but not those who are true believers.</u>

- **Luke 6:26**

"Woe unto you, when all men shall speak well of you! for so did their fathers to the false prophets."

<u>Be careful when everyone agrees with you.</u> This was true of the false prophets of the Old Testament.

2 Peter And Jude–Preaching Verse-by-Verse

- **Acts 13:6**
"And when they had gone through the isle unto Paphos, they found a certain sorcerer, a false prophet, a Jew, whose name *was* Barjesus:"

Paul found a false prophet, Barjesus, even on a lonely island.

- **1 John 4:1**
"Beloved, believe not every spirit, but try the spirits whether they are of God: because many false prophets are gone out into the world."

Every true Christian should test out and examine those who speak or write about spiritual things. Many of these speakers or writers are false prophets who should be rejected.

- **Revelation 16:13**
"And I saw three unclean spirits like frogs *come* out of the mouth of the dragon, and out of the mouth of the beast, and out of the mouth of the false prophet."

THE SATANIC TRINITY IS NAMED
Here is the satanic trinity:
  (1) the dragon,
  (2) the beast, and
  (3) the false prophet.

All three will be extremely active during the seven-year Tribulation.

- **Revelation 19:20**
"And the beast was taken, and with him the false prophet that wrought miracles before him, with which he deceived them that had received the mark of the beast, and them that worshipped his image. These both were cast alive into a lake of fire burning with brimstone."

THE BEAST AND FALSE PROPHET CAST INTO HELL
Both the satanic beast and his false prophet will be cast alive into Hell which is the Lake of Fire burning with fire and brimstone.

Verses On Heresies

- **Acts 24:14**
"But this I confess unto thee, that after the way which they call heresy, so worship I the God of my fathers, believing all things which are written in the law and in the prophets:"

> **PAUL & OTHERS FALSELY ACCUSED OF HERESY**
>
> Paul and other genuine Christians were accused of *"heresy"* (holding of certain views in this case, Paul held to true and unusual views) because the Christian faith was contrary to either Judaism or paganism.

- **1 Corinthians 11:19**
  "For there must be also heresies among you, that they which are approved may be made manifest among you."

> **THE MEANING OF THE GREEK WORD FOR "HERESY"**
>
> The meaning of the Greek Word for *"heresy"* is *"a holding of some position."* What is taught in this verse is that false "holdings" or "heresies" will appear so that it will be clear that those who hold to the truth of the Bible may be clearly manifested for all to see. The differences will be clear to those who are carefully listening. Some heretics are quiet and some are more outspoken. The outspoken ones show clearly that they are against the truth.

- **Galatians 5:19-21**
  "Now the works of the flesh are manifest, which are these; Adultery, fornication, uncleanness, lasciviousness, Idolatry, witchcraft, hatred, variance, emulations, wrath, strife, seditions, **heresies**, Envyings, murders, drunkenness, revellings, and such like: of the which I tell you before, as I have also told *you* in time past, that they which do such things shall not inherit the kingdom of God."

One category of the works of the flesh are *"heresies"* or false teachings.

Verses On Being Bought

- **1 Corinthians 6:20**
  "For ye are bought with a price: therefore glorify God in your body, and in your spirit, which are God's."

This verse is speaking of how the Lord Jesus Christ bought true Christians at Corinth out of the Devil's slave market of sin. The price of that purchase was the shedding of His blood on the cross. They believed in this Saviour with their hearts and minds and were made genuine Christians by that faith.

- **1 Corinthians 7:23**
  "Ye are bought with a price; be not ye the servants of men."

This is another verse referring to the price of salvation that was paid by the Lord Jesus Christ on the cross.

To sum up, Peter reminded his readers of the false teachers of both the Old and the New Testaments who denied God's truths. They were also bringing in damnable heresies.

Notice **how** these false teachers were bringing in their heresies. It was "*privily*" or secretly. It was also true that heresies didn't come all of a sudden–they don't come in immediately.

Heresy is what happened in the past and what is happening in our day in seminaries and colleges all around the world. Princeton Seminary, for example, started with light; now it's dark. Temple University, located close by in Philadelphia, as well as many, many other institutions began with much Bible truth. They **gradually** abandoned that beginning truth and substituted truth with all kinds of errors.

2 Peter 2:2

"And many shall follow their pernicious ways; by reason of whom the way of truth shall be evil spoken of."

This verse is a comment on the result of the false prophets and false teachers of Peter's day. He calls these false doctrines "*pernicious ways*."

THE MEANING OF THE GREEK WORD, "APOLEIA"

The Greek Word for "*pernicious*" is APOLEIA. Some of the meanings of this Greek Word are:

"*1) destroying, utter destruction; 1a) of vessels; 2) a perishing, ruin, destruction; 2a) of money; 2b) the destruction which consists of eternal misery in hell.*"

PERNICIOUS WAYS ABOUND IN OUR DAY AS WELL

Such "*pernicious ways*" had a huge following in Peter's day and have an even greater following in our day. Heresies against the Words of God abound around the world. Because of the prominence of such satanic heresies, the true doctrines and teachings of Biblical truth are laughed at, belittled, and scorned.

- Matthew 7:13

"Enter ye in at the strait gate: for wide *is* the gate, and broad *is* the way, that leadeth to destruction, and many there be which go in thereat:"

> **APOSTATE DOCTRINES IN ALL KINDS OF CHURCHES**
> The Lord Jesus Christ predicted that there would be many who would leave His straight gate of truth and Bible doctrines and enter into the destruction of Hell. *"Many"* false teachers are found in the Roman Catholic Church and apostate elements in Protestant groups including Methodists, Baptists, Lutherans, Presbyterians, Congregationalists and many others.

2 Peter 2:3

"And through covetousness shall they with feigned words make merchandise of you: whose judgment now of a long time lingereth not, and their damnation slumbereth not."

Those pastors, teachers, and individuals who have rejected the clear teachings and doctrines of the Words of God have been influenced by these false teachers and false prophets. Notice three things about false teachers in this verse:
> (1) their covetousness
> (2) their feigned words
> (3) their damnation

1. The Covetousness Of False Teachers. These false teachers were filled with covetousness in their manner.

Verses On Covetousness

> **THE MEANING OF THE GREEK WORD, "PLEONEXIA"**
> The Greek Word for *"covetousness"* is PLEONEXIA. Some of the meanings of this Greek Word are:
> > *"1) greedy desire to have more, covetousness, avarice"*

Here are some of the verses that explain the sin of covetousness:
- **Exodus 18:21**

"Moreover thou shalt provide out of all the people able men, such as fear God, men of truth, hating covetousness; and place *such* over them, *to be* rulers of thousands, *and* rulers of hundreds, rulers of fifties, and rulers of tens:"

This was the counsel to Moses from Jethro, his father-in-law. Though I can't assess the reliability of Jethro generally, in this instance he gave Moses some good advice. The helpers of Moses were to, especially, fear God, love truth, and hate covetousness.

- Habakkuk 2:9

"Woe to him that coveteth an evil covetousness to his house, that he may set his nest on high, that he may be delivered from the power of evil!"

> **WOE TO THOSE WHO PRACTICE COVETOUSNESS**
> The prophet Habakkuk pronounced a woe upon those who coveted an evil covetousness. They should have a good conscience, rather than one that is evil and wicked.

2. The Feigned Words Of False Teachers.
The words used by these false teachers were not true words, but feigned words.

> **THE MEANING OF THE GREEK WORD, "PLASTOS"**
> The Greek Word for "*feigned*" is PLASTOS. Some of the meanings of this Word are:
> "*1) moulded, formed, as from clay, wax, or stone; 2) feigned*"

We get our English word, "*plastic*" from this word. The words of these false teachers are like plastic, wax, or clay. They do not stand up, but can be twisted and changed at will. They are undependable words that cannot be trusted by anyone. They are not true and stable, but false and unstable.

3. The Damnation Of False Teachers. The end of these false teachers will be judgment by God which will end up in their well-deserved damnation.

2 Peter 2:4

"**For if God spared not the angels that sinned, but cast them down to hell, and delivered them into chains of darkness, to be reserved unto judgment;**"

Here are the first of three judgments by God mentioned in the next three verses (4-6):
- (1) the judgment of angels that sinned
- (2) the judgment of the old world
- (3) the judgment of Sodom and Gomorrha

1. The Judgment Of Angels That Sinned. God did not spare the angels that sinned, but cast them to Hell in chains of darkness to face final judgment.

Verses On Sinning Angels
- **Genesis 6:2**

"That the sons of God saw the daughters of men that they *were* fair; and they took them wives of all which they chose."

I believe that term, "*sons of God*" as used in the Old Testament refers to angels. I do not believe that the "*sons of God*" in Genesis 6 refer to the sons of Shem as some wrongly teach. <u>These fallen angelic beings took the form of men and sinned by marrying wives of the daughters of men.</u> From this union, a horrible race of monsters were made.

- **Genesis 6:4**

"There were giants in the earth in those days; and also after that, when the sons of God came in unto the daughters of men, and they bare *children* to them, the same *became* mighty men which *were* of old, men of renown."

The children of this wicked union were called "*giants*." The Hebrew Word for "***giants***" is NEPHALIM, which means "*fallen ones*." This is an apt description of these inhuman man-like beings whose existence was one of the reasons God destroyed the world with a flood.

God wiped out the whole world, lest this perverse mixture of Satanic giants, demons, and angels would cover the whole earth making impossible the birth of the Messiah and Saviour as a true human being <u>unmixed with these fallen ones</u>. God spared only eight people, Noah, his wife, their three sons, Shem, Ham, and Japheth and their three wives.

Some of the verses in Job show that the "*sons of God*" were angelic beings.

- **Job 1:6**

"Now there was a day when the sons of God came to present themselves before the LORD, and Satan came also among them."

<u>These "*sons of God*" were angels, including Satan, who were able to present themselves before the LORD.</u>

- **Job 2:1**

"Again there was a day when the sons of God came to present themselves before the LORD, and Satan came also among them to present himself before the LORD."

<u>Here is a second verse that identifies the "*sons of God*" as angels.</u>

2 Peter And Jude–Preaching Verse-by-Verse

- Job 38:7
"When the morning stars sang together, and all the sons of God shouted for joy?"

> **O.T. "SONS OF GOD" WERE ANGELS**
> Here is a third verse that identifies the *"sons of God"* as angels observing as God created the universe. Because of these three clear references in Job to the *"sons of God"* as angels, I believe the *"sons of God"* in Genesis 6 were also angels, though, in this case, fallen angels.

- Matthew 25:41
"Then shall he say also unto them on the left hand, Depart from me, ye cursed, into everlasting fire, prepared for the devil and his angels:"

> **THE DESTINY OF THE DEVIL–EVERLASTING HELL**
> The Lord Jesus Christ revealed the destiny of both the Devil and his evil angels. It is the everlasting fire of Hell. Those who do not genuinely receive the Lord Jesus Christ as their Saviour go to the Devil's place of everlasting fire also.

- 1 Corinthians 11:10
"For this cause ought the woman to have power on *her* head because of the angels."

Women were to have "*power*" on their heads. In verse 15 of this same chapter, her long hair is given to her as a "*covering*." Perhaps this is her "*power*" that would deliver her from the attack of the evil angels such as attacked women in Genesis Chapter six.

> "But ***if a woman have long hair***, *it is a glory to her: for **her hair is given her for a covering**.*" (1 Corinthians 11:15)

Though it's not clear, perhaps this long hair which is given to her as her "*covering*" is the "*power*" on her head.

- Jude 1:6
"And the angels which kept not their first estate, but left their own habitation, he hath reserved in everlasting chains under darkness unto the judgment of the great day."

This verse also makes me think of evil angels of Genesis six—which kept not their first estate, but came down to the earth, made themselves look like men, and then married women who brought forth "*giants*" or "*fallen ones*."

- 1 Corinthians 6:3
  "Know ye not that we shall judge angels? how much more things that pertain to this life?"

This verse indicates that genuine Christians will one day judge evil angels at a time and place and in the manner of God's choosing.

2 Peter 2:5

"And spared not the old world, but saved Noah the eighth person, a preacher of righteousness, bringing in the flood upon the world of the ungodly;"

NOAH WAS A PREACHER OF RIGHTEOUSNESS

God did not spare the angels that sinned. This verse tells us that God did not spare the old world of Noah's day. Noah was a preacher of righteousness who obeyed the Lord in whatever God told him to do. He found grace in the eyes of the Lord.

2. **The Judgment Of The Old World**.

GOD'S JUDGMENT OF THE UNIVERSAL FLOOD

This is the second judgment that Peter brings up in his letter. It is the judgment of the entire old world that ended up in the universal flood in Noah's day. God spared only eight people from that tragedy: Noah and his wife; Shem and his wife; Ham and his wife; and Japheth and his wife. Noah made an ark according to God's specifications, and God used that ark to save these eight people and the male and female pairs of all the species of insects, birds, and other animals. The judgment of the universal flood came because of the sins and debauchery of the people on the earth.

Verses On The Judgment Of The Flood
- Genesis 6:5
  "And GOD saw that the wickedness of man *was* great in the earth, and *that* every imagination of the thoughts of his heart *was* only evil continually."

THE PRE-FLOOD WORLD WAS CONTINUALLY EVIL

This is God's assessment of man's condition before the flood. It was great wickedness. It included not only external sins, but also the imaginations and thoughts of their hearts. It was a continual evil without cessation. The

wickedness was probably due, in large measure, because of this intermarriage of satanic spirits, demons, and angels with women.

- **Genesis 6:7-8**
"And the LORD said, I will destroy man whom I have created from the face of the earth; both man, and beast, and the creeping thing, and the fowls of the air; for it repenteth me that I have made them. But Noah found grace in the eyes of the LORD."

ONLY NOAH FOUND GRACE IN GOD'S EYES
God made it clear that he was going to destroy man whom He had created as well as beasts, creeping things, and the fowls of the air. <u>Just one man found grace in God's eyes</u>. His name was Noah. What a privilege and what a blessing!

- **Genesis 6:17**
"And, behold, I, even I, do bring a flood of waters upon the earth, to destroy all flesh, wherein *is* the breath of life, from under heaven; *and* every thing that *is* in the earth shall die."

This verse teaches, not a local flood, but a universal flood. It was a destruction of *"all flesh."* God promised that *"<u>everything that is in the earth shall die</u>."* Some Bible-believing Christians teach that Noah's flood was just a local flood. This is an error. From these and other verses, it is clear that this flood was a universal flood that covered the whole earth.

- **Genesis 7:21**
"And all flesh died that moved upon the earth, both of fowl, and of cattle, and of beast, and of every creeping thing that creepeth upon the earth, and every man:"

This is another clear verse showing this was a universal flood. Death came to *"all flesh"* including fowls, cattle, beasts, and every creeping thing as well as every man. I don't know how God could have said it any clearer.

Matthew 24:37-39
"But as the days of Noe *were*, so shall also the coming of the Son of man be. For as in the days that were before the flood they were eating and drinking, marrying and giving in marriage, until the day that Noe entered into the ark, And knew not until the flood came, and took them all away; so shall also the coming of the Son of man be."

BEFORE CHRIST'S RETURN–VERY GREAT EVIL

The Lord Jesus Christ taught his followers that the days before His return will be just like the days before Noah's flood. In that day, life carried on as usual, but ended with the sudden and unexpected coming of this universal flood of waters. The flood was sudden. They did not know it was coming, but when it did, it "*took them all away*." That signifies a universal flood very clearly.

- Luke 17:26-27

"And as it was in the days of Noe, so shall it be also in the days of the Son of man. They did eat, they drank, they married wives, they were given in marriage, until the day that Noe entered into the ark, and the flood came, and destroyed them all."

NOAH'S FLOOD WAS NOT LOCAL, BUT UNIVERSAL

This is similar to the verses in Matthew. When the flood came, it "*destroyed them all*." It was indeed a universal flood, despite what some pastors and teachers teach today.

2 Peter 2:6

"And turning the cities of Sodom and Gomorrha into ashes condemned them with an overthrow, making them an ensample unto those that after should live ungodly;"

[The Old Testament spelling of Gomorrah differs from that of the New Testament.]

3. **The Judgment Of Sodom And Gomorrah.**

GOD'S JUDGMENT AGAINST HOMOSEXUAL SODOMY

Here is the third example of God's just judgment. The first example was against the angels that sinned; the second example was against the people in the wicked world in Noah's day who sinned; this third example is against the people in the cities of Sodom and Gomorrah who sinned.

Verses On The Destruction Of Sodom And Gomorrah

- **Genesis 13:10**

"And Lot lifted up his eyes, and beheld all the plain of Jordan, that it *was* well watered every where, before the LORD

destroyed Sodom and Gomorrah, *even* as the garden of the LORD, like the land of Egypt, as thou comest unto Zoar." Abraham told Lot, his nephew, that he could choose whatever land he wanted for his cattle. Lot chose to go into the land of Sodom.
- **Genesis 13:13**
"But the men of Sodom *were* wicked and sinners before the LORD exceedingly."

It was clear that the men of Sodom were exceedingly wicked in the eyes of the LORD. May genuine Christians not choose to go to wicked places where wicked people are in charge.
- **Genesis 18:20**
"And the LORD said, Because the cry of Sodom and Gomorrah is great, and because their sin is very grievous;"

The sin of Sodom and Gomorrah was very grievous. It reached the ears of the LORD.
- **Genesis 19:24-25**
"Then the LORD rained upon Sodom and upon Gomorrah brimstone and fire from the LORD out of heaven; And he overthrew those cities, and all the plain, and all the inhabitants of the cities, and that which grew upon the ground."

> **GOD'S FIRE POURED OUT ON THE SODOMITES**
> **Because of the grievous and exceeding sinfulness of the inhabitants of Sodom and Gomorrah, the LORD rained brimstone and fire upon them in judgment.**

- **Genesis 19:28**
"And he looked toward Sodom and Gomorrah, and toward all the land of the plain, and beheld, and, lo, the smoke of the country went up as the smoke of a furnace."

The smoke of those cities rose up like the smoke of a furnace.
- **Genesis 19:30-32**
"And Lot went up out of Zoar, and dwelt in the mountain, and his two daughters with him; for he feared to dwell in Zoar: and he dwelt in a cave, he and his two daughters. And the firstborn said unto the younger, Our father *is* old, and *there is* not a man in the earth to come in unto us after the manner of all the earth: Come, let us make our father drink wine, and we will lie with him, that we may preserve seed of our father."

> **PERVERTED LOT WAS ALLOWED TO FLEE SODOM**
> **Lot was free to go out of Sodom. He was the nephew of Abraham. I assume that he had proper training in the past but, sadly, committed incest with his own two daughters.**

> They were both with child by their father. It was a perversion that he no doubt learned in the wicked city of Sodom.

- Luke 17:29

"But the same day that Lot went out of Sodom it rained fire and brimstone from heaven, and destroyed *them* all."

> **BY LOOKING BACK, LOT'S WIFE WAS DESTROYED**
>
> The Lord Jesus Christ described the judgment of Sodom. It happened the same day that Lot left the city. God sent fire and brimstone from heaven on Sodom, and on all the people; only Lot and his two daughters were spared. Lot's wife was also destroyed when she looked back in violation of God's orders.

The self-confessed lesbian, Virginia Ramey Mollenkott, wrote a book in which she lied about the wickedness and sins of Sodom and Gomorrah. She denied that Sodom was the headquarters of the sin of sodomy, lesbianism, and homosexuality based on a misinterpretation of verses in Ezekiel 16 (which uses the word, "Sodom" as a reference) to some of the nations around Jerusalem in Ezekiel's day. It is not a reference to the historical Sodom mentioned in Genesis. From what is mentioned in this reference in Ezekiel, <u>Mollenkott believed that those in Sodom were not homosexual sodomites and lesbians (like Mollenkott is), but were only uncharitable people.</u>

> **LESBIAN MOLLENKOTT'S FALSE VIEW OF SODOM**
>
> Mollenkott refuses to believe there was any sodomy and homosexuality in Sodom, only that they were uncharitable. How does Mollenkott explain the following verses from Genesis 19? The men of Sodom were homosexual sodomites without any question! *"And there came two angels to Sodom at even; and Lot sat in the gate of Sodom: and Lot seeing them rose up to meet them; and he bowed himself with his face toward the ground; And he said, Behold now, my lords, turn in, I pray you, into your servant's house, and tarry all night, and wash your feet, and ye shall rise up early, and go on your ways. And they said, Nay; but we will abide in the street all night. And he pressed upon them greatly; and they turned in unto him, and entered into his house; and he made them a feast, and did bake unleavened bread, and they did eat. But before*

> they lay down, the men of the city, even the men of Sodom, compassed the house round, both old and young, all the people from every quarter: And they called unto Lot, and said unto him, Where are the men which came in to thee this night? bring them out unto us, that we may know them. And Lot went out at the door unto them, and shut the door after him, And said, I pray you, brethren, do not so wickedly." (Genesis 19:1-7)

It was for the sin of homosexual sodomy that God destroyed Sodom and Gomorrah.

WHEN WILL GOD JUDGE PRO-SODOMITE AMERICA?

My question is this: At what point will God look at the United States of America and the rest of the world, where homosexualism and sodomy is not only freely practiced, but exalted, and judge them as He judged Sodom and Gomorrah? I don't know the answer to this question, but history might repeat itself in this matter.

Our current president, Obama, is not only favorable to homosexuals and homosexuality, but has pushed for homosexual marriages between two men and between two women. After the Rapture of true Christians before the Tribulation period, God will bring many kinds of judgments on the whole world as outlined in the book of Revelation.

In a recent Fox News program, they showed quotations from current textbooks used in our schools where sodomy and lesbianism are being pushed on our school children. I'm glad I am no longer a teacher in the School District of Philadelphia as I was for 19 years. I would not be able to stand by and let my students be taught that these sins are all right to practice.

2 Peter 2:7

"And delivered just Lot, vexed with the filthy conversation of the wicked:"

GOD CALLED LOT "JUST" THOUGH VERY SINFUL

Lot was delivered from God's righteous judgment on the cities of Sodom and Gomorrah. That was gracious of the Lord. God, through the Apostle Peter, called Lot *"just."* If it had not been written in the Bible, I would not have believed it because of all the unjust deeds Lot did when in Sodom and after leaving Sodom. God alone knows what's

> in the hearts of people, including Lot. Remember Lot's wicked and sinful suggestion that the sodomites, who wanted to have sexual relations with the angels who came to his door, could have sex with his own daughters.

- **Genesis 19:6-8**

"And Lot went out at the door unto them, and shut the door after him, And said, I pray you, brethren, do not so wickedly. Behold now, <u>**I have two daughters which have not known man; let me, I pray you, bring them out unto you, and do ye to them as** *is* **good in your eyes**</u>: only unto these men do nothing; for therefore came they under the shadow of my roof."

Though God calls him a *"just"* man, these actions of Lot in this instance are extremely unjust. <u>What kind of a father is this that would give his two daughters to these homosexual men</u>? He was a wicked, corrupt, and sinful father!

> **THE MEANING OF THE GREEK WORD, " KATAPONEO"**
>
> Lot was *"vexed with the filthy conversation of the wicked."* The Greek Word for *"vexed"* is KATAPONEO. Some of the meanings of this Greek Word are:
>
> > *"1) to tire down with toil, exhaust with labour; 1a) to afflict or oppress with evils; 1b) to make trouble for; 1c) to treat roughly."*
>
> Lot was adversely affected by the manner of living that he endured while in Sodom.

> **THE MEANING OF THE GREEK WORD, "ASELGEIA"**
>
> The Greek Word for *"filthy"* is ASELGEIA. Some of the meanings of this Word are:
>
> > *"1) unbridled lust, excess, licentiousness, lasciviousness, wantonness, outrageousness, shamelessness, insolence."*
>
> This word identifies the immorality, lasciviousness, and lust that prevailed in Sodom. All of this environment had an adverse influence upon Lot. He was not only *"in"* Sodom, but also, he was *"of"* Sodom. He partook of Sodom's sinful lifestyle.

2 Peter 2:8

"(For that righteous man dwelling among them, in seeing and hearing, vexed his righteous soul from day to day with their unlawful deeds;)"

Once again, God's Word not only called Lot *"just"* (2 Peter 2:7) but also *"righteous"* here in 2 Peter 2:8. Because this righteous and just man was dwelling among the wicked sinners in Sodom, by seeing their evil actions and hearing their evil words, he *"vexed"* his righteous soul.

THE MEANING OF THE GREEK WORD, "BASANIZO"

The Greek Word for *"vexed"* here is different from the Word used in verse 7. The Greek Word here is BASANIZO. Some of the meanings of that Word are:

"1) to test (metals) by the touchstone, which is a black siliceous stone used to test the purity of gold or silver by the colour of the streak produced on it by rubbing it with either metal; 2) to question by applying torture; 3) to torture; 4) to vex with grievous pains (of body or mind), to torment; 5) to be harassed, distressed; 5a) of those who at sea are struggling with a head wind."

You can see clearly that this Greek Word is very, very strong–much stronger than the Word used in verse 7 above. Lot's soul was tortured with grievous and tormenting pains as he lived among those evil profligates of Sodom and watched their wicked deeds which were contrary to God's standards. God again, calls him here, a righteous man. He doesn't seem too righteous with the way he is living. God only knows his heart.

Even in our world today, genuine Christians are *"vexed"* (though not necessarily tortured) by seeing and hearing what comes in on the radio, television, and Internet, as well as in books and magazines. The sins of the world are all around them. They must purpose to be separate from evil influences.

Lot apparently learned how to drink wine, be a drunkard, and be sexually immoral. That's how his two daughters were able to make him drunk and urge him to commit sexual incest with them,

giving them both children by him. Genuine Christians today must be very, very careful about their associations and companions lest they also fall into a wicked lifestyle.
- 1 Corinthians 15:33

"Be not deceived: evil communications corrupt good manners." "*Evil communications*" here means "*evil associations.*"

CHRISTIANS MUST AVOID EVIL ASSOCIATIONS

Such associations and companions corrupt Biblical morality and manners. True Christians must be on guard concerning such companions and associations. They must watch where they go, with whom they go, what happens when they go places, what they see, and what they hear. Everything that is evil around them can vex their hearts and souls. They can become like Lot if they are not very careful and do not read and heed the Words of God in the Bible!

2 Peter 2:9

"**The Lord knoweth how to deliver the godly out of temptations, and to reserve the unjust unto the day of judgment to be punished:**"

GOD CAN DELIVER THE JUST & PUNISH THE EVIL

The God of the Bible is in the business of deliverance. He delivers from sin and Hell's fire to those who truly trust in His Son as their Saviour. As this verse tells us, the Lord, in His wisdom, knows how to deliver those who are godly out of all their testings and trials.

Our God is perfectly able, as well, to reserve those who are unjust and unsaved for the judgment to be punished in Hell.

Verses On Deliverance
- **Galatians 1:4**

"Who gave himself for our sins, that he might deliver us from this present evil world, according to the will of God and our Father:"

CHRIST GAVE HIMSELF FOR THE WORLD'S SINS

Many people don't think anything is wrong with this world. Genuine Christians understand that Lord Jesus Christ gave Himself for their sins (and the sins of the whole

> world), and that He will deliver them from this present evil world. This includes all evil ways, actions, and beliefs of this unconverted world.

- **2 Timothy 4:18**

"And the Lord shall deliver me from every evil work, and will preserve *me* unto his heavenly kingdom: to whom *be* glory for ever and ever. Amen."

This was Paul's last letter. He was ready to die. That's why he said "*I have finished my course.*" He had run a good race for the Lord Jesus Christ. He knew that death by the Roman government was near. Tradition says Paul was beheaded by the short sword used by the Roman government for executing their enemies. He was not going to deny His Saviour or His Saviour's Words. He could have been "*delivered*" by a Roman pardon, but Paul chose to obey the Lord Jesus Christ who would "*deliver*" him from all evil and preserve him for Heaven for all eternity to come.

- **Hebrews 2:14**

"Forasmuch then as the children are partakers of flesh and blood, he also himself likewise took part of the same; that through death he might destroy him that had the power of death, that is, the devil;"

> **CHRIST DESTROYED SATAN AT THE CROSS**
>
> One of the purposes of the cross of Calvary was to destroy the one who had the power of death. Before the sacrifice of the Lord Jesus Christ at Calvary, Satan had the power of death.

- **Hebrews 2:15**

"And deliver them who through fear of death were all their lifetime subject to bondage."

> **CHRIST CAN DELIVER FROM SATAN'S BONDAGE**
>
> Deliverance from Satan's bondage, for those who are genuine Christians, was a second purpose of the death on Calvary of the Lord Jesus Christ.

Verses On Temptation

- **Mark 14:38**

"Watch ye and pray, lest ye enter into temptation. The spirit truly *is* ready, but the flesh *is* weak."

The three disciples, Peter, James and John, were asked by the Lord Jesus Christ to come to the garden of Gethsemane and pray with Him. This was just before the Jewish leader captured Him and took

Him to Jerusalem to be tried and then crucified. <u>Jesus told them to pray so they wouldn't enter into temptation.</u>
- **1 Corinthians 10:13**
"There hath no temptation taken you but such as is common to man: but God *is* faithful, who will not suffer you to be tempted above that ye are able; but will with the temptation also make a way to escape, that ye may be able to bear *it*."

GOD'S WAY TO ESCAPE WHEN FACING TEMPTATION
This is a wonderful verse for the child of God. God has promised born-again Christians that in any temptation that might come to them, He will provide a way to escape so that they can endure that temptation.

- **James 1:12**
"Blessed *is* the man that endureth temptation: for when he is tried, he shall receive the crown of life, which the Lord hath promised to them that love him."

TRUE CHRISTIANS MUST ENDURE TEMPTATIONS
Genuine Christians endure and put up with the temptations that come upon them. The special crown of life is promised to these Christians.

2 Peter 2:10

"But chiefly them that walk after the flesh in the lust of uncleanness, and despise government. Presumptuous are they, selfwilled, they are not afraid to speak evil of dignities."

FIVE SINS OF THOSE WALKING AFTER THE FLESH
The chief among the unjust that deserve severe judgment are those who walk after the flesh in these five characteristics:
    (1) they have the lust of uncleanness
    (2) they despise government
    (3) they are presumptuous
    (4) they are self-willed
    (5) they aren't afraid to speak evil of dignities

These five characteristics were present with:
    (1) the angels that sinned (2:4)
    (2) the old world of Noah's day (2:5)

(3) the people of Sodom and Gomorrah (2:6-8)
Sin seems to replicate itself no matter in what age or what locality.

THE MEANING OF THE GREEK WORD, "EPITHUMIA"
The Greek Word for *"lust"* is EPITHUMIA. Some of the meanings of this Greek Word are:
"1) desire, craving, longing, desire for what is forbidden, lust"

THE MEANING OF THE GREEK WORD, "MIASMOS"
The Greek Word for *"uncleanness"* is MIASMOS. Some of the meanings of this Greek Word are:
"1) the act of defiling, defilement, pollution"
In addition to their lust of uncleanness, the other four characteristics were also a part of the unjust thoughts and actions of these evil apostates.

Verses On Uncleanness
- **Matthew 23:27**

"Woe unto you, scribes and Pharisees, hypocrites! for ye are like unto whited sepulchres, which indeed appear beautiful outward, but are within full of dead *men's* bones, and of all uncleanness."

The Lord Jesus Christ told the Pharisees of His day that they were full of all uncleanness. They were like the dead and unclean bones of those who had been buried in the externally-whited tombs.

- **Romans 1:24**

"Wherefore God also gave them up to uncleanness through the lusts of their own hearts, to dishonour their own bodies between themselves:"

The heathen world was given up by God to uncleanness because of the lusts of their own hearts.

- **Colossians 3:5**

"Mortify therefore your members which are upon the earth; fornication, uncleanness, inordinate affection, evil concupiscence, and covetousness, which is idolatry:"

True Christians are commanded to mortify and put to death the members of their bodies including all kinds of uncleanness.

- **1 Thessalonians 4:7**

"For God hath not called us unto uncleanness, but unto holiness."

> **GENUINE CHRISTIANS ARE CALLED TO HOLINESS**
> Once people are born-again and saved, they receive a call to holiness, not to uncleanness.

One characteristic that was true of these false teachers was that they were self-willed. Here is a verse on not being self-willed.

- Titus 1:7
"For a bishop must be blameless, as the steward of God; not selfwilled, not soon angry, not given to wine, no striker, not given to filthy lucre;"

> **PASTORS-BISHOPS-ELDERS-NOT TO BE SELFWILLED**
> Unlike these apostate evil people, one of the qualifications of the pastors-bishops-elders was that they were not to be self-willed. If this is a part of their make-up, they should not be in pastoral ministries.
>
> These people are not afraid to speak evil of dignities, including the Lord Himself. Because of this, they don't care if they blaspheme the Name of the Lord Jesus Christ, using His Name in vain. This occurs today everywhere we go.

2 Peter 2:11

"Whereas angels, which are greater in power and might, bring not railing accusation against them before the Lord."

> **ANGELS-SUPERHUMAN, BUT NOT OMNIPOTENT**
> The angels seem to be superhuman, but they aren't omnipotent like God. They are not Deity. Their powers are greater than human beings, but they still do not bring railing accusation against these evil people before the Lord. The Lord is the only one Who can rebuke false teachers and rulers of people that speak evil of the just. The angels not rebuking is mentioned in the book of Jude as well.

- Jude 1:9
"Yet Michael the archangel, when contending with the devil he disputed about the body of Moses, durst not bring against him a railing accusation, but said, The Lord rebuke thee."

Michael is the leading angel. Of any angels who would have the power to rebuke these false teachers, it would be the angel Michael.

So here was Michael, the archangel, disputing about the body of Moses.

Though the details of this dispute are not clear, let's review briefly the death of Moses. God buried him in the land of Moab.

The book of Deuteronomy explains the death of Moses:
"And **Moses went up from the plains of Moab unto the mountain of Nebo**, to the top of Pisgah, that is over against Jericho. And the LORD shewed him all the land of Gilead, unto Dan . . . **So Moses the servant of the LORD died there in the land of Moab, according to the word of the LORD** . . . And Moses was an hundred and twenty years old when he died: his eye was not dim, nor his natural force abated. And the children of Israel wept for Moses in the plains of Moab thirty days: so the days of weeping and mourning for Moses were ended." (Deuteronomy 34:1, 5, 7-8)

Moses and Aaron both committed sins unto physical death (1 John 5:16-17). God told Moses very clearly to speak to the rock, and it would bring forth water for the people of Israel. Instead of this, Moses smote the rock twice (Numbers 20:11).

The following verses describe why God slew both Moses and Aaron because of this situation:
"And **Moses and Aaron** gathered the congregation together before the rock, and he said unto them, **Hear now, ye rebels; must we fetch you water out of this rock**? And Moses lifted up his hand, and with his rod he smote the rock twice: and the water came out abundantly, and the congregation drank, and their beasts also. **And the LORD spake unto Moses and Aaron, Because ye believed me not, to sanctify me in the eyes of the children of Israel, therefore ye shall not bring this congregation into the land which I have given them**." (Numbers 20:10-12)

In the Psalms, God gives a name to the sin of Moses:
"They angered him also at the waters of strife, so that **it went ill with Moses** for their sakes: Because they provoked his spirit, so that **he spake unadvisedly with his lips**."

(Psalms 106:32-33)

Apparently, there was a battle between the angel Michael and the Devil about the body of Moses. We're not told what the Devil wanted to do with Moses' body, but it would have been wrong. Michael didn't rebuke the Devil on this occasion, but had the Lord rebuke him.

2 Peter 2:12

"But these, as natural brute beasts, made to be taken and destroyed, speak evil of the things that they understand not; and shall utterly perish in their own corruption;"

These false teachers and apostate leaders were so evil that Peter describes them as *"natural brute beasts."* They were destined to be destroyed. They speak about things they do not even understand. They will perish in the Lake of Fire for all eternity because they have never received the Lord Jesus Christ as their Saviour and Redeemer. Notice what God says, first of all, "natural brute beasts."

THE MEANING OF THE GREEK WORD, "PHUSIKOS"

Notice the description of these false leaders. The Greek Word for *"natural"* is PHUSIKOS. Some of the meanings of this Greek Word are:

"1) produced by nature, inborn; 2) agreeable to nature; 3) governed by (the instincts of) nature."

They are just lost and unsaved people, who, though they might claim to be genuine Christians, are fake and phony preachers and teachers.

THE MEANING OF THE GREEK WORD, "ALOGOS"

They are called *"brute beasts."* The Greek Word for *"brute"* is ALOGOS. Some of the meanings of this Greek Word are:

"1) destitute of reason; 2) contrary to reason, absurd"

Verses On Beasts

- **Jude 1:10**

"But these speak evil of those things which they know not: but what they know naturally, as brute beasts, in those things they corrupt themselves."

Jude speaks of these false teachers as brute beasts. They are not genuine Christians. They have never truly trusted the Lord Jesus Christ as their Saviour.
- **Titus 1:12**
"One of themselves, *even* a prophet of their own, said, The Cretians *are* alway liars, evil beasts, slow bellies."

Here's another verse where people are called "*beasts*." That certainly isn't a very commendable name for these Cretian liars.

2 Peter 2:13

"And shall receive the reward of unrighteousness, as they that count it pleasure to riot in the day time. Spots they are and blemishes, sporting themselves with their own deceivings while they feast with you;"

FALSE TEACHERS MIXING WITH TRUE CHRISTIANS

These false teachers are unrighteous in every way parading themselves as being teachers of truth, and yet, their sermons and writings are full of error which brings in damnable heresies. Sadly, these false teachers are mixed in with genuine Christians which participate in their feasts as well as partake at the Lord's Table, which the Apostle Peter clearly describes in the above verse. As believers, we must be vigilant so that we can spot wolves in sheep's clothing in order to expose their erroneous teachings.

These wicked hypocrites are not clean and righteous, but are unclean spots and blemishes in the sight of the Lord. They also think it is pleasurable to riot. We have many rioters in our United States today and all over the world especially in these last days.

Verses On Riot
- **Titus 1:6**
"If any be blameless, the husband of one wife, having faithful children not accused of riot or unruly."

These evil false teachers riot. True Biblical pastors-bishops-elders cannot qualify Scripturally if they are accused of either rioting or being unruly. They are disqualified.
- **1 Peter 4:4**
"Wherein they think it strange that ye run not with *them* to the same excess of riot, speaking evil of *you*:"

TRUE CHRISTIANS HAVE CHANGED THEIR ACTIONS

Peter speaks of genuine Christians in his day who were once unsaved and worldly. Once they truly trusted in the Lord Jesus Christ as their Saviour, their former worldly friends thought they were strange because they no longer engaged in riotous behavior. Rioting was a thing of the past for these true Christians.

Verses On Spots
- **Ephesians 5:27**

"That he might present it to himself a glorious church, not having spot, or wrinkle, or any such thing; but that it should be holy and without blemish."

TRUE CHRISTIANS HAVE THEIR SPOTS REMOVED

After being made partakers of God's redemption by true faith in the Lord Jesus Christ, God gives to every one of them a position in Christ without having any spots, wrinkles, or blemishes. Their state down here on earth should strive to match their positional standing with the Lord.

- **1 Timothy 6:14**

"That thou keep *this* commandment without spot, unrebukeable, until the appearing of our Lord Jesus Christ:"
Genuine Christians are commanded to keep the commands of the Bible without any spot or deviation. This should be done by them until the Lord Jesus Christ returns in their Rapture, or until they meet Him in Heaven at their death.

- **Hebrews 9:14**

"How much more shall the blood of Christ, who through the eternal Spirit offered himself without spot to God, purge your conscience from dead works to serve the living God?"

CHRIST WAS IMPECCABLE–WITHOUT ANY SIN

The Lord Jesus Christ was without spot of any kind. He was and is sinless, perfect, and holy. He was impeccable. That is why He could bear the sins of the whole world in His body on the cross, shedding His blood for the forgiveness of those who put their genuine faith in Him as their Saviour.

2 Peter And Jude–Preaching Verse-by-Verse

- **2 Peter 3:14**

"Wherefore, beloved, seeing that ye look for such things, be diligent that ye may be found of him in peace, without spot, and blameless."

FALSE TEACHERS HAVE MANY BLEMISHES & SPOTS
These false teachers in Peter's day were full of spots and blemishes. True born-again Christians should be diligent that they may be found in Him, "*without spot, and blameless*" as they live for the Lord day by day.

- **Jude 1:12**

'These are spots in your feasts of charity, when they feast with you, feeding themselves without fear: clouds *they are* without water, carried about of winds; trees whose fruit withereth, without fruit, twice dead, plucked up by the roots;"

These unsaved and wicked people are spots to genuine Christians. There must be a clear separation from close fellowship with such people in order to avoid being contaminated with their sins and evil practices.

Verses On Blemishes
- **Exodus 12:5**

"Your lamb shall be without blemish, a male of the first year: ye shall take *it* out from the sheep, or from the goats:"

THE PASSOVER LAMB WAS WITHOUT ANY BLEMISH
The Passover lamb that the Israelites were to slay for each house was to be without blemish. It pictured the Lamb of God (John 1:29) Who was coming to take away the sins of the world. He was spotless, perfect, and without blemish. So the lamb for the Passover had to be as perfect as possible and without any blemishes.

- **Ephesians 5:27**

"That he might present it to himself a glorious church, not having spot, or wrinkle, or any such thing; but that it should be holy and without blemish."

The Lord Jesus Christ wants those who are regenerated Christians who are the "*church which is His Body*" (Ephesians 1:22-23) to be glorious and without spots, wrinkles, blemishes, or any such thing. He wants them to live holy lives.

- **1 Peter 1:18-19**

"Forasmuch as ye know that ye were not redeemed with corruptible things, *as* silver and gold, from your vain

conversation *received* by tradition from your fathers; But with the precious blood of Christ, as of a lamb without blemish and without spot:"
The Lord Jesus Christ, the Lamb of God, was without blemish or spot. He was and is perfectly sinless and holy.

THE MEANING OF THE
GREEK WORD, "SUNEUOCHEO"
The Greek Word for *"feast"* is SUNEUOCHEO. Some of the meanings of this Greek Word are:
"1) to entertain together; 2) to feast sumptuously with"

The problem with wolves in sheep's clothing with all their spots and blemishes is that they don't stay to themselves. Many times they enter into Bible-believing churches, groups, and other places. In so doing, they harm these groups that they have infiltrated with their poisonous views and actions.

2 Peter 2:14

"Having eyes full of adultery, and that cannot cease from sin; beguiling unstable souls: an heart they have exercised with covetous practices; cursed children:"

These false teachers commit adultery by looking on women with lust in their hearts.

Verses On Adultery

- **Exodus 20:14**

"Thou shalt not commit adultery."
This is not only a sin in the Old Testament, but also in the New Testament. Man's morality today does not agree with God's morality about this sin.

- **Leviticus 20:10**

"And the man that committeth adultery with *another* man's wife, *even he* that committeth adultery with his neighbour's wife, the adulterer and the adulteress shall surely be put to death."

ADULTERERS IN THE O.T. WERE TO BE KILLED

If adultery occurred in the Old Testament, both the adulterer and the adulteress would surely be put to death. This penalty is not given for this sin in the New Testament, but adultery is still a very heinous sin in the eyes of the God of the Bible.

- **Proverbs 6:32**

"*But* whoso committeth adultery with a woman lacketh understanding: he *that* doeth it destroyeth his own soul."

The sin of adultery is very destructive to a person's soul.

- **Jeremiah 23:14**

"I have seen also in the prophets of Jerusalem an horrible thing: they commit adultery, and walk in lies: they strengthen also the hands of evildoers, that none doth return from his wickedness: they are all of them unto me as Sodom, and the inhabitants thereof as Gomorrah."

O.T. FALSE PROPHETS PRACTICED ADULTERY

This sin of adultery was practiced by the false prophets in the Old Testament. God calls it a horrible thing. In this sexual immorality, they were acting like those in Sodom and Gomorrah.

- **Matthew 5:28**

"But I say unto you, That whosoever looketh on a woman to lust after her hath committed adultery with her already in his heart."

The Lord Jesus Christ defined adultery in the heart when a man, not just "*looked*" at a woman, but looked "*to lust after her.*"

- **Galatians 5:19**

"Now the works of the flesh are manifest, which are *these*; Adultery, fornication, uncleanness, lasciviousness,"

SOME TRUE CHRISTIANS WALK AFTER THEIR FLESH

Genuine Christians who are saved have their old flesh and sin nature just like the unsaved and lost people in this world. Their flesh, if uncontrolled by the Holy Spirit, is capable of committing any of these "*works of the flesh*" including adultery.

Verses On Beguiling

Peter mentions these false teachers also as having *"beguiling unstable souls."*

> **THE MEANING OF THE GREEK WORD, "DELEAZO"**
> The Greek Word for *"beguiling"* is DELEAZO. Some of the meanings of this Greek Word are:
> *"1) to bait, catch by a bait; 2) metaph. to beguile by banishments, allure, entice, deceive"*

- **Genesis 3:13**

"And the LORD God said unto the woman, What *is* this *that* thou hast done? And the woman said, The serpent beguiled me, and I did eat."

When asked by God, *"What is this that thou hast done?"* Eve's excuse for taking of the forbidden fruit was that Satan, the serpent, *"beguiled"* her. Satan is a great deceiver even today.

- **Genesis 29:25**

"And it came to pass, that in the morning, behold, it *was* Leah: and he said to Laban, What *is* this thou hast done unto me? did not I serve with thee for Rachel? wherefore then hast thou beguiled me?"

Laban beguiled Jacob about his choice for Rachel as his wife. Laban gave him Leah, thus deceiving him.

- **2 Corinthians 11:3**

"But I fear, lest by any means, as the serpent beguiled Eve through his subtilty, so your minds should be corrupted from the simplicity that is in Christ."

The beguiling of Satan is a real thing.

- **Colossians 2:4**

"And this I say, lest any man should beguile you with enticing words."

Paul warned true Christians in Colosse not to be beguiled by any enticing words that might be spoken.

- **Colossians 2:18**

"Let no man beguile you of your reward in a voluntary humility and worshipping of angels, intruding into those things which he hath not seen, vainly puffed up by his fleshly mind,"

> **TRUE CHRISTIANS SHOULD NOT WORSHIP ANGELS**
> The Colossians were warned again about being beguiled into worship of angels. These false teachers were

> not only beguiling people, but they were also unstable, without any firm foundation. All these trends apply equally today. False teachers change their theology and views.

Verses On Unstable
- **Genesis 49:4**

"Unstable as water, thou shalt not excel; because thou wentest up to thy father's bed; then defiledst thou *it*: he went up to my couch."

In blessing his sons, Jacob said that his oldest son, Reuben, was as unstable as water.

- **James 1:8**

"A double minded man *is* unstable in all his ways."

If anyone is double-minded, not knowing which idea is correct, they are unstable in all other ways as well. God does not want true Christians to be double-minded or unstable in any of their ways.

- **2 Peter 3:16**

"As also in all *his* epistles, speaking in them of these things; in which are some things hard to be understood, which they that are unlearned and unstable wrest, as *they do* also the other scriptures, unto their own destruction."

Peter is commending Paul's letters. He mentions that Paul's enemies who are unlearned and unstable twist and distort his words as they do to all other Scriptures.

In addition to all these other characteristics, these false teachers were filled with covetous practices.

Verses On Covetousness
- **Luke 16:14**

"And the Pharisees also, who were covetous, heard all these things: and they derided him."

The Pharisees were covetous. They wanted more power, more glory, more esteem, and more following.

- **1 Corinthians 5:11**

"But now I have written unto you not to keep company, if any man that is called a brother be a fornicator, or covetous, or an idolater, or a railer, or a drunkard, or an extortioner; with such an one no not to eat."

We should not keep company with covetous people even if they profess to be true Christians.

- **1 Timothy 3:3**

"Not given to wine, no striker, not greedy of filthy lucre; but patient, not a brawler, not covetous;"

> **PASTORS-BISHOPS-ELDERS-NOT COVETOUSNESS**
> One of the qualifications for the pastor-bishop-elder, is that he should not be covetous. He must not have *"the itch for more"* things.

Verses On Cursed

Another thing Peter mentions about these false teachers is that they are cursed children.

- **Jeremiah 17:5**

"Thus saith the LORD; Cursed *be* the man that trusteth in man, and maketh flesh his arm, and whose heart departeth from the LORD."

Those who trust in man and their flesh and whose heart departs from the Lord are cursed by the Lord.

- **Matthew 25:41**

"Then shall he say also unto them on the left hand, Depart from me, ye cursed, into everlasting fire, prepared for the devil and his angels:"

> **EVERLASTING FIRE FOR ALL NON-CHRISTIANS**
> At the judgment of the nations, those who have cursed God will be sent to the Lake of Fire in Hell which was prepared for the Devil and his angels.

These false teachers are specifically described as being cursed children.

2 Peter 2:15

"Which have forsaken the right way, and are gone astray, following the way of Balaam the son of Bosor, who loved the wages of unrighteousness;"

False teachers today, as in Peter's day, have gone astray, forsaking the right way given by God in His Words. They have done as Balaam did who was a false prophet for hire. The elders of Moab had hired Balaam to curse Israel as recorded in Numbers chapters 22-24 and 31. False teachers might get their financial reward in this life because of their motivation and love of money, but a day is coming when they will stand before the Lord Jesus Christ to be judged for their sins.

- **Revelation 2:14**
"But I have a few things against thee, because thou hast there them that hold the doctrine of Balaam, who taught Balac to cast a stumblingblock before the children of Israel, to eat things sacrificed unto idols, and to commit fornication."

2 Peter 2:16
"But was rebuked for his iniquity: the dumb ass speaking with man's voice forbad the madness of the prophet."

God did not let the iniquity of Balaam to go unpunished and unrecorded in the Bible.
- **Numbers 22:20-24**
"And God came unto Balaam at night, and said unto him, If the men come to call thee, rise up, *and* go with them; but yet the word which I shall say unto thee, that shalt thou do. And Balaam rose up in the morning, and saddled his ass, and went with the princes of Moab. And God's anger was kindled because he went: and the angel of the LORD stood in the way for an adversary against him. Now he was riding upon his ass, and his two servants *were* with him. And the ass saw the angel of the LORD standing in the way, and his sword drawn in his hand: and the ass turned aside out of the way, and went into the field: and Balaam smote the ass, to turn her into the way. But the angel of the LORD stood in a path of the vineyards, a wall *being* on this side, and a wall on that side."

On this occasion, the ass was not able to go forward. Balaam struck the animal because she turned out of the pathway.
- **Numbers 22:25-27**
"And when the ass saw the angel of the LORD, she thrust herself unto the wall, and crushed Balaam's foot against the wall: and he smote her again. And the angel of the LORD went further, and stood in a narrow place, where *was* no way to turn either to the right hand or to the left. And when the ass saw the angel of the LORD, she fell down under Balaam: and Balaam's anger was kindled, and he smote the ass with a staff."

BALAAM'S ASS WAS WISER THAN BALAAM

When the ass saw the angel of the LORD, she pushed Balaam's foot against the wall. Balaam hit her again. When the ass saw the angel of the LORD again, she fell down to the ground. Balaam hit her a third time.

- **Numbers 22:28**

"And the LORD opened the mouth of the ass, and she said unto Balaam, What have I done unto thee, that thou hast smitten me these three times?"

TWO ANIMALS IN THE O.T. WERE ABLE TO TALK

Then the LORD opened the mouth of the ass so she could speak. She asked Balaam why he had hit her. This miracle of speech by an animal was similar to when the serpent spoke to Eve in the Garden of Eden (Genesis 3:1-4).

- **Numbers 22:29-34**

"And Balaam said unto the ass, Because thou hast mocked me: I would there were a sword in mine hand, for now would I kill thee. And the ass said unto Balaam, *Am* not I thine ass, upon which thou hast ridden ever since *I was* thine unto this day? was I ever wont to do so unto thee? And he said, Nay. Then the LORD opened the eyes of Balaam, and he saw the angel of the LORD standing in the way, and his sword drawn in his hand: and he bowed down his head, and fell flat on his face. And the angel of the LORD said unto him, Wherefore hast thou smitten thine ass these three times? behold, I went out to withstand thee, because *thy* way is perverse before me: And the ass saw me, and turned from me these three times: unless she had turned from me, surely now also I had slain thee, and saved her alive. And Balaam said unto the angel of the LORD, I have sinned; for I knew not that thou stoodest in the way against me: now therefore, if it displease thee, I will get me back again."

BALAAM WAS REBUKED BY AN UNCLEAN ANIMAL

Balaam finally woke up to the fact that he was not in God's directive will for him to go and curse Israel. It took an animal--an unclean animal–to rebuke him and straighten him out.

False teachers in Peter's day were just as fake as Balaam was in his day. They also needed to be rebuked for their disobedience.

2 Peter 2:17

"These are wells without water, clouds that are carried with a tempest; to whom the mist of darkness is reserved for ever."

FALSE TEACHERS ARE AS WELLS AND CLOUDS
There are two figures of speech used here to describe these false teachers:
   (1) They are wells without any water
   (2) They are clouds carried with a tempest
Their judgment is reserved forever in the darkness of Hell.

What good is a well if it has no water? It is only for show. What good are rain clouds that are so driven by tempestuous winds that they do not send forth their water? So it is with these false teachers. They are useless and without any merit for genuine Christians.

Verses On Wells
- **Genesis 26:18**

"And Isaac digged again the wells of water, which they had digged in the days of Abraham his father; for the Philistines had stopped them after the death of Abraham: and he called their names after the names by which his father had called them."

Isaac dug wells in order to make water available to his family, his servants, and his animals. These false teachers were like the stopped wells made by the Philistines. There was nothing to refresh the body or the soul.

- **John 4:11**

"The woman saith unto him, Sir, thou hast nothing to draw with, and the well is deep: from whence then hast thou that living water?"

The Lord Jesus Christ asked for a drink from this Samaritan woman. He told her He would give her living water. She didn't understand what He meant. She told Him that he had nothing to draw the water with. He then told her that He was the Living Water.

- **John 4:10**

"Jesus answered and said unto her, If thou knewest the gift of God, and who it is that saith to thee, Give me to drink; thou wouldest have asked of him, and he would have given thee living water."

- **John 4:14**
"But whosoever drinketh of the water that I shall give him shall never thirst; but the water that I shall give him shall be in him a well of water springing up into everlasting life."

The well that the Lord Jesus Christ was talking about contained living water for spiritually-thirsty souls to partake of.

Verses On Clouds

- **Psalms 147:8**
"Who covereth the heaven with clouds, who prepareth rain for the earth, who maketh grass to grow upon the mountains."

God Himself made the clouds in the heavens for His own purposes and needs for His entire created universe.

- **Proverbs 25:14**
"Whoso boasteth himself of a false gift *is like* clouds and wind without rain."

BOASTING ABOUT FALSE GIFTS IS RIDICULOUS

It's bad enough to boast at all, but to boast about something a person doesn't possess is like clouds without any rain in them to water the ground. This is similar to the empty results that these false teachers bring with them.

- **Ecclesiastes 11:3**
"If the clouds be full of rain, they empty *themselves* upon the earth: and if the tree fall toward the south, or toward the north, in the place where the tree falleth, there it shall be."

These false teachers are like these empty clouds without any rain.

- **Isaiah 5:6**
"And I will lay it waste: it shall not be pruned, nor digged; but there shall come up briers and thorns: I will also command the clouds that they rain no rain upon it."

Before the HAARP changes in weather patterns, God was in undisputed control of the weather.

THE MEANING OF THE GREEK WORD, "LAILAPS"

These false teachers are like clouds carried with a tempest. The Greek Word for *"tempest"* is LAILAPS. Some of the meanings of this Greek Word are:

"1) a whirlwind, a tempestuous wind; 2) a violent attack of wind, a squall; 2a) never a single gust nor a steady blowing wind, however violent, but a storm breaking forth from black thunder clouds in furious gusts, with floods of rain, and throwing everything topsy-turvy"

> **FALSE TEACHERS ARE LIKE TEMPESTUOUS WINDS**
> That's what these false teachers are. They and their false doctrines are carried violently around the world, confusing people even more than they were before.

2 Peter 2:18

"For when they speak great swelling words of vanity, they allure through the lusts of the flesh, through much wantonness, those that were clean escaped from them who live in error."

> **FALSE TEACHERS SPEAK EMPTY & VAIN WORDS**
> These false teachers speak with vain words. These great words of vanity draw people to false beliefs and practices. They do this by means of the lusts of the flesh and wantonness. Their targets are people who had formerly escaped from errors and those who lived in these errors. This serious sin is evil.

Verses On Lusts

- **Romans 1:24**

"Wherefore God also gave them up to uncleanness through the lusts of their own hearts, to dishonour their own bodies between themselves:"

The uncleanness of the heathen world was caused by their lusts originated in their own hearts. Their heart-lusts led them to the dishonoring their own bodies between themselves by the sin of homosexuality. This is wicked and sinful behavior, even though President Obama, the Congress, the Supreme Court of the USA, and others consider it to be moral and acceptable!

- **Romans 6:12**

"Let not sin therefore reign in your mortal body, that ye should obey it in the lusts thereof."

These false teachers allure through lust. They teach that sinfulness is fine. Genuine Christians are commanded to stop letting sin reign in their mortal bodies to obey its lusts.

- **2 Timothy 2:22**

"Flee also youthful lusts: but follow righteousness, faith, charity, peace, with them that call on the Lord out of a pure heart."

> **OLDER PEOPLE MUST ALSO AVOID YOUTHFUL LUSTS**
> Even though a person may be old, they still have the lusts they had when they were younger. True Christians are commanded to flee such lusts and follow righteousness.
> This applies to people who believe that divorce and remarriage is all right. They lure and gather others to follow them in this unBiblical morality.

I think of people, for instance, like the late Pastor Peter Ruckman. He had a false view of the King James Bible and taught it to multitudes of followers. He had several wives and had been divorced and remarried many times. Because of his own sinful and unBiblical practices, he sanctioned this same lifestyle for others.

We had a man in the Dean Burgon Society, the very first year that we began (in 1978) who was divorced and remarried. He was a follower of Peter Ruckman in Ruckman's divorces and remarriages. He left the Dean Burgon Society because of his belief in Ruckman's false teachings about the King James Bible.

<u>Gail Riplinger, as of this writing, has had three marriages and two divorces. She also has followed Peter Ruckman's unBiblical views about the King James Bible and has even gone farther than Ruckman in his heresy. As the false teachers in Peter's day, these modern-day false teachers attract many people to follow their pernicious ways.</u>

> **THE MEANING OF THE GREEK WORD, "MATAIOTES"**
> False teachers of Peter's day used words of vanity to attract their followers. The Greek Word for *"vanity"* MATAIOTES. Some of the meanings of that Greek Word are:
> > *"1) what is devoid of truth and appropriateness; 2) perverseness, depravity; 3) frailty, want of vigour"*

Through these words of vanity, false teachers allure others to follow them.

THE MEANING OF THE GREEK WORD, "DELEAZO"

The Greek Word for *"allure"* is DELEAZO. Some of the meanings of that Word are:

"1) to bait, catch by a bait; 2) metaph. to beguile by banishments, allure, entice, deceive."

Even in our present day, false teachers and fake, make-believe Christians can allure many people by deceit. When those who have been allured and deceived find out these teachings are false, it is often too late and they are trapped.

THE MEANING OF THE GREEK WORD, "EPITHUMIA"

Not only is lust involved, but also wantonness. The Greek Word for *"lust"* is EPITHUMIA. Some of the meanings of that Greek Word are:

"1) desire, craving, longing, desire for what is forbidden, lust"

THE MEANING OF THE GREEK WORD, "ASELGEIA"

Wantonness is even stronger than lust. The Greek Word for *"wantonness"* is ASELGEIA. Some of the meanings of the Greek Word are:

"1) unbridled lust, excess, licentiousness, lasciviousness, wantonness, outrageousness, shamelessness, insolence"

This allurement is what false teachers use in our day as a means to get people to go along with their false thinking. Large churches pastored by Rick Warren and Bill Hybels allure people to follow them in various ways. I listened to a man who spoke at the Southwest Radio Church Ministries some time ago. He had a great video that I viewed. He quoted from Rick Warren's book and showed how he twisted the Scriptures right in the first ten pages of his book.

THE MEANING OF THE GREEK WORD, "PLANE"

Notice the last words of this verse in 2 Peter 2:18. He talked about people who live in "error." The Greek Word for *"error"* is PLANE. Some of the meanings of this Greek Word are:

"1) a wandering, a straying about; 1a) one led astray from the right way,

> *roams hither and thither; 2) metaph. 2a) mental straying 2a1) error, wrong opinion relative to morals or religion; 2b) error which shows itself in action, a wrong mode of acting; 2c) error, that which leads into error, deceit or fraud"*

We get our word, *"planet"* from this Greek Word. A *"planet"* is a heavenly body that wanders about the skies. It does not remain in a fixed place in the heavens. This is a very apt description of what false teachings do. They cause those who accept them to wander and to stray hither and thither away from the Bible's clear truths.

2 Peter 2:19

"While they promise them liberty, they themselves are the servants of corruption: for of whom a man is overcome, of the same is he brought in bondage."

These false teachers promise their hearers or readers liberty and freedom, yet they themselves are slaves of corruption.

THE MEANING OF THE GREEK WORD, "PHTHORA"

The Greek Word for *"corruption"* is PHTHORA. Some of the meanings of that Greek Word are:

> *"1) corruption, destruction, perishing; 1a) that which is subject to corruption, what is perishable; 1b) in the Christian sense, eternal misery in hell; 2) in the NT, in an ethical sense, corruption i.e. moral decay"*

False teachers are slaves to all kinds of corruption, and their pupils are overcome and conquered by their false teachings. They do not receive the promise of *"liberty."* Instead, they are brought into bondage by these erroneous teachings.

THE MEANING OF THE GREEK WORD, "DOULOO"

The Greek Word for *"bondage"* is DOULOO. Some of the meanings for this Greek Word are:

> *"1) to make a slave of, reduce to bondage; 2) metaph. give myself wholly to one's needs and service, make myself a bondman to him"*

It is sad indeed to be brought into this enslavement.

Verses On Bondage
- **Galatians 2:4**

"And that because of false brethren unawares brought in, who came in privily to spy out our liberty which we have in Christ Jesus, that they might bring us into bondage:"

FALSE TEACHERS BRING PEOPLE INTO BONDAGE

False teachers today want to bring as many people as possible into bondage. In Paul's day, there were false brethren who wanted to bring genuine Christians in Galatia back into the bondage under the Mosaic law. The New Testament makes it clear that true Christians are not under any part of the law of Moses.

"*For sin shall not have dominion over you: for **ye are not under the law**, but under grace. What then? shall we sin, because **we are not under the law**, but under grace? God forbid.*" (Romans 6:14-15)

"*But now **we are delivered from the law**, that being dead wherein we were held; that we should serve in newness of spirit, and not in the oldness of the letter.*" (Romans 7:6)

- **Galatians 5:1**

"Stand fast therefore in the liberty wherewith Christ hath made us free, and be not entangled again with the yoke of bondage." That's what false teachers wanted those in Peter's day to do. It is also what many false teachers today want genuine Christians to do. They try to entangle Christians with the bondage of the law of Moses.

2 Peter 2:20

"**For if after they have escaped the pollutions of the world through the knowledge of the Lord and Saviour Jesus Christ, they are again entangled therein, and overcome, the latter end is worse with them than the beginning.**"

Notice the picture here. Once people genuinely trust the Lord Jesus Christ as their Saviour, in God's sight, they have escaped the pollutions and judgments due to this world. Once freed by the Lord Jesus Christ from the bondage and judgments of this world, if they follow their flesh and go back into the practices of the world, that end is worse than before they were saved. If they are genuinely saved, they will not lose their salvation, but God will judge them for their carnality and worldliness. Though it is not certain as to what God might do in this case, He may even take them Home to Heaven if they have committed a sin unto physical death spoken of in 1 John 5:16:

> *"If any man see his brother sin a sin which is not unto death, he shall ask, and he shall give him life for them that sin not unto death. There is a sin unto death: I do not say that he shall pray for it."*

2 Peter 2:21

"For it had been better for them not to have known the way of righteousness, than, after they have known it, to turn from the holy commandment delivered unto them."

This verse seems to be referring to people who have known the way to everlasting life by genuine faith in the Lord Jesus Christ. According to the following verse, they seem to be true Christians, but are only pretending to be so. They seem to have had a smattering of truth and light, but later turned from that light that had been delivered unto them.

"PROFESSING-ONLY CHRISTIANS" ARE PHONY

These so-called professing Christians do not seem to be possessing Christians. Their mouths talk about the Christian faith, but their hearts have not received it. God wants people's hearts to be in line with their mouths.

Verses On The Mouth Related To The Heart

- **Psalms 62:4**

"They only consult to cast *him* down from his excellency: they delight in lies: they bless with their mouth, but they curse inwardly. Selah."

This is the essence of fake Christians. They bless the Lord with their mouths, but curse Him inwardly.

- **Psalms 78:36**

"Nevertheless they did flatter him with their mouth, and they lied unto him with their tongues."

These people flattered with their mouths, but lied to the Lord with their tongues.

- **Psalms 78:37**

"For their heart was not right with him, neither were they stedfast in his covenant."

Their heart was not right. This is important to the Lord. He looks

on the heart of people rather than only what they say with their mouth.
- **Isaiah 29:13**
"Wherefore the Lord said, Forasmuch as this people draw near *me* with their mouth, and with their lips do honour me, but have removed their heart far from me, and their fear toward me is taught by the precept of men:"

FAKE & PHONY PEOPLE ABOUND IN OUR WORLD

This is an accurate description of phony people. Their mouths and lips are antagonistic to their heart which is far from the Lord. God looks at the heart of people regardless of what their mouths and lips utter.

- **Ezekiel 33:31**
"And they come unto thee as the people cometh, and they sit before thee *as* my people, and they hear thy words, but they will not do them: for with their mouth they shew much love, *but* their heart goeth after their covetousness."

Here is another verse that shows a mouth-and-heart disengagement. This is the essence of false Christianity and make-believe Christians. It defines fake Christianity and fake preachers.

- **Matthew 15:7-8**
"Ye hypocrites, well did Esaias prophesy of you, saying, This people draweth nigh unto me with their mouth, and honoureth me with *their* lips; but their heart is far from me."

The Lord Jesus Christ exposed the hypocritical Pharisees of His day by a quotation from Isaiah. Their mouth and lips honor the Lord, but their heart is a far distance away from Him.

Verses On Repentance

- **Matthew 11:20**
"Then began he to upbraid the cities wherein most of his mighty works were done, because they repented not:"

The Lord Jesus Christ scolded the cities where He performed many miracles because they did not repent of their evil ways.

- **Matthew 11:21-22**
"Woe unto thee, Chorazin! woe unto thee, Bethsaida! for if the mighty works, which were done in you, had been done in Tyre and Sidon, they would have repented long ago in sackcloth and ashes. But I say unto you, It shall be more tolerable for Tyre and Sidon at the day of judgment, than for you."

These cities were reproved by the Lord Jesus Christ because they did not repent. Because of this lack of repentance when the Saviour Himself reproved them, it'll be more tolerable for Tyre and Sidon at judgment day than for them. This shows that, evidently, there will be gradations of judgment among those who go to the Lake of Fire in Hell.

2 Peter 2:22

"But it is happened unto them according to the true proverb, The dog is turned to his own vomit again; and the sow that was washed to her wallowing in the mire."

This is a true proverb regarding those who profess some knowledge of religion, but have no internal change. They are not true Christians. Both dogs and pigs were classed as unclean animals in the Old Testament.

Those who are phony and pretending to be Christians are likened to unclean dogs returning to their vomit. They are also like unclean pigs that had external washing and yet return to their pig lifestyle of wallowing in the mire. Washing doesn't change the nature of a pig. Nor does lip-service change the heart of those who only profess, but don't possess God's eternal salvation by genuine faith in the Lord Jesus Christ as their Saviour.

Verses On True Divine Washing

- **1 Corinthians 6:11**

"And such were some of you: but ye are washed, but ye are sanctified, but ye are justified in the name of the Lord Jesus, and by the Spirit of our God."

GENUINE CHRISTIANS HAVE BEEN WASHED BY GOD

This verse talks about people who were wicked sinners before they were saved, but they have been washed by genuine faith in the Lord Jesus Christ as their Saviour. They were washed and cleansed by the blood of the Lord Jesus Christ.

- **Revelation 1:5**

"And from Jesus Christ, *who is* the faithful witness, *and* the first begotten of the dead, and the prince of the kings of the earth. Unto him that loved us, and washed us from our sins in his own blood,"

CHRIST LOVES EVERYONE & WANTS THEM SAVED

Here's another verse showing that the Lord Jesus Christ loved every sinner in the world and washed them from their sins in His own blood. Now, they need to receive that washing and genuinely receive Him as their Saviour. Then and only then can this washing avail for them.

2 Peter
Chapter Three

2 Peter 3:1

"This second epistle, beloved, I now write unto you; in both which I stir up your pure minds by way of remembrance:"

PETER WANTED TO STIR UP PURE MINDS

Peter is writing to his readers a second time. He wanted to stir up their pure minds. The Greek Word for *"stir up"* is DIEGEIRO. Some of the meanings of that Greek Word are:

> *"1) to wake up, awaken, arouse (from sleep); 1a) of the sea, which begins to be agitated, to rise; 1b) metaph.; 1b1) to arouse the mind; 1b2) stir up, render active."*

He wanted to stir up their minds in order for them to get a good understanding about the ways of the Lord. He said that his readers had "pure" minds.

THE MEANING OF THE GREEK WORD, "HEILIKRINES"

The Greek Word for *"pure"* is HEILIKRINES. Some of the meanings of that Greek Word are:

> *"1) pure, sincere, unsullied; 2) found pure when unfolded and examined by the sun's light"*

May the minds of all genuine Christians in our day have this kind of purity!

Verses On Purity
- **Psalms 12:6**

"The words of the LORD *are* pure words: *as* silver tried in a furnace of earth, purified seven times."

VERBAL, PLENARY PRESERVED WORDS NEEDED

God's Words are as pure as purified silver. <u>This is why we must be certain that we have the verbal, plenary, inspired Words of the Hebrew, Aramaic, and Greek originals that have also been verbally plenarily preserved to our present day.</u> It is from these Words that we must make accurate translations into all languages of the world, even as our King James Bible translators did in 1604 to 1611.

- **Psalms 18:26**

"With the pure thou wilt shew thyself pure; and with the froward thou wilt shew thyself froward."

<u>God respects those who are pure. Every true Christian should be pure in heart, soul, body, and actions.</u>

- **Matthew 5:8**

"Blessed *are* the pure in heart: for they shall see God."

<u>God wants people to be pure in their hearts. This is only possible after they have genuinely trusted in the Lord Jesus Christ as their Saviour</u>, and begin to walk in the power of God the Holy Spirit.

- **1 Timothy 1:5**

"Now the end of the commandment is charity out of a pure heart, and *of* a good conscience, and *of* faith unfeigned:"

NEED FOR A PROPER HEART, CONSCIENCE, & FAITH

To be Biblically proper, charity and love must come out of a pure heart, a good conscience, and an unfeigned faith in the Words of God in the Bible.

- **2 Timothy 2:22**

"Flee also youthful lusts: but follow righteousness, faith, charity, peace, with them that call on the Lord out of a pure heart."

<u>Pastor Timothy admonished the child of God to flee youthful lusts.</u> Hearts must be pure to please the Lord.

- **1 Peter 1:22**

"Seeing ye have purified your souls in obeying the truth through the Spirit unto unfeigned love of the brethren, *see that ye* love one another with a pure heart fervently:"

Fellow Christians should have unfeigned love for one another with fervent and pure hearts.

Verses On The Mind

It is very important that the minds of true Christians should be properly functioning before the Lord.

- Acts 14:2

"But the unbelieving Jews stirred up the Gentiles, and made their minds evil affected against the brethren."

> **MINDS EVILLY AFFECTED AGAINST CHRISTIANS**
>
> Minds could be easily affected for evil against genuine Christians in the New Testament as well as in our day. Minds can be stirred up to hate people. We need pure minds, not like those unbelieving Jews in the book of Acts.

- Philippians 4:7

"And the peace of God, which passeth all understanding, shall keep your hearts and minds through Christ Jesus."

True Christians, all of whom are indwelt by the Holy Spirit, are able to partake of the peace of God which can keep and guard their minds.

Verses On Remembering

- Luke 23:42

"And he said unto Jesus, Lord, remember me when thou comest into thy kingdom."

One of the thieves being crucified on the cross next to the Lord Jesus Christ trusted Him as his Saviour and asked to be remembered by Him.

- 1 Corinthians 4:17

"For this cause have I sent unto you Timotheus, who is my beloved son, and faithful in the Lord, who shall bring you into remembrance of my ways which be in Christ, as I teach every where in every church."

Timothy accompanied Paul in many places on his missionary journeys. He saw Paul's "ways" firsthand. He would bring those ways to remembrance for those in Corinth.

- 2 Peter 1:12

"Wherefore I will not be negligent to put you always in remembrance of these things, though ye know *them*, and be established in the present truth."

Peter wanted his readers to remember the things that would establish them in the truth.

- **2 Peter 1:15**

"Moreover I will endeavour that ye may be able after my decease to have these things always in remembrance."

Peter wanted his readers to remember the truths that he was taught. Thus he wrote both 1 and 2 Peter.

2 Peter 3:2

"That ye may be mindful of the words which were spoken before by the holy prophets, and of the commandment of us the apostles of the Lord and Saviour:"

OLD TESTAMENT AND NEW TESTAMENT WRITINGS

Peter wanted his readers to be mindful of two classes of Bible materials:

(1) the writings of the holy prophets of the Old Testament, and

(2) the writings of the writers of the New Testament. The only way this could happen was to insure both the verbal, plenary inspiration of the Hebrew and Aramaic Words of the Old Testament as well as the verbal, plenary preservation of the Greek of the New Testament.

The Old Testament Hebrew and Aramaic Words and the New Testament Greek Words underlying the King James Bible are the verbally, plenarily inspired and preserved Words.

8,000 DIFFERENCES IN N.T. GREEK TEXTS

The false Gnostic Critical Greek New Testament Text by either Westcott and Hort, Nestle-Aland, or the United Bible Society have in the New Testament more than 8,000 differences from the Traditional Received Greek New Testament. This evidence is found in Dr. Jack Moorman's book, *8,000 Differences Between The Critical Text And The Received Greek Text* (BFT #3084 @ $20.00 + $8.00 S&H).

356 FALSE DOCTRINAL PASSAGES IN GREEK TEXTS

Of the 8,000 differences in the Greek New Testament Texts, there are 356 passages where false doctrine is taught. 2 Peter 3:2 is one of these 356 false doctrine passages. In the phrase, *"of us the apostles,"*

> these false Gnostic Critical Greek Texts merely say "*of the apostles*" and omit the Greek Word, HEMON, which means "*of us.*" By eliminating "*of us,*" these false Gnostic Greek Texts are denying that Peter was one of the apostles of the Lord Jesus Christ.

This is a serious doctrinal aberration, fallacy, and apostasy. Most definitely, Simon Peter was not only one of the apostles, but was among the leading three apostles–Peter, James, and John.

Verses Of Personal Words From One Of The Apostles
Peter wanted his readers to be mindful of the words of **us** (including himself) the apostles. Here are a few of such words from the apostle Paul that Peter wanted his readers to bear in mind.
- **Acts 20:27**

"For I have not shunned to declare unto you all the counsel of God."

The Apostle Paul wanted to tell his listeners all of God's counsel without eliminating any part of it.
- **Acts 20:29-30**

"For I know this, that after my departing shall grievous wolves enter in among you, not sparing the flock. Also of your own selves shall men arise, speaking perverse things, to draw away disciples after them."

The Apostle Paul warned about apostate teachers who, like grievous wolves, would speak perverse doctrines and draw away many of the flock of the Lord Jesus Christ after them.
- **Acts 20:32**

"And now, brethren, I commend you to God, and to the word of his grace, which is able to build you up, and to give you an inheritance among all them which are sanctified."

In this verse, the Apostle Paul commended his listeners to God Himself and His Words. He said that God's Words would not only build them up, but also give them an inheritance.
- **2 Timothy 3:1-5**

"This know also, that in the last days perilous times shall come. For men shall be lovers of their own selves, covetous, boasters, proud, blasphemers, disobedient to parents, unthankful, unholy, Without natural affection, trucebreakers, false accusers, incontinent, fierce, despisers of those that are good, Traitors, heady, highminded, lovers of pleasures more than lovers of God; Having a form of godliness, but denying the power thereof: from such turn away."

> **WARNINGS OF THINGS IN THE LAST DAYS**
>
> In these verses to Pastor Timothy, the Apostle Paul, in his last letter before his execution by the Roman government, warned about many things. Today, we are really in such "*last days*" where these things Paul warned about are taking place.

- 1 Timothy 4:1-2

"Now the Spirit speaketh expressly, that in the latter times some shall depart from the faith, giving heed to seducing spirits, and doctrines of devils; Speaking lies in hypocrisy; having their conscience seared with a hot iron;"

Paul is once again speaking of things that will happen in the latter times. It is also true that many have now departed from the doctrinal faith of the Bible. The other things mentioned have also been evident.

> **BE MINDFUL OF GOD'S PRESERVED WORDS**
>
> So it is important, says Peter, to be mindful of the words, not only spoken by the holy prophets in the Old Testament, but also "of the commandment of us the apostles of our Lord and Saviour" in the New Testament.
>
> If the Lord had not preserved the inspired Hebrew, Aramaic and Greek Words of the Old and New Testaments, no one could be "*mindful*" of them.

It's a shame that many of our fundamentalist brethren have selected the false Gnostic Critical Greek Texts which distort over 356 doctrinal passages. This false teaching has been, and is being, led among Fundamentalists, by Bob Jones University, Detroit Baptist Seminary, the now-closed Calvary Seminary, Central Seminary, Pillsbury Baptist Bible College, and other schools and seminaries.

2 Peter 3:3

"Knowing this first, that there shall come in the last days scoffers, walking after their own lusts,"

From what is happening in our day, it seems like we are in the last of these last days. Both Peter and Paul mentioned the last days in the New Testament, over two thousand years ago. If it was the last days then; what about today?

Verses On Last Days

- **Acts 2:17**

"And it shall come to pass in the **last days**, saith God, I will pour out of my Spirit upon all flesh: and your sons and your daughters shall prophesy, and your young men shall see visions, and your old men shall dream dreams:"

This is one of the things that will happen in the last days. It is a quotation from the prophecy of Joel 2:28. The Pentecostals and the Charismatics often use this verse to justify their unBiblical speaking in "*tongues*" and other things.

- **2 Timothy 3:1-7**

"This know also, that in the **last days** perilous times shall come. For men shall be lovers of their own selves, covetous, boasters, proud, blasphemers, disobedient to parents, unthankful, unholy, Without natural affection, trucebreakers, false accusers, incontinent, fierce, despisers of those that are good, Traitors, heady, highminded, lovers of pleasures more than lovers of God; Having a form of godliness, but denying the power thereof: from such turn away. For of this sort are they which creep into houses, and lead captive silly women laden with sins, led away with divers lusts, Ever learning, and never able to come to the knowledge of the truth."

In these verses, Paul told Pastor Timothy what would happen in the last days. To a greater or lesser extent, every one of these things mentioned is happening today. These signs are with us now.

SCOFFERS ARE MANY IN THESE LAST DAYS

Peter mentions that scoffers and unbelievers will come who will be walking after their own lusts. From the verses that follow, they will be evolutionists, denying the creation of the universe by God.

THE MEANING OF THE GREEK WORD, "EMPAIKTES"

The Greek Word for "*scoffers*" is EMPAIKTES. Some of the meanings of this Greek Word are:

"*1) a mocker, a scoffer*"

They will be mocking and deriding those of us who believe the Bible to be God's Words--true and trustworthy. They will also be filled with their own lusts.

> **THE MEANING OF THE GREEK WORD, "EPITHUMIA"**
> The Greek Word for *"lusts"* is EPITHUMIA. Some of the meanings of this Greek Word are:
> > *"1) desire, craving, longing, desire for what is forbidden, lust"*
>
> Many, if not most, of the apostate clergy today are justifying the homosexual lifestyle and homosexual marriages. In fact, many church groups today think it is all right to have homosexual ministers who are walking after their own lusts.

2 Peter 3:4

"And saying, Where is the promise of his coming? for since the fathers fell asleep, all things continue as they were from the beginning of the creation."

> **THE FALSE UNIFORMITARIAN VIEW OF CREATION**
> They believe in a continuous *uniformitarianism* from the beginning of creation. That means that everything is the same and does not change. This *uniformitarianism* belief is false. Change does happen in the universe (whether major or minor) while some things stay the same. God's Person, nature, plans, and predictions do not change; neither do His Words in the Bible change.

In this verse, Peter mentions that some of these false teachers deny the promise of the *"coming"* of the Lord Jesus Christ.

Below are ten verses that promise the second coming of the Lord Jesus Christ. Some verses speak of **the first phase of His second coming** in the Rapture of all genuinely-saved Christians, whether dead or alive. Their bodies will be instantly transformed into glorified bodies like that of the Lord Jesus Christ.

Other verses speak of **the second phase of His coming** to earth with true Christians (who were raptured seven years before) to set up his thousand-year reign in the Millennium. I will indicate for each verse whether it refers to the first phase or the second phase of His coming.

Verses On Christ's Second Coming--In Two Phases

- **1 Corinthians 1:7**

"So that ye come behind in no gift; waiting for the coming of our Lord Jesus Christ:"

This refers to the first phase of Christ's coming at the Rapture.

- **1 Corinthians 15:23**

"But every man in his own order: Christ the firstfruits; afterward they that are Christ's at his coming."

This refers to the first phase of Christ's coming at the Rapture.

- **1 Thessalonians 2:19**

"For what *is* our hope, or joy, or crown of rejoicing? *Are* not even ye in the presence of our Lord Jesus Christ at his coming?"

This refers to the first phase of Christ's coming at the Rapture.

- **1 Thessalonians 3:13**

"To the end he may stablish your hearts unblameable in holiness before God, even our Father, at the coming of our Lord Jesus Christ with all his saints."

This refers to the second phase of Christ's coming.

- **1 Thessalonians 4:15**

"For this we say unto you by the word of the Lord, that we which are alive *and* remain unto the coming of the Lord shall not prevent them which are asleep."

This refers to the first phase of Christ's coming at the Rapture.

- **1 Thessalonians 5:23**

"And the very God of peace sanctify you wholly; and *I pray God* your whole spirit and soul and body be preserved blameless unto the coming of our Lord Jesus Christ."

This refers to the first phase of Christ's coming at the Rapture.

- **2 Thessalonians 2:1**

"Now we beseech you, brethren, by the coming of our Lord Jesus Christ, and *by* our gathering together unto him,"

This refers to the first phase of Christ's coming at the Rapture.

- **2 Thessalonians 2:8**

"And then shall that Wicked be revealed, whom the Lord shall consume with the spirit of his mouth, and shall destroy with the brightness of his coming:"

This refers to the second phase of Christ's coming.

- **James 5:8**

"Be ye also patient; stablish your hearts: for the coming of the Lord draweth nigh."

This refers to the first phase of Christ's coming at the Rapture.

- 1 John 2:28

"And now, little children, abide in him; that, when he shall appear, we may have confidence, and not be ashamed before him at his coming."

This refers to the first phase of Christ's coming at the Rapture.

The apostate unbelievers in Peter's day and in our day deny both the first phase and the second phase of the coming of our Lord Jesus Christ.

2 Peter 3:5

"For this they willingly are ignorant of, that by the word of God the heavens were of old, and the earth standing out of the water and in the water:"

FALSE TEACHERS CALLED "WILLINGLY IGNORANT"

These apostates and false teachers were willingly ignorant of what the Words of God had to say about creation. These mockers are willingly ignorant. It's one thing to be ignorant of something, but to be willingly ignorant is to be ignorant on purpose. It seems like it's planned ignorance. Let's look at some other uses in the Bible of the term, *"willingly."*

Verses On Willingly

- Exodus 25:2

"Speak unto the children of Israel, that they bring me an offering: of every man that giveth it willingly with his heart ye shall take my offering."

All offerings to the Lord's work should be made willingly and from the heart.

- Proverbs 31:13

"She seeketh wool, and flax, and worketh willingly with her hands."

THE VIRTUOUS WOMAN WORKS WILLINGLY

The virtuous woman in Proverbs 31 works willingly with her hands. No one needs to force her to do these needed tasks.

- 1 Peter 5:2

"Feed the flock of God which is among you, taking the oversight *thereof*, not by constraint, but willingly; not for filthy lucre, but of a ready mind;"

BIBLICAL QUALITIES NEEDED FOR PASTORS
Biblically-qualified and motivated pastors (who are also called bishops and elders) should preach God's Words and take the oversight as a bishop-elder over their churches willingly. It should be neither by constraint or force, nor for money. It should be done with a ready and a willing mind.

Verses On Ignorant
Though these false teachers were ignorant of God's truths about His creation and His care, true Christians should never be ignorant, willingly or unwillingly, of and about God's Words or any other truths.

- **Romans 1:13**

"Now I would not have you ignorant, brethren, that oftentimes I purposed to come unto you, (but was let hitherto,) that I might have some fruit among you also, even as among other Gentiles."

PAUL WANTED TO VISIT THE CHRISTIANS IN ROME
Paul did not want the brethren at Rome to be ignorant that he often purposed to come to them, but had been hindered. He wanted to have some spiritual fruit among them.

- **Romans 10:3**

"For they being ignorant of God's righteousness, and going about to establish their own righteousness, have not submitted themselves unto the righteousness of God."

RECEIVING RIGHTEOUSNESS BEFORE GOD
The Jews of Paul's day (and probably even today) were ignorant of God's righteousness that was and is bestowed on those who truly trust in His Son, the Lord Jesus Christ, as their Saviour.

Such righteousness with God can never be established by the works and deeds of men and women. <u>God considers all people to be sinners and totally unable to establish a righteous standing with God by themselves without the Lord Jesus Christ as their Saviour.</u>

- **Romans 11:25**

"For I would not, brethren, that ye should be ignorant of this mystery, lest ye should be wise in your own conceits; that blindness in part is happened to Israel, until the fulness of the Gentiles be come in."

Paul didn't want those at Rome to be ignorant of the fact that blindness in part had happened to Israel as a nation. At a later time, the blindness would be taken away.

- **1 Corinthians 14:38**

"But if any man be ignorant, let him be ignorant."

Paul has been discussing many things in this chapter. He is saying that if people don't want to learn these things, let them remain in their ignorance.

- **2 Corinthians 2:11**

"Lest Satan should get an advantage of us: for we are not ignorant of his devices."

Paul was not ignorant of the various strategies, devices, schemes, and plots of Satan.

- **1 Thessalonians 4:13**

"But I would not have you to be ignorant, brethren, concerning them which are asleep, that ye sorrow not, even as others which have no hope."

Paul did not want genuine Christians in Thessalonica to be ignorant of the place where their fellow Christians were who had died. They are with the Lord Jesus Christ in Heaven.

Verses On Creation

As far as the creation of the heavens and the earth are concerned, these false mockers had only guesswork to go on without any true and proper knowledge of how it all came about.

- **Genesis 1:1**

"In the beginning God created the heaven and the earth."

This is how creation came about. God did it by His wonderful and omnipotent power.

- **Genesis 1:9-10**

"And God said, Let the waters under the heaven be gathered together unto one place, and let the dry *land* appear: and it was so. And God called the dry *land* Earth; and the gathering together of the waters called he Seas: and God saw that *it was* good."

These false teachers were concerned about the earth and the water. These verses tell that story clearly. God separated between the water and the earth. The earth was standing out of the water.

2 Peter 3:6

"Whereby the world that then was, being overflowed with water, perished:"

FALSE TEACHERS TEACH MANY FALSE DOCTRINES

The universal flood is one more thing of which false teachers are willingly ignorant. The same is true of those in our day who refuse to accept the Traditional Received New Testament Greek Text that underlies the King James Bible's New Testament. Though these teachers are well- educated, they have accepted the false views originated by the apostate Anglican leaders, Westcott and Hort, from their 1881 Greek text.

Verses On The Flood

- Genesis 6:17

"And, behold, I, even I, do bring a **flood of waters upon the earth, to destroy all flesh, wherein *is* the breath of life**, from under heaven; *and* every thing that *is* in the earth shall die."

NOAH'S FLOOD WAS UNIVERSAL, NOT LOCAL

This verse makes it clear that the flood in Noah's time was a universal flood. Many Christian leaders today have doubted this. They maintain that it was only a local flood. Many of our brethren don't believe in the universal flood; they just say it was a local flood.

- Luke 17:27

"They did eat, they drank, they married wives, they were given in marriage, until the day that Noe entered into the ark, and **the flood came, and destroyed them all**."

The Lord Jesus Christ, in this verse, also made it quite clear that the flood destroyed all human beings upon the earth at that time **except** Noah, his wife, and their sons, Shem, Ham, and Japheth with their wives.

2 Peter 3:7

"But the heavens and the earth, which are now, by the same word are kept in store, reserved unto fire against the day of judgment and perdition of ungodly men."

THE PERDITION OF UNGODLY MEN WILL BE BY FIRE

In contrast to God's judgment of this world by the universal flood, Peter wrote, that in the end times, God will judge this world by fire against ungodly people. The heavens and earth are kept in store, according to God's Words, and reserved unto fire.

Verses On Fire

- 1 Corinthians 3:13

"Every man's work shall be made manifest: for the day shall declare it, because it shall be revealed by fire; and the fire shall try every man's work of what sort it is."

<u>This describes the judgment seat of Christ for every genuine Christian.</u> Though it is applied to Christians in a figurative sense, the illustration of fire burning up hay, wood, and stubble and purifying gold, silver, and precious stones is literally how fire affects these materials.

- 1 Corinthians 3:15

"If any man's work shall be burned, he shall suffer loss: but he himself shall be saved; yet so as by fire."

This is what happens when real fire is applied to the materials in this context.

- 2 Thessalonians 1:7-8

"And to you who are troubled rest with us, when the Lord Jesus shall be revealed from heaven with his mighty angels, In flaming fire taking vengeance on them that know not God, and that obey not the gospel of our Lord Jesus Christ:"

ENEMIES AT ARMAGEDDON--DESTROYED BY FIRE

This verse refers to the second phase of the return of the Lord Jesus Christ. It will occur after the seven-year Tribulation during the Battle of Armageddon. This is the battle where thousands, even millions of warriors, will gather together in Israel in order to take over that country and nation. This coming of the Lord Jesus

Christ will be in flaming fire and will destroy those who don't know Him--having rejected His gospel.
- **Hebrews 12:29**
"For our God *is* a consuming fire."

Purifying fire is a part of God's nature. That's why we mortals cannot go near Him unless we are *"in Christ"* and genuinely saved. Only then can people have close fellowship with Him.
- **2 Peter 3:12**
"Looking for and hasting unto the coming of the day of God, wherein the heavens being on fire shall be dissolved, and the elements shall melt with fervent heat?"

This verse is clear that one day in the future, fire shall melt the elements of our universe with fervent heat. The elements shall be dissolved.
- **Revelation 20:10**
"And the devil that deceived them was cast into the lake of fire and brimstone, where the beast and the false prophet *are*, and shall be tormented day and night for ever and ever."

HELL IS GENUINE, REAL, AND EVERLASTING FIRE

Hell is called *"the Lake of Fire."* In Hell there is real, genuine, and literal fire. This is where the beast and the false prophet will still be after they have been in the Lake of Fire for 1,000 years during the Millennium. The Devil will be cast in that same Lake of Fire at the end of the Millennium as well.

THE SATANIC TRINITY WILL BE SENT TO HELL

The entire satanic trinity will be in conscious, continuous suffering and torment for all eternity to come. This will likewise be the fate of all those who have not truly received the Lord Jesus Christ as their Saviour.

MANY TRUE CHRISTIANS DENY THE LITERAL HELL

It is sad, but true, that many who call themselves fundamental Bible-believing Christians have removed the literal fire out of Hell. They teach that Hell is just a place of suffering without any fire. Others of this group are teaching that Hell and God's eternal punishment for the satanic trinity and all lost people is not eternal and everlasting. They say this in spite of the Bible verses that describe it clearly as *"everlasting."*

"Wherefore if thy hand or thy foot offend thee, cut them off, and cast them from thee: it is better for thee to enter into life halt or maimed, rather than having two hands or two feet to be cast into **_everlasting fire_**." (Matthew 18:8)

"Then shall he say also unto them on the left hand, Depart from me, ye cursed, into **_everlasting fire_**, prepared for the devil and his angels:" (Matthew 25:41)

"Who shall be punished with **_everlasting_** destruction from the presence of the Lord, and from the glory of his power;" (2 Thessalonians 1:9)

"And the angels which kept not their first estate, but left their own habitation, he hath reserved in **_everlasting_** chains under darkness unto the judgment of the great day." (Jude 1:6)

Some people deny that there is judgment of any kind for those who are not genuine Christians. This is also a great error.

2 Peter 3:8

"But, beloved, be not ignorant of this one thing, that one day is with the Lord as a thousand years, and a thousand years as one day."

Because the Greek Words for "_be not ignorant_" are in the Greek present tense, and it is a prohibition, it means to stop an action already in progress. It means, therefore, that they were to "_stop being ignorant._"

MEANING OF PROHIBITIONS IN THE AORIST TENSE

If it were in the Greek aorist tense, it would mean don't even begin to be ignorant.

Apparently, Peter's readers were ignorant of God's Person and nature as well as the nature of an endless eternity. Peter declared that "_one day is with the Lord as a thousand years, and a thousand years as one day._"

Just think of eternity. Think of the thousands of years that have passed since the creation of our earth. Then, go way back before that time and think of the millions and millions of years that God the Father, God the Son, and God the Holy Spirit existed. When you have thought about past eternity, think of future eternity of more millions and millions of years. Each thousand-year period, God considers as only one single day.

Some authors, teachers, and pastors wrongly interpret the "*day*" of this verse with the Hebrew Word, "*day*" in Genesis Chapter one. They seek to prove the error of evolution with this erroneous interpretation of "*day.*" Notice the last sentence of Genesis 1:5:

> "And God called the light Day, and the darkness he called Night. **And the evening and the morning were the first day**."
> (Genesis 1:5)

The first part of those words are repeated every day of the six days of creation. The only changes are the substitution of the words "*second,*" "*third,*" "*fourth,*" "*fifth,*" and "*sixth*" before the word, "*day.*" These are very clearly solar days and not thousands of years as some so-called "Christian" evolutionists falsely teach.

Peter doesn't want his readers to be ignorant of what the Bible teaches about God's eternity. He had an eternal past, and He will have an eternal future.

2 Peter 3:9

"The Lord is not slack concerning his promise, as some men count slackness; but is longsuffering to us-ward, not willing that any should perish, but that all should come to repentance."

There are three important themes in this verse:
 (1) slackness;
 (2) longsuffering; and
 (3) Christ's unlimited atonement. The Lord is "*not slack concerning His promise.*"

THE MEANING OF THE GREEK WORD, "BRADUNO"

The Greek Word for "*slack*" is BRADUNO. Some of the meanings of this Greek Word are:

> "*1) to delay, be slow; 1a) to render slowly, retard; 1b) to be long, to tarry, loiter*"

When the Lord promises something, He will fulfill it. He doesn't delay, or hesitate to carry out these promises. You can count on Him.

Verses On Slackness

- **Deuteronomy 7:9-10**

"Know therefore that the LORD thy God, he *is* God, the faithful God, which keepeth covenant and mercy with them that love him and keep his commandments to a thousand generations; And repayeth them that hate him to their face, to destroy them: he will not be slack to him that hateth him, he will repay him to his face."

God is not slack or delayed in meting out judgment for those people who hate Him.

- **Joshua 18:3**

"And Joshua said unto the children of Israel, How long *are* ye slack to go to possess the land, which the LORD God of your fathers hath given you?"

Joshua reproved the Israelites because they were slack and delayed in their entrance into the land of promise which the LORD had given them.

MEANING OF THE GREEK WORD, "MAKROTHUMIA"

One of the attributes of the Lord is His longsuffering. The Greek Word for *"longsuffering"* is MAKROTHUMIA. Some of the meanings of this Greek Word are:

> *"1) to be of a long spirit, not to lose heart; 1a) to persevere patiently and bravely in enduring misfortunes and troubles; 1b) to be patient in bearing the offenses and injuries of others; 1b1) to be mild and slow in avenging; 1b2) to be longsuffering, slow to anger, slow to punish."*

This is a very meaningful attribute of every Person of our Triune God–the Father, the Son, and the Holy Spirit. Because of His longsuffering, He has not yet judged this wicked world for all their apostasies and sins.

Verses On Longsuffering
- **Exodus 34:6**

"And the LORD passed by before him, and proclaimed, The LORD, The LORD God, merciful and gracious, longsuffering, and abundant in goodness and truth,"

GOD'S LONGSUFFERING IS VERY IMPORTANT
God's longsuffering is an important attribute mentioned in the Old Testament. He is also merciful, gracious, and has an abundance of goodness and truth.

- **Numbers 14:17-18**

"And now, I beseech thee, let the power of my Lord be great, according as thou hast spoken, saying, The LORD *is* longsuffering, and of great mercy, forgiving iniquity and transgression, and by no means clearing *the guilty*, visiting the iniquity of the fathers upon the children unto the third and fourth *generation*."

The LORD is longsuffering and also of great mercy and forgiveness. He also judges the sins of all.

- **Psalms 86:15**

"But thou, O Lord, *art* a God full of compassion, and gracious, longsuffering, and plenteous in mercy and truth."

Longsuffering is only one of the important attributes of the Bible's only True God.

- **2 Corinthians 6:4-6**

"But in all *things* approving ourselves as the ministers of God, in much patience, in afflictions, in necessities, in distresses, In stripes, in imprisonments, in tumults, in labours, in watchings, in fastings; By pureness, by knowledge, by longsuffering, by kindness, by the Holy Ghost, by love unfeigned,"

Genuine Christians should exercise longsuffering by the power of the indwelling Holy Spirit.

- **Galatians 5:19-22**

"Now the works of the flesh are manifest, which are *these*; Adultery, fornication, uncleanness, lasciviousness, Idolatry, witchcraft, hatred, variance, emulations, wrath, strife, seditions, heresies, Envyings, murders, drunkenness, revellings, and such like: of the which I tell you before, as I have also told *you* in time past, that they which do such things shall not inherit the kingdom of God. But the fruit of the Spirit is love, joy, peace, longsuffering, gentleness, goodness, faith,"

LONGSUFFERING–A FRUIT OF THE HOLY SPIRIT

Longsuffering is one of the nine fruits of God the Holy Spirit Who indwells every born-again Christian. When they are controlled by God's Holy Spirit, longsuffering can be manifested.

- **Ephesians 4:1-3**

"I therefore, the prisoner of the Lord, beseech you that ye walk worthy of the vocation wherewith ye are called, With all lowliness and meekness, with longsuffering, forbearing one another in love; Endeavouring to keep the unity of the Spirit in the bond of peace."

The walk of genuine Christians should be guided by lowliness, meekness, and longsuffering.

- **Colossians 1:11**

"Strengthened with all might, according to his glorious power, unto all patience and longsuffering with joyfulness;"

God's glorious power can strengthen true Christians with might, patience, and joyful longsuffering.

- **Colossians 3:12**

"Put on therefore, as the elect of God, holy and beloved, bowels of mercies, kindness, humbleness of mind, meekness, longsuffering;"

LONGSUFFERING--PUT ON LIKE A GARMENT

Longsuffering is to be put on like a garment by genuine Christians who are walking with the Lord.

- **1 Timothy 1:16**

"Howbeit for this cause I obtained mercy, that in me first Jesus Christ might shew forth all longsuffering, for a pattern to them which should hereafter believe on him to life everlasting."

PAUL TO BE A PATTERN OF LONGSUFFERING

After Paul's conversion, he said he had obtained mercy from the Lord to show forth God's longsuffering as a pattern for others who should later become saved.

- **2 Timothy 3:10**

"But thou hast fully known my doctrine, manner of life, purpose, faith, longsuffering, charity, patience,"

Pastor Timothy had been with Paul on many of his missionary journeys. He was a witness, not only of Paul's doctrine, manner of life, and other things, but also of his longsuffering.

- **2 Timothy 4:2**
"Preach the word; be instant in season, out of season; reprove, rebuke, exhort with all longsuffering and doctrine."
Along with preaching the Words of God, as I seek to do in each of our three weekly services, I seek to include longsuffering along with the other elements mentioned here of reproof, rebuke, exhortation, and doctrine.
- **1 Peter 3:20**
"Which sometime were disobedient, when once the longsuffering of God waited in the days of Noah, while the ark was a preparing, wherein few, that is, eight souls were saved by water."

From other verses, there were apparently about one hundred and twenty years that God waited, in His longsuffering while Noah built the ark. After that, He sent the universal flood as His judgment upon the earth that took all except eight people.

The Heresy Of Hyper-Calvinism

HYPER-CALVINISM IS AN UNBIBLICAL HERESY

The last part of this ninth verse mentions that God was *"not willing that any should perish, but that all should come to repentance."* This verse destroys the heresy of hyper-Calvinism which teaches, among other false things, that God really **IS** willing for the "non-elect" to perish. It also teaches falsely that God is not willing that **ALL** should come to repentance, but only a few that they entitle *"the elect."*

The hyper-Calvinists also teach the heresy of a "limited atonement" of the Lord Jesus Christ. That is, they believe that He died not for the sins of the entire world, but only for the sins of what they call "the elect." The Bible is very clear in its teachings of an "unlimited atonement" by the Lord Jesus Christ. That is, He died for every person who ever lived on this earth, not only for the small group they call "the elect." There are many verses that teach this truth.

Verses Against Hyper-Calvinism
- **John 3:16**
"For God so loved the world, that he gave his only begotten Son, that whosoever believeth in him should not perish, but have everlasting life."

> **SOME HYPER-CALVINISTS ADD TO JOHN 3:16**
> Some, if not all, of the hyper-Calvinists understand this as *"God so loved the world OF THE ELECT."* How can they add those three words of that phrase and violate God's Word by so doing?! This verse clearly teaches that the objects of God's love are the whole *"world."* No one is exempted.

Another part of the heresy of hyper-Calvinist teachings is that only the ones that they term "the elect" can believe on the Lord Jesus Christ and be saved. All the "non-elect" ones cannot believe in and receive Him as their Saviour. This part of their heresy is clearly refuted by the words, *"that **whosoever believeth** in him should not perish, but have everlasting life."* Those who believe in the Lord Jesus Christ as their Saviour are not limited to "the elect" as heretical hyper-Calvinists believe. God's salvation is available to "***whosoever believeth***." That means genuine heart belief, not merely intellectual belief.

- **1 Peter 2:24**

"Who his own self bare our sins in his own body on the tree, that we, being dead to sins, should live unto righteousness: by whose stripes ye were healed."

> **CHRIST BORE THE WORLD'S SINS ON THE CROSS**
> On the cross at Calvary, God the Father laid upon His own Son the sins of the whole world. He bore those sins in His own perfectly holy and righteous body. The *"our"* in this verse refers to every human being of Adam's race, whether man, woman, or child, who ever lived. It does not refer only to "the elect."

- **Isaiah 53:5**

"But he *was* wounded for our transgressions, *he was* bruised for our iniquities: the chastisement of our peace *was* upon him; and with his stripes we are healed."

Isaiah was speaking of the Messiah, the Lord Jesus Christ, Who would one day come to this earth and die for the sins of all the people who ever lived. The three uses of *"our"* in this verse refer to all humanity, whether Jews or Gentiles, not just to "the elect."

- **Isaiah 53:6**

"All we like sheep have gone astray; we have turned every one to his own way; and the LORD hath laid on him the iniquity of us all."

This verse also speaks about a universal, unlimited atonement for the sins of the whole world. The two uses of *"we,"* and the one use of *"us,"* include all the members of the human race.
- 1 John 2:2
"And he is the propitiation for our sins: and not for ours only, but also for *the sins of* the whole world."

MEANING OF THE GREEK WORD, "HILASMOS"
The Greek Word for *"propitiation"* is HILASMOS. Some of the meanings of that Greek Word are:
"1) an appeasing, propitiating; 2) the means of appeasing, a propitiation"

CHRIST'S PROPITIATION FOR EVERYONE'S SINS
The Lord Jesus Christ's death on the cross was the appeasing satisfaction on the part of God, not only for the sins of true Christians, but also for the sins of *"the whole world."* That is a very clear refutation of the heresy of hyper-Calvinists who teach that the death of the Lord Jesus Christ was only for "the elect." This means that, in dying for their sins, He made provision for the whole world. People must genuinely believe on the Lord Jesus Christ as their Saviour before Christ's death is applied to them. But the provision for their salvation and the offer of eternal life is open for all to receive and accept.

UNIVERSALISM HELD BY MANY IS SERIOUS HERESY
Sometimes the hyper-Calvinists accuse those of us who hold to this position that we are teaching a universalism in the sense that 100% of the people in the world are automatically saved. That is not what the Bible teaches. The Bible teaches that the Lord Jesus Christ died for the sins of the whole world. He made provision for them to be forgiven, but, they must trust and receive Him as their personal Saviour for this provision to be applied to their own lives. If people do not come to Him in genuine and believing faith, they do not receive salvation, but will perish in the Lake of Fire in Hell.

2 Peter 3:10

"But the day of the Lord will come as a thief in the night; in the which the heavens shall pass away with a great noise, and the elements shall melt with fervent heat, the earth also and the works that are therein shall be burned up."

> **THE BEGINNING OF THE DAY OF THE LORD**
> <u>I believe the day of the Lord starts with the Tribulation period. It includes many judgments upon this earth. It also includes the heavens passing away and the elements melting with fervent heat.</u> The earth will be burned up at the very end of the Millennium. At the end of the Millennium, there will also be the Great White Throne Judgment, where all the sinners of all the world will be judged and cast into the Lake of Fire.
>
> This verse shows that the <u>Day of the LORD</u> will come in an unexpected and surprising manner. It will "*come as a thief in the night.*" The expression, the "*day of the LORD*" is found a total of twenty-three times in our King James Bible.

Verses On The "Day Of The LORD"

- **Isaiah 13:6**

"Howl ye; for the day of the LORD *is* at hand; it shall come as a destruction from the Almighty."

In the Tribulation Period, there is going to be much destruction.

- **Isaiah 13:7-11, 13**

"Therefore shall all hands be faint, and every man's heart shall melt: And they shall be afraid: pangs and sorrows shall take hold of them; they shall be in pain as a woman that travaileth: they shall be amazed one at another; their faces *shall be as* flames. Behold, the day of the LORD cometh, cruel both with wrath and fierce anger, to lay the land desolate: and he shall destroy the sinners thereof out of it. For the stars of heaven and the constellations thereof shall not give their light: the sun shall be darkened in his going forth, and the moon shall not cause her light to shine. And I will punish the world for *their* evil, and the wicked for their iniquity; and I will cause the arrogancy of the proud to cease, and will lay low the haughtiness of the terrible. . . . Therefore

I will shake the heavens, and the earth shall remove out of her place, in the wrath of the LORD of hosts, and in the day of his fierce anger."

THE DAY OF THE LORD BRINGS PUNISHMENT

Many people think that *"the day of the LORD"* sounds like a very fine and pleasant thing. This is not correct. In the above verses, there are some things which will transpire in the *"day of the LORD"* and there are some of things that will happen during the Tribulation period and at other later times. The day of the LORD is part of God's punishment for the sins of mankind.

- **Jeremiah 46:10**

"For this *is* the day of the Lord GOD of hosts, a day of vengeance, that he may avenge him of his adversaries: and the sword shall devour, and it shall be satiate and made drunk with their blood: for the Lord GOD of hosts hath a sacrifice in the north country by the river Euphrates."

This verse makes it clear that the day of the LORD is a day of vengeance when the LORD will avenge Himself on His adversaries.

- **Ezekiel 13:5**

"Ye have not gone up into the gaps, neither made up the hedge for the house of Israel to stand in the battle in the day of the LORD."

We see in this verse that the day of the LORD will be a time of battle.

- **Joel 1:15**

"Alas for the day! for the day of the LORD *is* at hand, and as a destruction from the Almighty shall it come."

The day of the LORD is not a pleasant day, it is a day of destruction.

- **Joel 2:30-32**

"And I will shew wonders in the heavens and in the earth, blood, and fire, and pillars of smoke. The sun shall be turned into darkness, and the moon into blood, before the great and the terrible day of the LORD come. And it shall come to pass, *that* whosoever shall call on the name of the LORD shall be delivered: for in mount Zion and in Jerusalem shall be deliverance, as the LORD hath said, and in the remnant whom the LORD shall call."

Some of these judgments are mentioned in the book of Revelation. During the seven-year Tribulation period, many will call upon His Name and be saved. The Antichrist will kill their bodies, but their souls will be immediately taken to Heaven.

- **Joel 3:13-16**

"Put ye in the sickle, for the harvest is ripe: come, get you down; for the press is full, the fats overflow; for their wickedness *is* great. Multitudes, multitudes in the valley of decision: for the day of the LORD *is* near in the valley of decision. The sun and the moon shall be darkened, and the stars shall withdraw their shining. The LORD also shall roar out of Zion, and utter his voice from Jerusalem; and the heavens and the earth shall shake: but the LORD *will be* the hope of his people, and the strength of the children of Israel."

These are literal fulfillments that will take place. The sun and the moon will be darkened, and the stars will withdraw their shining.

- **Amos 5:18**

"Woe unto you that desire the day of the LORD! to what end *is* it for you? the day of the LORD *is* darkness, and not light."

Some people even today mistakenly desire the day of the LORD. That's a very bad choice, because it will be a day of darkness rather than light.

- **Zephaniah 1:14-15**

"The great day of the LORD *is* near, *it is* near, and hasteth greatly, *even* the voice of the day of the LORD: the mighty man shall cry there bitterly. That day *is* a day of wrath, a day of trouble and distress, a day of wasteness and desolation, a day of darkness and gloominess, a day of clouds and thick darkness,"

Again the day of the LORD is described as a day of wrath, trouble, distress, wasteness, desolation, darkness, gloominess, clouds, and thick darkness. How could such a day be worthy of being looked forward to?

- **Zephaniah 1:17-18**

"And I will bring distress upon men, that they shall walk like blind men, because they have sinned against the LORD: and their blood shall be poured out as dust, and their flesh as the dung. Neither their silver nor their gold shall be able to deliver them in the day of the LORD'S wrath; but the whole land shall be devoured by the fire of his jealousy: for he shall make even a speedy riddance of all them that dwell in the land."

SEVERE PUNISHMENT DURING THE TRIBULATION

God will pour out His judgment in this Tribulation period. If people come to the Lord Jesus Christ before that judgment happens, they will be saved--they will be born-again--and go to Heaven. God will judge the heathen. Their blood shall be poured out like dust. Only through genuine faith in the Lord Jesus Christ can people be delivered. Silver and gold can't buy deliverance.

- Zechariah 14:1-4

"Behold, the day of the LORD cometh, and thy spoil shall be divided in the midst of thee. For I will gather all nations against Jerusalem to battle; and the city shall be taken, and the houses rifled, and the women ravished; and half of the city shall go forth into captivity, and the residue of the people shall not be cut off from the city. Then shall the LORD go forth, and fight against those nations, as when he fought in the day of battle. And his feet shall stand in that day upon the mount of Olives, which *is* before Jerusalem on the east, and the mount of Olives shall cleave in the midst thereof toward the east and toward the west, *and there shall be* a very great valley; and half of the mountain shall remove toward the north, and half of it toward the south."

Here the battle of Armageddon is described. These verses describe the second phase of the coming of the Lord Jesus Christ. They tell about when He will set his feet upon the mount of Olives. The mount of Olives will cleave in the midst making half of the mountain move to the north and half to move toward the south. This will open up a valley from east to west, and will allow living waters to flow from Jerusalem into the desert which shall blossom as the rose.

- Zechariah 14:6-8

"And it shall come to pass in that day, *that* the light shall not be clear, *nor* dark: But it shall be one day which shall be known to the LORD, not day, nor night: but it shall come to pass, *that* at evening time it shall be light. And it shall be in that day, *that* living waters shall go out from Jerusalem; half of them toward the former sea, and half of them toward the hinder sea: in summer and in winter shall it be."

This day is another reference to the day of the LORD. My mother sent Mrs. Waite and me to the holy land in the 1980's. We stayed at a hotel located on that Mount of Olives. We can understand very clearly how this prophecy will be fulfilled and how this Mount can move to the north and to the south opening up a valley running east and west.

- **Acts 2:19-20**

"And I will shew wonders in heaven above, and signs in the earth beneath; blood, and fire, and vapour of smoke: The sun shall be turned into darkness, and the moon into blood, before that great and notable day of the Lord come:"

The New Testament repeats here what was predicted in the Old Testament about these signs that would occur before the coming of the day of the Lord.

- **Revelation 16:14-16**

"For they are the spirits of devils, working miracles, *which* go forth unto the kings of the earth and of the whole world, to gather them to the battle of that great day of God Almighty. Behold, I come as a thief. Blessed *is* he that watcheth, and keepeth his garments, lest he walk naked, and they see his shame. And he gathered them together into a place called in the Hebrew tongue Armageddon."

This describes the Battle of Armageddon that will take place in the great day of God Almighty. It will happen in the valley of Jezreel.

It says here, in 2 Peter 3:10, that *"the elements shall melt with fervent heat."*

THE MEANING OF THE GREEK WORD, "STOICHEION"

The Greek Word for *"elements"* is STOICHEION. Some of the meanings of that Greek Word are:

"1) any first thing, from which the others belonging to some series or composite whole take their rise, an element, first principal; 1a) the letters of the alphabet as the elements of speech, not however the written characters, but the spoken sounds; 1b) the elements from which all things have come, the material causes of the universe; 1c) the heavenly bodies, either as parts of the heavens or (as others think) because in them the elements of man, life and destiny were

> *supposed to reside; 1d) the elements, rudiments, primary and fundamental principles of any art, science, or discipline; 1d1) i.e. of mathematics, Euclid's geometry"*

This Greek Word would include the elements that make up our entire universe. According to an Internet link I looked up the other day, [https://en.wikipedia.org/wiki/Periodic_table], there were then 118 elements on the most recent Periodic Table. When this Bible prophecy is fulfilled, all of these elements will melt and be destroyed.

THE MEANING OF THE GREEK WORD, "LUO"

The Greek Word for *"melt"* is LUO. Some of the meanings of that Greek Word are:

"1) to loose any person (or thing) tied or fastened; 1a) bandages of the feet, the shoes, 1b) of a husband and wife joined together by the bond of matrimony; 1c) of a single man, whether he has already had a wife or has not yet married; 2) to loose one bound, i.e. to unbind, release from bonds, set free; 2a) of one bound up (swathed in bandages); 2b) bound with chains (a prisoner), discharge from prison, let go 3) to loosen, undo, dissolve, anything bound, tied, or compacted together; 3a) an assembly, i.e. to dismiss, break up; 3b) laws, as having a binding force, are likened to bonds; 3c) to annul, subvert; 3d) to do away with, to deprive of authority, whether by precept or act; 3e) to declare unlawful; 3f) to loose what is compacted or built together, to break up, demolish, destroy; 3g) to dissolve something coherent into parts, to destroy; 3h) metaph., to overthrow, to do away with"

GOD WILL CREATE A NEW HEAVEN AND NEW EARTH

The Lord Who created the heavens and the earth, made all of the elements that are contained in it. God will destroy this old earth and create what is called a *"new heaven and a new earth."*

This is referred to in four Bible verses:
"*For, behold, I create new heavens and a new earth: and the former shall not be remembered, nor come into mind.*" (Isaiah 65:17)

"*For as the new heavens and the new earth, which I will make, shall remain before me, saith the LORD, so shall your seed and your name remain.*" (Isaiah 66:22)

"*Nevertheless we, according to his promise, look for new heavens and a new earth, wherein dwelleth righteousness.*" (2 Peter 3:13)

"*And I saw a new heaven and a new earth: for the first heaven and the first earth were passed away; and there was no more sea.*" (Revelation 21:1)

The creation of the new heaven and the earth will probably take place at the end of the Millennial Reign of the Lord Jesus Christ.

When this takes place, as it says in the verse, "*the works that are therein shall be burned up.*" When I was teaching at Shelton College in Cape May, New Jersey, many years ago, one of the teachers held a different view of the "*works*" of this world. <u>He believed, contrary to the Bible, that all the beautiful cultural works such as beautiful music, art work, and other such things, will be preserved in Heaven.</u> This verse shows clearly that this is not a Biblical position.

THE MEANING OF THE GREEK WORD, "KATAKAIO"

All these "*works,*" however important, will be burned up. The Greek Word for "*burned up*" is KATAKAIO. Some of the meanings of this Greek Word are:

"*1) to burn up, consume by fire*"

All that men honor and exalt will be done away with.

2 Peter 3:11

"Seeing then that all these things shall be dissolved, what manner of persons ought ye to be in all holy conversation and godliness,"

Since all of the fine things of this world will be dissolved and pass away, genuine Christians must be pure and holy in their lives.

Verses On Purity And Holiness

- **1 John 3:2-3**

"Beloved, now are we the sons of God, and it doth not yet appear what we shall be: but we know that, when he shall appear, we shall be like him; for we shall see him as he is. And every man that hath this hope in him purifieth himself, even as he is pure."

The hope that true Christians have, in being made like unto the Lord Jesus Christ when He comes, should cause them to be pure and holy in their living.

- **Romans 6:19**

"I speak after the manner of men because of the infirmity of your flesh: for as ye have yielded your members servants to uncleanness and to iniquity unto iniquity; even so now yield your members servants to righteousness unto holiness."

GOD WANTS TO USE CHRISTIANS' BODIES

Once people have become genuine Christians, they are urged to yield their members to the Lord Jesus Christ. Their members would include their hands, eyes, legs, ears, mouths, and hearts. The Lord wants them to be holy in every part of their bodies.

- **2 Corinthians 7:1**

"Having therefore these promises, dearly beloved, let us cleanse ourselves from all filthiness of the flesh and spirit, perfecting holiness in the fear of God."

BOTH FLESH AND SPIRIT SHOULD BE CLEANSED

True Christians still have their old sinful nature. They must cleanse themselves from filthiness, not only of their flesh, but also of the spirit. God wants them to live holy lives.

- **1 Thessalonians 4:7**

"For God hath not called us unto uncleanness, but unto holiness."

God has called every genuine born-again Christian to holiness–not uncleanness. That must be their goal.

This holiness must be manifested in all holy conversation and godliness.

> **MEANING OF THE GREEK WORD, "ANASTROPHE"**
>
> The Greek Word for *"conversation"* here is ANASTROPHE. Some of the meanings of that Greek Word are:
>
> *"1) manner of life, conduct, behaviour, deportment"*
>
> Purity and holiness must be seen in the lives of all true Christians.

2 Peter 3:12

"Looking for and hasting unto the coming of the day of God, wherein the heavens being on fire shall be dissolved, and the elements shall melt with fervent heat?"

In the Bible, the prophetic order of events is:
(1) the Rapture of all true Christians
(2) the seven-year Tribulation Period
(3) the 1,000-year Millennial Reign of the Lord Jesus Christ
(4) the judgment of all unsaved people at the Great White Throne judgment
(5) all the unsaved people being cast into the Lake of Fire of Hell
(6) God's creation of a new heaven and a new earth

This verse has some similar information to that found in 2 Peter 3:10. It states that *"the heavens being on fire shall be dissolved."*

> **THE MEANING OF THE GREEK WORD, "LUO"**
>
> The Greek Word for *"dissolved"* is LUO. That is the same word used in verse ten for the word, *"melt."* I urge you to go back to verse ten for the many meanings of the Greek Word for both *"dissolved"* and for *"melt."*

The Greek Word for *"elements"* in this verse is the same Greek Word **STOICHEION** used above in verse ten. I suggest you go back to that verse for the many meanings of that Greek Word.

> **THE MEANING OF THE GREEK WORD, "TEKO"**
> In this verse, the Greek Word for *"melt"* used here is TEKO. Some of the meanings of that Greek Word are:
> *"1) to make liquid; 2) to become liquid, to melt; 3) to perish or become destroyed by melting"*

The making of these elements to melt will be done by means of *"fervent heat."*

> **THE MEANING OF THE GREEK WORD, "KAUSAOO"**
> The Greek Word for *"fervent heat"* is KAUSAOO. Some of the meanings of this Greek Word are:
> *"1) to burn up, set fire to; 2) to suffer with feverish burning, be parched with fever."*

To accomplish this, it will take a powerful Divine miracle. Nothing that man could come up with would be able to make this happen. It will have to be from the Lord Himself.

2 Peter 3:13

"Nevertheless we, according to his promise, look for new heavens and a new earth, wherein dwelleth righteousness."

We have previously seen four verses about the new heavens and the new earth in verse ten mentioned earlier. There will be a new heaven and a new earth, according to God's promise. Righteousness alone will dwell there.

> **THE CREATION OF THE NEW HEAVENS AND EARTH**
> This process of God's creating the new heavens and new earth will likely take place at the end of the Millennial Reign of the Lord Jesus Christ after the Great White Throne Judgment of the lost who will be sent to the Lake of Fire in Hell.

In the phrase *"new heavens"* and *"new earth,"* it is important to understand the meaning of the Greek Word for *"new."*

> **THE MEANING OF THE GREEK WORD, "KAINOS"**
>
> The Greek Word here is not NEOS, but KAINOS. Some of the meanings of this Greek Word for "*new*" are:
>
>> "*1) new; 1a) as respects form; 1a1) recently made, fresh, recent, unused, unworn; 1b) as respects substance; 1b1) of a new kind, unprecedented, novel, uncommon, unheard of.*"

This Greek Word gives the idea of "*fresh*," "*novel*," and "*of new kind*." It is a different kind of newness than NEOS.

> **THE MEANING OF THE GREEK WORD, "NEOS"**
>
> Some of the meanings of the Greek Word for "*new*" (NEOS), are:
>
>> "*1) recently born, young, youthful; 2) new*"

To be "recently born" would speak of originality, not just "*recent*" or "*fresh*." When a boy or girl is born, he or she is "*brand new*," as they say, and never existed before conception.

Since the Greek Word (KAINOS) is used, the new heavens and new earth will be "*recent*," but also "*a fresh*" and "*new kind*" of heaven and earth. They will be changed, but they will not be created from the beginning. They will not have a "*rebirth*," but a refreshing and a change from what they were before.

Let me illustrate these differences in a practical and down-to-earth way. A few years ago, a lady that I knew wanted to get a new (KAINOS) car. She didn't necessarily want to get a new (NEOS) car because they cost too much. So she bought a 1998 car that was new (KAINOS) to her, yet not brand-new (NEOS).

2 Peter 3:14

"Wherefore, beloved, seeing that ye look for such things, be diligent that ye may be found of him in peace, without spot, and blameless."

Since these genuine Christians were looking for this new heavens and new earth, Peter is asking them to be diligent so they might be found by the Lord Jesus Christ in peace, without spot, and blameless.

> **THE MEANING OF THE GREEK WORD, "PROSDOKAO"**
> The Greek Word for *"look"* used here is PROSDOKAO. Some of the meanings of this Greek Word are:
>> *"1) to expect (whether in thought, in hope, or in fear); 2) to look for, wait for"*

This would be a look of expectancy. It would mean they were looking forward to this new situation. While looking, waiting, and expecting this promise, Peter wanted these true Christians to be in peace, without any spots, and blameless.

> **THE MEANING OF THE GREEK WORD, "AMOMETOS"**
> The Greek Word for *"blameless"* is AMOMETOS. Some of the meanings of this Greek Word are:
>> *"1) that cannot be censured, blameless"*
>
> It doesn't necessarily mean "perfect." False charges against a person do not take away a person's otherwise blameless character.

Verses On Blameless

- Philippians 2:14-15

"Do all things without murmurings and disputings: That ye may be blameless and harmless, the sons of God, without rebuke, in the midst of a crooked and perverse nation, among whom ye shine as lights in the world;"

Once they are truly saved, God wants Christians to cease their murmurings and disputings and be blameless, without rebuke. They should shine as lights in the midst of the crooked and perverted world.

- 1 Thessalonians 5:23

"And the very God of peace sanctify you wholly; and *I pray God* your whole spirit and soul and body be preserved blameless unto the coming of our Lord Jesus Christ."

> **EVERY HUMAN BEING IS TRIPARTITE**
> Every human being is tripartite. Each person has three parts—a spirit, a soul, and a body. If they are true Christians, God wants them completely set apart to Him. He wants them to be preserved blameless in all three parts of their bodies until they die and go to Heaven, or

until the Lord Jesus Christ returns in the Rapture to take them Home to Heaven.

THE MEANING OF THE GREEK WORD, "ASPILOS"

Peter also wanted the lives of Christians to whom he was writing to be "*without spot*." The Greek Word for this is ASPILOS. Some of the meanings of this Greek Word are:

> "*1) spotless; 2) metaph. 2a) free from censure, irreproachable; 2b) free from vice, unsullied*"

All true Christians should aim at that goal in order to please the Lord Jesus Christ, their Saviour.

2 Peter 3:15

"And account that the longsuffering of our Lord is salvation; even as our beloved brother Paul also according to the wisdom given unto him hath written unto you;"

Our Lord is truly longsuffering. For verses on longsuffering and its meaning, I invite you to look back at our comments on 2 Peter 3:9. That longsuffering leads many to come to a true and Biblical salvation from their sins and from Hell.

Peter not only declares here that he knows the Apostle Paul, but:

    (1) he calls him a "*beloved brother*";
    (2) he says that Paul has written to his readers as well; and
    (3) he says that Paul's writings were from the wisdom "*given unto him.*"

This implies that he wrote Words that were inspired by the Holy Spirit. In any event, Peter held Paul in high esteem.

Verses From Paul On Salvation

- **Romans 1:16**

"For I am not ashamed of the gospel of Christ: for it is the power of God unto salvation to every one that believeth; to the Jew first, and also to the Greek."

SALVATION THROUGH GENUINE FAITH IN CHRIST

Paul's teaching on the reception of God's salvation is very clear in this verse. The gospel of the Lord Jesus

Christ is the good news that He died for the sins of the world. That substitutionary death on the cross can bring salvation only to those who genuinely believe in Him as their Saviour, regardless of their racial or religious background.

- Romans 10:10

"For with the heart man believeth unto righteousness; and with the mouth confession is made unto salvation."

BELIEF IN CHRIST FROM THE HEART NEEDED

In this verse, Paul makes it clear that genuine belief in the Lord Jesus Christ must be from the heart, not just acceptance from the head. Saved, born-again Christians should testify as they share with others about the genuineness of their salvation.

- 2 Corinthians 6:2

"(For he saith, I have heard thee in a time accepted, and in the day of salvation have I succoured thee: behold, now *is* the accepted time; behold, now *is* the day of salvation.)"

THE ACCEPTED TIME FOR SALVATION IS "NOW"

In this verse, Paul speaks about the accepted time for people to receive salvation by true faith in the Lord Jesus Christ. The accepted time is right now. It is to be an immediate acceptance of the Saviour. There should be no delay. A person might die today and be ushered into Hell's fires. The only acceptable time is right now because *"now is the day of salvation."* Tomorrow might be too late. People should never put off making sure of their acceptance of the Bible's only way of salvation.

2 Peter 3:16

"As also in all his epistles, speaking in them of these things; in which are some things hard to be understood, which they that are unlearned and unstable wrest, as they do also the other scriptures, unto their own destruction."

Again in this verse, Peter mentions Paul's epistles and likens them to *"the other scriptures,"* thus identifying his letters as Scripture. Peter acknowledged that in some of Paul's letters were things that were hard to be understood. However, that is no reason for unlearned and unstable people to wrest and twist God's Words as they do other Scriptures.

> **THE MEANING OF THE GREEK WORD, "STREBLOO"**
> The Greek Word for *"wrest"* is STREBLOO. Some of the meanings of that Greek Word are:
> *"1) to twist, turn awry; 2) to torture, put to the rack; 3) metaph. to pervert, of one who wrests or tortures language in a false sense"*

Even today, there are many seminaries, schools, churches, publications, writers, church leaders, pastors, and others who are unmercifully twisting and perverting the clear teachings of the Words of God. This perverting is done by both those who are unlearned and unstable, as well as by those who are learned and stable. They know exactly what they are doing to pervert the Scriptures that God has given to us by His verbal, plenary **inspiration**; He has preserved for us, up to this very day, His Words by His verbal, plenary **preservation**. Let's look at some verses that speak about God's Scriptures.

Verses On The Scriptures
- **Matthew 22:29**

"Jesus answered and said unto them, Ye do err, not knowing the scriptures, [GRAPHE] nor the power of God."

The Lord Jesus Christ rebuked the Sadducees who denied any resurrection. They erred because they knew neither the Scriptures nor the mighty power of God. When used in the Bible, the word, *"Scripture,"* (the Greek Word is GRAPHE), always refers to the original language Words of Hebrew, Aramaic, and Greek which have been preserved for us today and forevermore. The followers of Peter Ruckman and Gail Riplinger teach that this word refers to the King James Bible. They apply it to 2 Timothy 3:16-17 in a wrong attempt to prove that the King James Bible was *"given by inspiration of God"* or God-Breathed. This is a serious doctrinal and Scriptural error.

- **Matthew 26:56**

"But all this was done, that the scriptures [GRAPHE] of the prophets might be fulfilled. Then all the disciples forsook him, and fled."

This is a *second reference* to the Scriptures as the Hebrew and Aramaic Words of the Old Testament.

- **Luke 24:27**
"And beginning at Moses and all the prophets, he expounded unto them in all the scriptures [GRAPHE] the things concerning himself."

This is a *third reference* to the Scriptures as being the Hebrew and Aramaic Words of the Old Testament.

- **Luke 24:32**
"And they said one to another, Did not our heart burn within us, while he talked with us by the way, and while he opened to us the scriptures [GRAPHE]?"

This is a *fourth reference* to the Scriptures as being the Hebrew and Aramaic Words of the Old Testament.

- **Luke 24:45**
"Then opened he their understanding, that they might understand the scriptures [GRAPHE],"

This is a *fifth reference* to the Scriptures as being the Hebrew and Aramaic Words of the Old Testament.

- **John 5:39**
"Search the scriptures [GRAPHE]; for in them ye think ye have eternal life: and they are they which testify of me."

This is a *sixth reference* to the Scriptures as being the Hebrew and Aramaic Words of the Old Testament.

- **Acts 17:2**
"And Paul, as his manner was, went in unto them, and three sabbath days reasoned with them out of the scriptures [GRAPHE],"

This is a *seventh reference* to the Scriptures as being the Hebrew and Aramaic Words of the Old Testament.

- **Acts 17:10-11**
"And the brethren immediately sent away Paul and Silas by night unto Berea: who coming thither went into the synagogue of the Jews. These were more noble than those in Thessalonica, in that they received the word with all readiness of mind, and searched the Scriptures [GRAPHE] daily, whether those things were so."

This is a *eighth reference* to the Scriptures as being the Hebrew and Aramaic Words of the Old Testament.

My wife and I went to high school in Berea, Ohio. We are Bereans in that sense, but also in the sense of this verse in that we do search the Scriptures daily.

- **Acts 18:24**

"And a certain Jew named Apollos, born at Alexandria, an eloquent man, *and* mighty in the Scriptures [GRAPHE], came to Ephesus."

This is a *ninth reference* to the Scriptures as being the Hebrew and Aramaic Words of the Old Testament.

- **2 Timothy 3:16**

"All scripture [GRAPHE] *is* given by inspiration of God, and *is* profitable for doctrine, for reproof, for correction, for instruction in righteousness:"

This is a *tenth reference* to the Scriptures as being the Hebrew and Aramaic Words of the Old Testament.

"GIVEN BY INSPIRATION OF GOD"=THEOPNEUSTOS

The five words, *"given by inspiration of God"* are translations of the one Greek Word, THEOPNEUSTOS. This compound Word comes from THEOS ("God") and PNEUSTOS from PNEO ("to breathe"). It literally means "God-breathed."

As I mentioned before, Peter Ruckman, Gail Riplinger, and their many followers, use the word ("Scripture") to refer to the King James Bible rather than to the proper reference of the Hebrew, Aramaic, and Greek Words. They are teaching serious heresy.

THE KING JAMES BIBLE, NOT "GOD-BREATHED"

God did not "breathe-out" the words of the King James Bible. Those English words were man's words, accurately and skillfully translated from God's Words–the original Hebrew, Aramaic and Greek Words --by well-equipped men. When people fail to make this vital distinction they get themselves into many theological errors.

- **Romans 15:4**

"For whatsoever things were written aforetime were written for our learning, that we through patience and comfort of the scriptures [GRAPHE] might have hope."

This is a *eleventh reference* to the Scriptures as being the Hebrew and Aramaic Words of the Old Testament.

- **2 Timothy 3:15**

"And that from a child thou hast known the holy scriptures [GRAPHE], which are able to make thee wise unto salvation through faith which is in Christ Jesus."

This is a *twelfth reference* to the Scriptures as being the Hebrew and Aramaic Words of the Old Testament. Timothy knew the Hebrew Scriptures.

HEBREW, ARAMAIC, & GREEK WORDS PRESERVED
It is very important to see, that we have, preserved by God to this very day, the Scriptures which were originally given to us by God Himself in the languages of Hebrew, Aramaic, and Greek. Translations of those Scriptures (into any language in the world today) should be done carefully and accurately as the translators of the King James Bible did.

2 Peter 3:17
"Ye therefore, beloved, seeing ye know these things before, beware lest ye also, being led away with the error of the wicked, fall from your own stedfastness."

Since Peter's readers knew how these false teachers were twisting and perverting God's Words, he warned them to beware.

THE MEANING OF THE GREEK WORD, "PHULASSO"
The Greek Word for *"beware"* is PHULASSO. Some of the meanings of that Greek Word are:

> *"1) to guard; 1a) to watch, keep watch; 1b) to guard or watch, have an eye upon: lest he escape; 1c) to guard a person (or thing) that he may remain safe; 1c1) lest he suffer violence, be despoiled, etc. to protect; 1c2) to protect one from a person or thing; 1c3) to keep from being snatched away, preserve safe and unimpaired; 1c4) to guard from being lost or perishing; 1c5) to guard one's self from a thing; 1d) to guard i.e. care for, take care not to violate; 1d1) to observe; 2) to observe for one's self something to escape; 2a) to avoid, shun flee from; 2b) to guard for one's self (i.e. for one's safety's sake) so as not to violate, i.e. to keep,*

> observe (the precepts of the Mosaic law)"

All genuine Christians today must also beware in the full sense of this Greek Word in view of the many wicked and false errors of doctrine that abound around the world.
- **Colossians 2:8**
  "Beware lest any man spoil you through philosophy and vain deceit, after the tradition of men, after the rudiments of the world, and not after Christ."

This same Greek Word is used in this verse with the definition listed above. True Christians must be guarded against all sorts of philosophy and vain deceit that is being promulgated in schools, on the radio, on TV, and across the world through the Internet.

ERROR AND FALSE DOCTRINE SHOULD BE EXPOSED

Without the trait of awareness of what evils surround Christians in our time, they would not be able to effectively expose and correct the errors which are rampant today. They must not fall from their own steadfast and Biblical positions.

2 Peter 3:18

"But grow in grace, and in the knowledge of our Lord and Saviour Jesus Christ. To him be glory both now and for ever. Amen."

Peter did not want his readers to be spiritually immature. He wanted them to grow in grace and in the knowledge of the Lord Jesus Christ.

THE MEANING OF THE GREEK WORD, "AUXANO"

The Greek word for "*grow*" is AUXANO. Some of the meanings of this Greek Word are:

> "1) to cause to grow, augment; 2) to increase, become greater; 3) to grow, increase; 3a) of plants; 3b) of infants; 3c) of a multitude of people; 3d) of inward Christian growth"

If true Christians are to be effective for the Lord Jesus Christ, they must heed this imperative command of the Apostle Peter. Notice the two objects of that growth. There must be growth in grace and in "*knowledge of their Lord and Saviour Jesus Christ.*"

> **THE MEANING OF THE GREEK WORD, "CHARIS"**
>
> The Greek Word for *"grace"* is CHARIS. Some of the meanings of that Greek Word are:
>
> *"1) grace; 1a) that which affords joy, pleasure, delight, sweetness, charm, loveliness: grace of speech; 2) good will, loving-kindness, favour; 2a) of the merciful kindness by which God, exerting his holy influence upon souls, turns them to Christ, keeps, strengthens, increases them in Christian faith, knowledge, affection, and kindles them to the exercise of the Christian virtues; 3) what is due to grace; 3a) the spiritual condition of one governed by the power of divine grace; 3b) the token or proof of grace, benefit; 3b1) a gift of grace; 3b2) benefit, bounty; 4) thanks, (for benefits, services, favours), recompense, reward"*

The application of this definition of grace is a challenge for every genuine Christian. Only by the power of God the Holy Spirit, Who indwells them, can these Christians grow and increase in all the aspects of God's grace.

As far as Christians growing in the knowledge of the Lord Jesus Christ, this is essential if they really want to please their Saviour. The only place where this knowledge can be found is in the Old and New Testaments of the Bible. The Saviour is found throughout His Word. To increase in the knowledge of Him necessitates a continual reading and heeding of the Bible.

The Lord Jesus Christ deserves and should receive glory both now and forevermore.

> **THE MEANING OF THE GREEK WORD, "DOXA"**
>
> The Greek Word for *"glory"* is DOXA. Some of the meanings of that Greek Word are:
>
> *"1) opinion, judgment, view; 2) opinion, estimate, whether good or bad concerning someone; 2a) in the NT always a good opinion concerning one,*

> *resulting in praise, honour, and glory; 3) splendour, brightness; 3a) of the moon, sun, stars; 3b) magnificence, excellence, preeminence, dignity, grace; 3c) majesty; 3c1) a thing belonging to God; 3c1) the kingly majesty which belongs to Him as supreme ruler, majesty in the sense of the absolute perfection of the deity; 3c2) a thing belonging to Christ; 3c2a) the kingly majesty of the Messiah; 3c2b) the absolutely perfect inward or personal excellency of Christ; the majesty; 3c3) of the angels; 3c3a) as apparent in their exterior brightness; 4) a most glorious condition, most exalted state; 4a) of that condition with God the Father in heaven to which Christ was raised after He had achieved his work on earth; 4b) the glorious condition of blessedness into which is appointed and promised that true Christians shall enter after their Saviour's return from heaven"*

CHRIST DESERVES ALL MAJESTY AND GLORY

The Lord Jesus Christ truly deserves all the majesty, blessedness, brightness, and glory that true Christians should give Him. He is worthy of such glory as being perfect Man and perfect God Who is now seated at the right hand of God the Father.

THE MEANING OF THE GREEK WORD, "AMEN"

The last word of the book of 2 Peter is "*Amen.*" Some of the meanings of the Greek Word are:

> "*1) firm; 1a) metaph. faithful; 2) verily, amen; 2a) at the beginning of a discourse - surely, truly, of a truth; 2b) at the end - so it is, so be it, may it be fulfilled. It was a custom, which passed over from the synagogues to the Christian assemblies, that when he*

> who had read or discoursed, had offered up solemn prayer to God, the others responded Amen, and thus made the substance of what was uttered their own."

It is interesting to note that the word, "*Amen*," is almost a universal Word that is known and used in many of the languages of the world. The author who gave the definition of "*Amen*" says this about its universality:

> **THE USE OF "AMEN" AROUND THE WORLD**
>
> "*The word "amen" is a most remarkable word. It was transliterated directly from the Hebrew into the Greek of the New Testament, then into Latin and into English and many other languages, so that it is practically a universal word. It has been called the best known word in human speech. The word is directly related--in fact, almost identical--to the Hebrew Word for "believe" (amam), or faithful. Thus, it came to mean "sure" or "truly", an expression of absolute trust and confidence.*"

When we use the word, "*Amen*," we should understand its meaning. It indicates something with which we agree and believe.

Jude
Chapter One

Jude 1:1

"Jude, the servant of Jesus Christ, and brother of James, to them that are sanctified by God the Father, and preserved in Jesus Christ, and called:"

This little book was written by Jude, but it is not clear which Jude it was since there are several mentioned in the New Testament. It is clear that he was a servant of the Lord Jesus Christ and that he was the brother of one of the several men named James. As I have looked at this problem, there seemed to be eight different possibilities for Jude. One of the eight possibilities being that Jude was the half brother of the Lord Jesus Christ.

I'd like to think the half-brother of Jesus wrote this, but it could be the apostle Jude or Judas. In the New Testament, there are four different men named James.

SOME OF THE PEOPLE NAMED "JUDE" OR "JUDAS"

Here is what is found under the name of Jude (or otherwise known as Judas as it is sometimes spelled):

"1) the fourth son of Jacob; 2) an unknown ancestor of Christ; 3) a man surnamed the Galilean, who at the time of the census of Quirinus, excited the revolt in Galilee, Acts 5:37; 4) a certain Jew of Damascus, Acts 9:11; 5) a prophet surnamed Barsabas, of the church at Jerusalem, Acts 15:22,27,32; 6) the apostle, Jn 14:22, who was surnamed Lebbaeus or Thaddaeus, and according to opinion wrote the Epistle of Jude; 7) the half-brother of Jesus, Mt. 13:55; 8) Judas Iscariot, the apostle who betrayed Jesus"

From this list of various names for either Jude or Judas, you can see that the person who wrote this book is not clear. It certainly was not Judas Iscariot. We know that for certain.

Jude wrote to those who were sanctified, preserved in the Lord Jesus Christ, and called.

THE MEANING OF THE GREEK WORD, "HAGIAZO"

The Greek Word for *"sanctified"* is HAGIAZO. Some of the meanings of that Greek Word are:

"1) to render or acknowledge, or to be venerable or hallow; 2) to separate from profane things and dedicate to God; 2a) consecrate things to God; 2b) dedicate people to God; 3) to purify; 3a) to cleanse externally; 3b) to purify by expiation: free from the guilt of sin; 3c) to purify internally by renewing of the soul"

This verb is in the Greek perfect tense. As such, it means those who have been purified and set apart for God in the past, who remain purified in the present, and who will continue to be purified in the future. These genuine Christians will never lose their salvation and their standing with God as being set apart from the world and set apart unto Him.

Verses With The Name, Jude Or Judas

- **Luke 6:13**

"And when it was day, he called *unto him* his disciples: and of them he chose twelve, whom also he named apostles;"

The Lord began choosing His apostles in this verse. In verse 16, Judas (or Jude) is listed.

- **Luke 6:16**

"And Judas *the brother* of James, and Judas Iscariot, which also was the traitor."

There are two Judases that were apostles, Judas (or Jude) who was the brother of James, and Judas Iscariot.

- **John 14:22**

"Judas saith unto him, not Iscariot, Lord, how is it that thou wilt manifest thyself unto us, and not unto the world?"

This was Judas (or Jude) the apostle who asked this question at the last supper.

- Acts 1:13

"And when they were come in, they went up into an upper room, where abode both Peter, and James, and John, and Andrew, Philip, and Thomas, Bartholomew, and Matthew, James *the son* of Alphaeus, and Simon Zelotes, and Judas *the brother* of James."

So Judas (or Jude) the brother of James is one of the apostles who were gathered into the upper room on that occasion.

Verses On Sanctify

Jude was writing to people who had been sanctified by genuine faith in the Lord Jesus Christ.

- 1 Corinthians 6:11

"And such were some of you: but ye are washed, but ye are sanctified, but ye are justified in the name of the Lord Jesus, and by the Spirit of our God."

By true faith in the Lord Jesus Christ, people can be washed, sanctified, and justified.

- John 17:19

"And for their sakes I sanctify myself, that they also might be sanctified through the truth."

SANCTIFIED BY GOD'S WORDS

The Lord Jesus Christ sanctified Himself so that those who have genuinely trusted Him might be sanctified (or set apart) through the truth of God's Words found in the Bible.

- Acts 20:32

"And now, brethren, I commend you to God, and to the word of his grace, which is able to build you up, and to give you an inheritance among all them which are sanctified."

Those who are thus "sanctified" have an inheritance awaiting them in Heaven.

Jude 1:2

"Mercy unto you, and peace, and love, be multiplied."

This is Jude's greeting. He wants mercy, peace, and love to be multiplied in his readers.

> **THE MEANING OF THE GREEK WORD, "ELEOS"**
>
> The Greek Word for *"mercy"* is ELEOS. Some of the meanings of this Greek Word are:
>
> > *"1) mercy: kindness or good will towards the miserable and the afflicted, joined with a desire to help them; 1a) of men towards men: to exercise the virtue of mercy, show one's self merciful; 1b) of God towards men: in general providence; the mercy and clemency of God in providing and offering to men salvation by Christ; 1c) the mercy of Christ, whereby at his return to judgment he will bless true Christians with eternal life"*

Such mercy can come only from the God of Heaven. It was evidenced by His sending His Son from Heaven to die for the sins of the world so that whoever trusts in Him might have everlasting life.

God's peace is another gift that He gives those who have truly trusted in the Lord Jesus Christ as their Saviour.

> **THE MEANING OF THE GREEK WORD, "EIRENE"**
>
> The Greek Word for *"peace"* is EIRENE. Some of the meanings of that Greek Word are:
>
> > *"1) a state of national tranquillity; 1a) exemption from the rage and havoc of war; 2) peace between individuals, i.e. harmony, concord; 3) security, safety, prosperity, felicity, (because peace and harmony make and keep things safe and prosperous); 4) of the Messiah's peace; 4a) the way that leads to peace (salvation); 5) of Christianity, the tranquil state of a soul assured of its*

> *salvation through Christ, and so fearing nothing from God and content with its earthly lot, of whatsoever sort that is; 6) the blessed state of devout and upright men after death"*

God gives His peace to those who have genuinely accepted His Son as their Saviour. This peace is made possible by the indwelling of God the Holy Spirit in every true Christian.

GOD'S LOVE SUMMED UP IN JOHN 3:16

It is God's love that made both His mercy and His peace possible for sinful human beings. This love is summed up in John 3:16:

> *"For God so loved the world, that he gave his only begotten Son, that whosoever believeth in him should not perish, but have everlasting life."* (John 3:16)

Jude 1:3

"Beloved, when I gave all diligence to write unto you of the common salvation, it was needful for me to write unto you, and exhort you that ye should earnestly contend for the faith which was once delivered unto the saints."

You can see, from this verse, that when Jude gave diligence to write to his readers about their common salvation, he realized the need to first exhort them to *"earnestly contend for the faith which was once delivered unto the saints."*

"THE FAITH" REFERS TO BIBLE DOCTRINES

The phrase, *"the faith,"* (TEI PISTEI) has the definite article in the Greek. As such, it refers to the doctrines of the Faith found in the Bible.

THE MEANING OF THE GREEK WORD, "SPOUDE"

The Greek Word for *"diligence"* is SPOUDE. Some of the meanings of this Greek Word are:

> *"1) haste, with haste; 2) earnestness, diligence; 2a) earnestness in accomplishing, promoting, or striving*

> *after anything; 2b) to give all diligence, interest one's self most earnestly"*

This shows that Jude is very much in earnest when writing to his readers regarding the doctrines of the Faith. The doctrines are very important to him.

The Greek verb used for the phrase, "***earnestly contend***," is EPIAGONIZOMAI. It is in the Greek present tense and means to continue this action without let up. This is a compound verb made up of EPI plus AGONIZOMAI. The preposition, EPI, added to AGONIZOMAI, is used, in Greek syntax, as an intensive. This is why the word, "*earnestly*" is added to the word, "*contend.*"

In 1 Timothy 6:12, the phrase, "***fight the good fight*** of Faith," the same Greek root is used twice. The verb, "*fight*" is AGONIZOMAI. The word for "*fight*," in the phrase "*the good fight*," is AGON. Since the same Greek root is included in "*contend*" as well as "*fight*," it is clear that the word, "*contend,*" is a synonym for "*fight.*"

WE MUST CONTEND FOR THE BIBLE'S DOCTRINES

The Bible's Faith and doctrine that were "*once delivered unto the saints*" are what must be contended and fought for. To know the exact Faith and doctrine that was once delivered, we must know the Greek Words that were originally given to the saints. This is why we contend for the Traditional Received Greek Words that underlie the King James Bible so we can know the exact Faith and doctrine for which we must contend and fight.

Verses On Contending

- **Nehemiah 13:11**

"Then contended I with the rulers, and said, Why is the house of God forsaken? And I gathered them together, and set them in their place."

Nehemiah contended with the rulers because they forsook the house of God.

- **Nehemiah 13:17**

"Then I contended with the nobles of Judah, and said unto them, What evil thing *is* this that ye do, and profane the sabbath day?"

Nehemiah contended with the nobles of Judah because they profaned God's Sabbath day.

- **Nehemiah 13:25**

"And I contended with them, and cursed them, and smote certain of them, and plucked off their hair, and made them swear by God, *saying*, Ye shall not give your daughters unto their sons, nor take their daughters unto your sons, or for yourselves."

Nehemiah contended with the people of Judah, cursed them, smote some of them, plucked off their hair, and made them promise not to intermarry with the heathen. He certainly was a fighter and a contender.

- **Proverbs 28:4**

"They that forsake the law praise the wicked: but such as keep the law contend with them."

Those who were keeping the law of Moses contended with the wicked. They did not praise them.

Verses On The Faith As Bible Doctrine

Let me repeat what I wrote above about *"the faith"*:

*"The phrase, "the faith," (TEI PISTEI) has the definite article in the Greek. As such, it refers to the **doctrines of the faith found in the Bible**."*

IMPORTANCE OF THE DOCTRINES OF THE FAITH

The importance of all the doctrines of "the Faith" is repeated many times in the New Testament. We must not underestimate its value and importance as many are doing today.

- **Acts 14:22**

"Confirming the souls of the disciples, *and* exhorting them to continue in the faith, and that we must through much tribulation enter into the kingdom of God."

CONTINUE IN THE DOCTRINES OF THE BIBLE

Paul exhorted all of those he led to the Lord Jesus Christ to continue in the Faith, with the whole body of Christian doctrine taught in the Bible.

- **Acts 16:5**

"And so were the churches established in the faith, and increased in number daily."

CHRISTIANS MUST BE ESTABLISHED IN THE BIBLE
Paul saw to it that the churches he founded were established and made firm in the Faith. He didn't want them to be immature Christians.

- **1 Corinthians 16:13**

"Watch ye, stand fast in the faith, quit you like men, be strong."

Once true Christians had the Bible Faith, they were to hold it fast without wavering or changing it as most of our Bible versions and translations have done. This is because they have been based on false Gnostic Critical Greek Texts rather than on the Traditional Received Greek Text on which our King James Bible is based.

- **Ephesians 4:13**

"Till we all come in the unity of the faith, and of the knowledge of the Son of God, unto a perfect man, unto the measure of the stature of the fulness of Christ:"

I believe the unity of all the doctrines of the Faith will only come when genuine Christians are in Heaven. It would appear to be impossible while here on earth.

- **Colossians 2:7**

"Rooted and built up in him, and stablished in the faith, as ye have been taught, abounding therein with thanksgiving."

God wants every true Christian to be established firmly in the doctrines of the Bible.

- **1 Timothy 4:1**

"Now the Spirit speaketh expressly, that in the latter times some shall depart from the faith, giving heed to seducing spirits, and doctrines of devils;"

This verse predicted that in the latter times some shall depart from the Faith. We are living in the last days. and many of these predictions have come true. There is a departure from the Faith all around the world--in the apostate Protestant churches, also in Roman Catholicism, in cults, in New Evangelicalism, and with many who are in the so-called fundamentalist world. All these departures are a disgrace to God and His Bible doctrines!

- **1 Timothy 6:10**

"For the love of money is the root of all evil: which while some coveted after, they have erred from the faith, and pierced themselves through with many sorrows."

The love of money often leads pastors and others to err from the Faith found in the Bible. God promises that many sorrows will result if this occurs, regardless of how much money is received.

- **2 Timothy 4:7**
"I have fought a good fight, I have finished *my* course, I have kept the faith:"

> **PAUL GUARDED BIBLE DOCTRINES–SO SHOULD WE**
> Paul looked back on his entire ministry for the Lord Jesus Christ and could honestly say that he kept and guarded the doctrinal Faith of the Bible. May genuine Christians be able to say this as well as they depart this life!

- **Titus 1:13**
"This witness is true. Wherefore rebuke them sharply, that they may be sound in the faith;"

Speaking of the deceivers in Titus 1:10, Paul wanted them to be rebuked sharply. He hoped rebuke would get them to be sound in the Bible doctrines of the Faith.

- **1 Peter 5:9**
"Whom resist stedfast in the faith, knowing that the same afflictions are accomplished in your brethren that are in the world."

This verse (Jude 1:3) refers back to Satan who must be resisted steadfastly in order to keep within the Faith and doctrines of the Bible.

When Jude wrote in the present verse to earnestly contend and battle for the Faith, he meant it. I'm glad for those Bible-believing fundamentalists who are battling for all the doctrines of the Faith. I wish they would contend for the Faith that is found in the Hebrew, Aramaic, and Greek Words that underlie the King James Bible.

> **356 FALSE DOCTRINAL PASSAGES IN NEW BIBLES**
> This Faith is different from that of the modern Bible versions in over 356 doctrinal passages because of their use of the wrong Hebrew, Aramaic, and Greek Words as their foundation.
>
> If a Bible translation (in any language in the world) is based on the wrong Hebrew Words, the wrong Aramaic Words, and the wrong Greek Words, these translations will contain many doctrinal, historical, and grammatical errors.

The Faith and doctrines for which we today must contend are the same that were *"once delivered unto the saints."* The *"saints"* in the New Testament always refers to genuine born-again

Christians, not to those defined by the Roman Catholic Church. To contend for this Faith which was *"once delivered,"* we must have the same Greek Words that were delivered to the early Christians. These Words are those found in the Traditional Received Greek Text that underlies the King James Bible.

ONCE DELIVERED WORDS--NOT IN NEW BIBLES

These *"once delivered"* words are not the Greek Words that underlie the modern Bible versions such as the NASV, the RSV, the NRSV, the NIV, the TEV, the ESV, or any of the other modern perversions. We must not, as these modern versions do, change in any way what was originally given to true Christians of apostolic times.

It must be pointed out that a man or woman who *"earnestly contends,"* in these days in which we live, for *"the faith once delivered unto the saints"* will find themselves in a heated battle with those who war against the Faith. These people support the modern Bible versions which pervert at least 356 doctrinal passages. I have listed some of these above. Those who contend for the original doctrinal Faith should be prepared to be called all sorts of names and insults. But these names and insults should never dissuade them from continuing to *"earnestly contend"* for that Faith!

Jude 1:4

"For there are certain men crept in unawares, who were before of old ordained to this condemnation, ungodly men, turning the grace of our God into lasciviousness, and denying the only Lord God, and our Lord Jesus Christ."

This verse sheds much light on the kind of false teachers about whom Jude was writing.

(1) they were creepers;
(2) they came in unawares;
(3) they were of old ordained to condemnation;
(4) they were ungodly men;
(5) they turned God's grace into lasciviousness;
(6) they denied the only Lord God; and
(7) they denied the Lord Jesus Christ.

THE MEANING OF THE GREEK WORD, "PAREISDUNO"

The Greek Word for *"crept in unawares"* is PAREISDUNO. Some of the meanings for this expression are:

*"1) to enter secretly, slip in stealthily;
2) to steal in"*

UNGODLY MEN CREPT INTO CHURCHES SECRETLY

These ungodly men crept in secretly so that no one would detect that they were false teachers. This is exactly what the apostate modernists and liberals have done. They have first slipped in secretly to Christian colleges and seminaries. Then those who attended these unbelieving schools, adversely influenced by them, became pastors. Then these unbelieving heretical pastors stole quietly into the churches and poisoned them with their unbelief. These ungodly men posed as being godly. However, they were merely wolves dressed in sheep's clothing.

One of the things that these ungodly men did was to turn God's grace into lasciviousness.

THE MEANING OF THE GREEK WORD, "ASELGEIA"

The Greek Word for *"lasciviousness"* is ASELGEIA. Some of the meanings of this Greek Word are:

"1) unbridled lust, excess, licentiousness, lasciviousness, wantonness, outrageousness, shamelessness, insolence"

This is a grievous thing to do to the grace of God. This is one of the many evil fruits of all ungodly people. Sad to say that lasciviousness is often shown by genuine Christians who are walking after their sinful flesh rather than being guided by the indwelling Holy Spirit. Tragically, a carnal Christian might act in an ungodly manner, just like one who has never been saved, so people observing would not be able to tell the difference.

> *"Now the works of the flesh are manifest, which are these; Adultery, fornication, uncleanness, **lasciviousness**, Idolatry, witchcraft, hatred, variance, emulations, wrath, strife, seditions, heresies, Envyings, murders, drunkenness, revellings, and such*

> like: of the which I tell you before, as I have also told you in time past, that they which do such things shall not inherit the kingdom of God." (Galatians 5:19-21)

The tense of the word, "*do*," is a Greek present tense. This means a continual and uninterrupted lifestyle committing such actions mentioned in the verses above.

Jude 1:5

"I will therefore put you in remembrance, though ye once knew this, how that the Lord, having saved the people out of the land of Egypt, afterward destroyed them that believed not."

These ungodly men were condemned to spend all eternity in the Lake that burns with fire and brimstone. Jude speaks of four judgments by God (verses 5, 6, 7 and 11) which are analyzed at length in the following pages.

1. God's Judgment On The Egyptians

This is the first of God's judgments. It happened in Moses' day.
- **Exodus 12:29-30**

"And it came to pass, that at midnight the LORD smote all the firstborn in the land of Egypt, from the firstborn of Pharaoh that sat on his throne unto the firstborn of the captive that was in the dungeon; and all the firstborn of cattle. And Pharaoh rose up in the night, he, and all his servants, and all the Egyptians; and there was a great cry in Egypt; for *there was* not a house where *there was* not one dead."

God destroyed the firstborn of all the Egyptians as He had promised to do. This was the tenth plague that the LORD mentioned in these verses.
- **Exodus 12:13**

"And the blood shall be to you for a token upon the houses where ye *are*: and when I see the blood, I will pass over you, and the plague shall not be upon you to destroy *you*, when I smite the land of Egypt."

GOD DID NOT DESTROY FAITHFUL ISRAELITES

God was also gracious to the Israelites who followed His instructions and put the blood of a lamb on the top and side posts of their doors. He did not destroy the faithful Israelites.

PHARAOH WANTED TO ENSLAVE ISRAEL AGAIN

After Pharaoh told Moses and the Israelites to leave Egypt, Pharaoh changed his mind. He sent hundreds of soldiers and many chariots to capture these Jews and bring them back into Egypt to put them in slavery again. This attempt ended with the Egyptian army being drowned in the Red Sea and Israel escaping without any harm whatsoever.

Jude 1:6

"And the angels which kept not their first estate, but left their own habitation, he hath reserved in everlasting chains under darkness unto the judgment of the great day."

2. God's Judgment On Evil Angels

MANY EVIL ANGELS FOLLOWED SATAN

These angels in this verse did not keep their first estate, but left their former dwelling in Heaven with the Lord. These angels followed the lead angel, Lucifer, when he sinned against God.

- **Isaiah 14:12**

"How art thou fallen from heaven, O Lucifer, son of the morning! *how* art thou cut down to the ground, which didst weaken the nations!"

Apparently, Lucifer, or Satan, led many other disobedient and evil angels with him when he was cut down to the ground.

- **Matthew 25:31**

"When the Son of man shall come in his glory, and all the holy angels with him, then shall he sit upon the throne of his glory:"

This refers to the many angels who were the holy angels. They did not follow Satan in his rebellion against God.

- **Matthew 25:41**

"Then shall he say also unto them on the left hand, Depart from me, ye cursed, into everlasting fire, prepared for the devil and his angels:"

This verse tell us two things: (1) It tells us that the Devil and all of his angels will be sent to everlasting fire in Hell. (2) It also tells why this everlasting fire of Hell was prepared. It was not specifically prepared for those who reject the Lord Jesus Christ as

their Saviour though they will be sent there, but it was prepared especially for the Devil and his angels.
- **2 Peter 2:4**
"For if God spared not the angels that sinned, but cast *them* down to hell, and delivered *them* into chains of darkness, to be reserved unto judgment;"

This refers to these evil angels that sinned. They will be cast down to Hell and delivered to judgment in chains of darkness.
- **Revelation 12:7**
"And there was war in heaven: Michael and his angels fought against the dragon; and the dragon fought and his angels,"

God's archangel, Michael, fought against Satan (who is called the dragon here) and the angels who followed him.
- **Revelation 12:9**
"And the great dragon was cast out, that old serpent, called the Devil, and Satan, which deceiveth the whole world: he was cast out into the earth, and his angels were cast out with him."

In this verse, both Satan and his evil angels were cast into the earth.
- **Genesis 6:2**
"That the sons of God saw the daughters of men that they *were* fair; and they took them wives of all which they chose."

GENESIS 6 "SONS OF GOD" WERE EVIL ANGELS

I believe firmly that the *"sons of God"* in this verse were evil angels who took the bodies of human beings and cohabited with women who were on the earth. Jude's statement, *"the angels which kept not their first estate, but left their own habitation,"* would back up the conclusion that these angels performed evil acts leading to the sub-humans or *"fallen ones."* If left alone, there would be no pure race left to provide for the birth of the Lord Jesus Christ. This led God to slay the entire human race except for Noah and seven of his family members to continue the pure race that God originally had created.

- **Genesis 6:4**
"There were giants in the earth in those days; and also after that, when the sons of God came in unto the daughters of men, and they bare *children* to them, the same *became* mighty men which *were* of old, men of renown."

Children were born as a result of these sinful actions between the *"sons of God"* and the daughters of men. The Hebrew Word for

"*giants*" is NEPHALIM. They were "*fallen ones.*" The reason I believe these "*sons of God*" were angels is because of the use of this term in the book of Job.
- **Job 1:6**
  "Now there was a day when the sons of God came to present themselves before the LORD, and Satan came also among them."

These "*sons of God*" were before the LORD along with Satan. Both Satan and these "*sons of God*" were angels.
- **Job 2:1**
  "Again there was a day when the sons of God came to present themselves before the LORD, and Satan came also among them to present himself before the LORD."

This verse also identifies the "*sons of God*" as angels.
- **Job 38:7**
  "When the morning stars sang together, and all the sons of God shouted for joy?"

Judging by the context of Job 38:4-6, this is a reference to the "*sons of God*" as angels being present at the creation of the world.
- **1 Corinthians 11:10**
  "For this cause ought the woman to have power on *her* head because of the angels."

This seems to be saying that Christian women should have proper length hair in submission to their own husbands and to the Lord Jesus Christ so that evil angels would not have any occasion to be tempted to do to them as they did to women in Genesis 6. Dr. M. R. DeHaan also believed that this is the reason for the phrase in this verse "*because of the angels.*"
- **1 Corinthians 6:3**
  "Know ye not that we shall judge angels? how much more things that pertain to this life?"

Though the time of this judgment is not specified, Christians will judge these evil angels someday.

Jude 1:7

"Even as Sodom and Gomorrha, and the cities about them in like manner, giving themselves over to fornication, and going after strange flesh, are set forth for an example, suffering the vengeance of eternal fire."

Remember these four judgments mentioned by Jude:
    (1) God judged the Egyptians;
    (2) God judged evil angels; and in this verse, we see that
    (3) God judged Sodom and Gomorrah.
    (4) God judged Cain, Balaam, and Korah.

3. God's Judgment On Sodom And Gomorrah

The wickedness and sin of Sodom and Gomorrah and the cities around them involved fornication and going after strange flesh. Their judgment by God is suffering the vengeance of eternal fire.

THE MEANING OF THE GREEK WORD, "PORNEIA"

The Greek Word for *"fornication"* is PORNEIA. Some of the meanings of this Greek Word are:

"1) illicit sexual intercourse; 1a) adultery, fornication, homosexuality, lesbianism, intercourse with animals etc.; 1b) sexual intercourse with close relatives; Lev. 18; 1c) sexual intercourse with a divorced man or woman; Mk. 10:11,12; 2) metaph. the worship of idols; 2a) of the defilement of idolatry, as incurred by eating the sacrifices offered to idols"

Our normal use of the word *"fornication"* relates primarily to sexual relations by someone who is unmarried. However, as you can see, the technical Greek definition of PORNEIA, also includes *"homosexuality, lesbianism, intercourse with animals, and sexual intercourse with close relatives."* I believe that every one of these sins were present in Sodom, Gomorrah, and the surrounding cities.

THE MEANING OF THE GREEK WORD, "HETEROS"

"*Going after strange flesh*" is illustrative of their sins as well. The Greek Word for "*strange*" is HETEROS. Some of the meanings of this Greek Word are:

"*1) the other, another, other; 1a) to number; 1a1) to number as opposed to some former person or thing; 1a2) the other of two; 1b) to quality; 1b1) another: i.e. one not of the same nature, form, class, kind, different*"

That sin would include their having sexual relations with strange flesh of animals, being involved with bestiality.

Abraham's plea to God to spare Sodom and Gomorrah was that if He could find ten righteous people in those cities, then God would not destroy them. But, not even ten could be found. Because of this, God utterly destroyed both cities lest their wickedness would spread around the world.

MALE AND FEMALE SODOMITES ARE INCREASING

It is indeed sad to say, but sodomites of both the male and the female variety are on the increase in the United States of America as well as in the nations around the world. I wonder if God will also judge America and other nations for their sodomite sins?

Jude 1:8

"Likewise also these filthy dreamers defile the flesh, despise dominion, and speak evil of dignities."

Jude is still speaking about those false teachers who crept in unawares (verse four). He calls them "*filthy dreamers*" in this verse. They are apostates, unbelievers, and heretics.

MEANING OF THE GREEK WORD, "ENUPNEAZOMAI"

The Greek Word for "*filthy dreamers*" is ENUPNEAZOMAI. It is in the Greek present tense and signifies a continuous activity. Some of the meanings of this Greek Word are:

"*1) to dream (divinely suggested) dreams; 2) metaph., to be beguiled with sensual images and carried away to an impious course of conduct*"

These false teachers continuously think of immoral sexual activities in which they can take part. This fits in with *"defiling the flesh"* as well.

THE SIN OF HOMOSEXUALITY IS ON THE INCREASE

When people leave the standards and doctrines taught in the Bible, they become filthy in their moral standards. Many of these who are in the apostasy even today teach that it is all right to practice homosexuality and to have homosexual marriages. They teach that it is all right to commit fornication, adultery, and even bestiality as well. Homosexual practices once forbidden in the military are now accepted. Even bestiality has been mentioned recently to be put into the UCMJ (the Universal Code of Military Justice) and being permitted by military personnel.

THE MEANING OF THE GREEK WORD, "MIANO"

These false teachers defile the flesh. The Greek Word for *"defile"* is MIANO. Some of the meanings of this Greek Word are:

> *"1) to dye with another colour, to stain;*
> *2) to defile, pollute, sully, contaminate,*
> *soil; 2a) to defile with sins"*

Due to the filthy dreams of these false teachers, they defile and contaminate their flesh with various immoral practices.

Not only that, but these teachers will *"speak evil of dignities."*

MEANING OF THE GREEK WORD, "BLASPHEMEO"

The Greek Word for *"speak evil"* is BLASPHEMEO. Some of the meanings of this Greek Word are:

> *"1) to speak reproachfully, rail at,*
> *revile, calumniate, blaspheme; 2) to be*
> *evil spoken of, reviled, railed at"*

THE MEANING OF THE GREEK WORD, "KURIOTES"

These false teachers revile and rail at dignities. The Greek Word for *"dignities"* is KURIOTES. Some of the meanings of this Greek Word are:

> *"1) dominion, power, lordship; 2) in the*
> *NT: one who possesses dominion"*

This would indicate that they will blaspheme and speak evil of the Lord God of Heaven and earth Who possesses dominion over the entire world.

Jude 1:9

"Yet Michael the archangel, when contending with the devil he disputed about the body of Moses, durst not bring against him a railing accusation, but said, The Lord rebuke thee."

This verse is referring to what took place between Michael the archangel and Satan regarding the burial of the body of Moses. Michael didn't argue with the Devil at this time, but told him that the Lord would rebuke him.

> **MOSES KEPT OUT OF CANAAN BECAUSE OF HIS SIN**
>
> **Because of Moses and Aaron's sin mentioned in Deuteronomy 34 about smiting the rock twice instead of speaking to it as God told him, Moses was not able to go into the land of promise, but only to view it from Mount Nebo where he died.**

On that occasion, the verse below tells us another sin that Moses committed:
- **Psalms 106:33**

"Because they provoked his spirit, so that he [that is, Moses] **spake unadvisedly** with his lips."
Moses and Aaron took credit for bringing forth the water rather than giving the credit to the Lord for this miracle. Notice what Moses said to the people on that occasion:
- **Numbers 20:10**

"And Moses and Aaron gathered the congregation together before the rock, and he said unto them, Hear now, ye rebels; **must we fetch you water out of this rock**?"
Moses was taking credit for himself and Aaron for the miracle of bringing forth water from the rock for the people of Israel rather than giving glory to the Lord for performing it. His words also indicated that he was very angry.

Verses About The Burial Of Moses
- **Deuteronomy 34:5-6**

"So Moses the servant of the LORD died there in the land of Moab, according to the word of the LORD. And he buried him in a valley in the land of Moab, over against Bethpeor: but no man knoweth of his sepulchre unto this day."

Though Moses committed a grievous sin against the LORD, he was still called "*the servant of the LORD*." The specific location of the grave of Moses is not told to us.

Verses About Michael

- **Daniel 10:13**

"But the prince of the kingdom of Persia withstood me one and twenty days: but, lo, Michael, one of the chief princes, came to help me; and I remained there with the kings of Persia."

Michael was one of the chief princes. He is a leader of the angels.

- **Daniel 10:21**

"But I will shew thee that which is noted in the scripture of truth: and *there is* none that holdeth with me in these things, but Michael your prince."

Michael the archangel is called a prince here.

- **Daniel 12:1**

"And at that time shall Michael stand up, the great prince which standeth for the children of thy people: and there shall be a time of trouble, such as never was since there was a nation *even* to that same time: and at that time thy people shall be delivered, every one that shall be found written in the book."

Michael was a great prince and a special angel who was to defend and protect the nation of Israel.

- **Revelation 12:7**

"And there was war in heaven: Michael and his angels fought against the dragon; and the dragon fought and his angels,"

This verse speaks of a war in heaven between Michael and his angels and the dragon (the Devil) and his angels. We know that Michael and his angels will win that battle when it takes place in the future.

Jude 1:10

"But these speak evil of those things which they know not: but what they know naturally, as brute beasts, in those things they corrupt themselves."

APOSTATES CAN'T UNDERSTAND THE BIBLE

These apostates and unbelievers were speaking evil of those things they don't understand or know about. The Scriptures are clear that men and women who are not genuine Christians can't understand the Bible. The verse below is very clear on this.

- 1 Corinthians 2:14

"But the natural man receiveth not the things of the Spirit of God: for they are foolishness unto him: neither can he know *them*, because they are spiritually discerned."

THE MEANING OF THE GREEK WORD, "PSUCHIKOS"

The Greek for "*natural*" is PSUCHIKOS. Some of the meanings of that Greek Word are:

"*1) of or belonging to breath; 1a) having the nature and characteristics of the breath; 1a1) the principal of animal life, which men have in common with the brutes; 1b) governed by breath; 1b1) the sensuous nature with its subjection to appetite and passion.*"

You can say from the meaning of this Greek Word that "*natural*" refers only to the physical life of a man or woman. It has nothing to do with their spiritual life or being a genuine Christian.

These apostates have that which is in common with beasts. The name "*brute beasts*" is a fitting title for them.

THE MEANING OF THE GREEK WORD, "ALOGOS"

The Greek Word for "*brute*" is ALOGOS. Some of the meanings of this Greek Word are:

"*1) destitute of reason; 2) contrary to reason, absurd.*"

This is true of animals. In effect, Jude is calling these apostate unbelievers animals who are destitute of reason.

You might wonder if it is proper to refer to people as animals. If you remember, the Lord Jesus Christ referred to some people as being like animals.

CHRIST CALLED HEROD A FOX

Referring to Herod, the Lord Jesus Christ called him a "*fox.*"

"*And he said unto them, Go ye, and tell that fox, Behold, I cast out devils, and I*

> do cures to day and to morrow, and the third day I shall be perfected." (Luke 13:32)

Referring to the Pharisees and Sadducees of His day, the Lord Jesus Christ called them *"vipers"* or snakes.

> *"But when he saw many of the Pharisees and Sadducees come to his baptism, he said unto them, O generation of vipers, who hath warned you to flee from the wrath to come?"* (Matthew 3:7)

This term is also repeated in Luke 3:7 and Matthew 12:34. In Matthew 23:33, the Lord Jesus Christ refers to the scribes and Pharisees as *"vipers"* as well as *"serpents."*

BIBLICAL MORALITY SCOFFED AT BY THE LOST

It is also said in Jude 1:10 that in the things they do not understand in the Bible, they corrupt themselves. They not only corrupt themselves in all kinds of sensual and sexual sins, but they corrupt others by their apostasy and liberalism. They take away, add to, and change many of the verses and doctrines of the Bible. Once this is done, all Biblical morality is maligned and scoffed at. We see that this has taken place in an ever-increasing measure in the United States of America because of many generations of religious apostasy.

Jude 1:11

"Woe unto them! for they have gone in the way of Cain, and ran greedily after the error of Balaam for reward, and perished in the gainsaying of Core."

"Korah" is the Old Testament spelling for the New Testament spelling of "Core."

4. God's Judgment On Cain, Balaam, And Korah

This is the last of specific judgments by God mentioned by Jude (verses 5, 6, and 7)

Jude likens the judgment of these apostate leaders to that of Cain, Balaam, and Korah.

Verses On Cain's Judgment
- **Hebrews 11:4**

"By faith Abel offered unto God a more excellent sacrifice than Cain, by which he obtained witness that he was righteous, God testifying of his gifts: and by it he being dead yet speaketh."

By faith, Abel followed God's clear directives about offerings. He offered a blood offering of one of his clean animals. Cain, on the other hand, violated God's rules and offered a bloodless offering of some of his vegetables.

Blood offerings were important to God in the Old Testament. They prefigured the shedding of the blood of the Lamb of God, the Lord Jesus Christ, Who would one day come into the world and offer Himself for the sins of mankind.

The blood offering is important. That's the serious heresy of John MacArthur. He despises the blood offering of the Lord Jesus Christ. He said *"blood"* doesn't mean *"blood"* but that it is only a metonym or figure of speech for *"death."* I encourage our readers to order *"Fourteen Biblical Effects of Christ's Literal Blood"* **(BFT #2548-T @ 10/$2.00 + S&H)**. In this 6-page leaflet, you will see exactly the specific Biblical effects that the literal blood of the Lord Jesus Christ performs. John MacArthur is a heretic on every one of these fourteen effects on the blood of Christ which God reveals in the Bible regarding what Christ's blood does. To put *"death"* in place of all these fourteen effects that talk about *"blood"* is heresy in the extremist sense.

It is a very sad thing that not only the apostates and the neo-evangelicals agree with MacArthur's heresy on the blood of the Lord Jesus Christ, but also many Bible-believing fundamentalists are following his heresy on this major doctrine.

- **1 John 3:12**

"Not as Cain, *who* was of that wicked one, and slew his brother. And wherefore slew he him? Because his own works were evil, and his brother's righteous."

Not only did Cain reject God's principles of blood offerings in the Old Testament, but he also committed the first murder in history, killing his own brother Abel.

Verses On Balaam's Judgment

Another person that these apostate false teachers follow is the false prophet Balaam who was looking for personal rewards.

- **Numbers 22:6-7**

"Come now therefore, I pray thee, curse me this people; for they *are* too mighty for me: peradventure I shall prevail, *that* we may smite them, and *that* I may drive them out of the land: for I wot that he whom thou blessest *is* blessed, and he whom thou cursest is cursed. And the elders of Moab and the elders of Midian departed with the rewards of divination in their hand; and they came unto Balaam, and spake unto him the words of Balak."

Balaam was called by the Moabite king, Balak, to come and curse the people of Israel. Moab's elders visited Balaam with rewards and money to pay him to curse Israel.

- **Joshua 13:22**

"Balaam also the son of Beor, the soothsayer, did the children of Israel slay with the sword among them that were slain by them."

Because Balaam took up residence in pagan territory, he was slain when Joshua fought against that land.

- **Nehemiah 13:2**

"Because they met not the children of Israel with bread and with water, but hired Balaam against them, that he should curse them: howbeit our God turned the curse into a blessing."

BALAAM WAS A FALSE PROPHET FOR HIRE

Notice Nehemiah's phrase, how Moab *"hired Balaam."* He was a prophet for hire. So are many liberal apostate ministers around the world. They fashion their sermons to appeal to the greatest donors in their congregations rather than to stick to the Bible's truths. It is often not what they say, but what Bible doctrines and truths they leave out.

My mother-in-law, Gertrude Grace Sanborn, often said "*listen for the absent note*" when listening to the sermons of many ministers. What is **not** said is often more important than what **is** said.

- **2 Peter 2:15**

"Which have forsaken the right way, and are gone astray, following the way of Balaam *the son* of Bosor, who loved the wages of unrighteousness;"

BALAAM LOVED WAGES OF UNRIGHTEOUSNESS

The apostle Peter described Balaam in crystal-clear language. He *"loved the wages of unrighteousness,"* and many in Peter's day, as in our day, have forsaken the right way and have gone astray for the love of money.

- **Revelation 2:14**
"But I have a few things against thee, because thou hast there them that hold the doctrine of Balaam, who taught Balac to cast a stumblingblock before the children of Israel, to eat things sacrificed unto idols, and to commit fornication."

In addition to all the other evils of Balaam mentioned above, he taught Israel to sacrifice to idols and commit the sin of fornication.

Verses On Korah's Judgment

The third judgment Jude mentions in this verse is those who perished in the "*gainsaying of Core*" (or Korah). Numbers 16 gives us some information about Korah who was after power and prestige. He was the son of Levi, who wanted to be a priest rather than remain as a Levite who helped priests.

- **Numbers 16:2-3**
"And they rose up before Moses, with certain of the children of Israel, two hundred and fifty princes of the assembly, famous in the congregation, men of renown: And they gathered themselves together against Moses and against Aaron, and said unto them, *Ye take* too much upon you, seeing all the congregation *are* holy, every one of them, and the LORD *is* among them: wherefore then lift ye up yourselves above the congregation of the LORD?"

Korah was one of the rebellious people who asked why the priests lifted themselves up above the other Israelites. This was the case because God made the rules.

- **Numbers 16:5**
"And he spake unto Korah and unto all his company, saying, Even to morrow the LORD will shew who *are* his, and *who is* holy; and will cause *him* to come near unto him: even *him* whom he hath chosen will he cause to come near unto him."

Moses answered Korah and those who were with him. He told them to get some censors and go into the tabernacle to see what the Lord would tell them to do.

- **Numbers 16:16-17**
"And Moses said unto Korah, Be thou and all thy company before the LORD, thou, and they, and Aaron, to morrow: And take every man his censer, and put incense in them, and bring ye before the LORD every man his censer, two hundred and fifty censers; thou also, and Aaron, each of *you* his censer."

There were a total of two hundred and fifty with Korah's rebellion against God's order for the Aaronic priesthood.

- **Numbers 16:23-26**
"And the LORD spake unto Moses, saying, Speak unto the congregation, saying, Get you up from about the tabernacle of Korah, Dathan, and Abiram. And Moses rose up and went unto Dathan and Abiram; and the elders of Israel followed him. And he spake unto the congregation, saying, Depart, I pray you, from the tents of these wicked men, and touch nothing of theirs, lest ye be consumed in all their sins."

The Lord told Moses to speak to the congregation of Israel to separate themselves from Korah and his company lest they be consumed and judged as well.

- **Numbers 16:29-30**
"If these men die the common death of all men, or if they be visited after the visitation of all men; *then* the LORD hath not sent me. But if the LORD make a new thing, and the earth open her mouth, and swallow them up, with all that *appertain* unto them, and they go down quick into the pit; then ye shall understand that these men have provoked the LORD."

The LORD told Moses that Korah's judgment would not be a common death, but that the earth would open and swallow him up with all two hundred and fifty men.

- **Numbers 16:32-35**
"And the earth opened her mouth, and swallowed them up, and their houses, and all the men that *appertained* unto Korah, and all *their* goods. They, and all that *appertained* to them, went down alive into the pit, and the earth closed upon them: and they perished from among the congregation. And all Israel that *were* round about them fled at the cry of them: for they said, Lest the earth swallow us up *also*. And there came out a fire from the LORD, and consumed the two hundred and fifty men that offered incense."

The LORD kept His promise and consumed all two hundred and fifty men by casting them into the opened earth and burning them with fire because they offered incense like only priests were to do.

- **Numbers 16:49**
"Now they that died in the plague were fourteen thousand and seven hundred, beside them that died about the matter of Korah."

> **GOD SLEW OVER 15,000 JEWS DUE TO THEIR SINS**
> Many in Israel murmured against Moses and Aaron because of God's punishment of Korah and the 250 princes. God caused a plague among them that killed 14,750 of the complainers in addition to Korah and the 250 princes who followed him.

We have analyzed these four types of judgments spoken of by Jude in verses 5, 6, 7, and here in 11 (pages 150-164.) These people were judged. Those living in our day doing similar things will be judged as well.

Jude 1:12

"These are spots in your feasts of charity, when they feast with you, feeding themselves without fear: clouds they are without water, carried about of winds; trees whose fruit withereth, without fruit, twice dead, plucked up by the roots;"

> **UNBELIEVERS--LIKE SPOTS, CLOUDS AND TREES**
> <u>Jude is referring to unbelievers and apostates living in his day</u>. The same can be said of apostates in our day. Notice what he calls them:
> (1) spots feeding without fear alongside believers
> (2) clouds without water blown about by winds
> (3) trees without fruit, twice dead

<u>First of all, these genuine Christians in Jude's day did not separate from apostate unbelievers, but let them eat together at the Lord's Supper.</u> Spots on someone's clothing or on someone's wall would be unwanted and unclean marks. They should not have close fellowship with such spots and should separate from them.

<u>Secondly, unbelievers and apostates are clouds without water.</u> If they have no water, what is their purpose? Yet these waterless clouds are moving around by winds without any permanency. Normally clouds have rain to water the crops and plants on the earth as well as bringing drinking water to people. <u>This is a picture of unbelieving apostate ministers and pastors today who are in many churches around the world. They talk a good game, but they are as dry clouds without giving out the pure Water of Life and eternal salvation through genuine faith in the</u>

Lord Jesus Christ's finished work at Calvary. These clouds without rain are found among cults, Roman Catholic churches, and in many Protestant churches as well.

FALSE TEACHERS--TREES WITH WITHERED FRUIT
The third thing about these false teachers who have crept in unawares is that they are likened either to *"trees whose fruit withereth"* or to having no fruit or roots at all. The Lord was displeased with such fruitless ministries in Jude's day and He is likewise displeased with them in our own day. They are like dry, leafless, fruitless, and worthless trees.

Jude 1:13
"Raging waves of the sea, foaming out their own shame; wandering stars, to whom is reserved the blackness of darkness for ever."

FALSE TEACHERS ARE LIKE WAVES AND STARS
In this verse, Jude gives his readers two more word pictures of these false teachers.

(1) They are raging waves of the sea; people cannot survive in raging waves, nor can ships travel safely in them.

(2) They are wandering stars doomed to darkness forever; these stars wander off course in doctrine and morality.

THE MEANING OF THE GREEK WORD, "AGRIOS"
The Greek Word for *"raging"* is AGRIOS. Some of the meanings for that Greek Word are:

> *"1) living or growing in the fields or woods; 1a) of animals, wild, savage; 1b) of countries, wild, uncultivated, unreclaimed; 2) of men and animals in a moral sense, wild savage, fierce; 2a) boorish, rude; 2b) of any violent passion, vehement, furious"*

These apostate false teachers are oftentimes filled with wild, savage, and violent passion against Bible-believing Christians.

The second picture in this verse shows these false teachers as wandering stars whose end will be the blackness and darkness of Hell.

> **THE MEANING OF THE GREEK WORD, "PLANETES"**
> The Greek Word for "*star*" is PLANETES. Some of the meanings of this Greek Word are:
> "*1) a wanderer: wandering stars*"
> We get the word "*planet*" from this Greek Word. Normal stars are stable.

Navigators can guide their ships by fixed stars, but not by wandering planets. A mariner knows the position of a star, at a certain time and at a certain latitude and longitude. By these facts, he can know exactly where his ship is located.

> **FALSE LEADERS UNDEPENDABLE FOR GUIDANCE**
> These apostate and false religious leaders in Jude's day and in our day cannot be depended on for guidance in any way. They keep changing their theological beliefs like these wandering stars.

This is why Jude urges his readers to earnestly contend for the doctrinal Faith of our Bibles which was once delivered unto the New Testament saints. This is so important in our day because most of the ministers have forsaken that Biblical doctrinal Faith. This is why our **Bible For Today Baptist Church** earnestly contends for the doctrinal Faith, despite the many who fight against us for doing so.

Jude 1:14

"**And Enoch also, the seventh from Adam, prophesied of these, saying, Behold, the Lord cometh with ten thousands of his saints,**"

Enoch is seventh from Adam. Genesis gives us the line. (1) Adam, (2) Seth, (3) Enos, (4) Cainan, (5) Mahalaleel, (6) Jared, and (7) Enoch. Enoch, a man who walked with God (Genesis 5:24), prophesied concerning these false teachers who were like the raging waves and wandering stars. The book of Enoch is not one of our canonical books, but Jude quotes Enoch as saying that the Lord will come back to earth with ten thousands of his saints who have been previously raptured to Heaven. He will be coming to judge these apostate teachers.

- **Genesis 5:24**
"And Enoch walked with God: and he *was* not; for God took him."
It is also recorded that he walked with God in Genesis 5:22.
- **Hebrews 11:5**
"By faith Enoch was translated that he should not see death; and was not found, because God had translated him: for before his translation he had this testimony, that he pleased God."

TRANSLATION–OF ENOCH AND OF THE BIBLE

That word, *"translation,"* is a good word. It means that God took him bodily up to Heaven. Every part of Enoch's body was taken to Heaven. Nothing was left upon the earth. An accurate Bible translation must take every single one of the plenarily (full), verbally inspired, and preserved Hebrew, Aramaic, and Greek Words and bring them over into whatever language they are being placed. This is what the King James Bible English translation has done. Translators must not add to the Words, or take away from the Words.

Verses On Christ's Coming With His Saints
- **Revelation 19:11**
"And I saw heaven opened, and behold a white horse; and he that sat upon him *was* called Faithful and True, and in righteousness he doth judge and make war."

GLORIFIED CHRISTIANS RETURN WITH CHRIST

This refers to the second phase of the coming of the Lord Jesus Christ. The first phase will be the Rapture of all genuine Christians into the air. The second phase of His coming will be His return to earth with all those true Christians in their resurrected bodies.

- **Revelation 19:14**
"And the armies *which were* in heaven followed him upon white horses, clothed in fine linen, white and clean."

This is a clear reference regarding Christians which will be in Heaven to follow their Saviour when He comes to judge these evil and false teachers, and all the ungodly.

Jude 1:15

"To execute judgment upon all, and to convince all that are ungodly among them of all their ungodly deeds which they have ungodly committed, and of all their hard speeches which ungodly sinners have spoken against him."

<u>The purpose of the first coming</u> of the Lord Jesus Christ in His incarnation was to offer eternal life to all those who genuinely receive Him as their Saviour.
- John 1:11-12

"He came unto his own, and his own received him not. But as many as received him, to them gave he power to become the sons of God, *even* to them that believe on his name:"

Verses On The Second Coming Of Christ To Earth

Jude refers, in this verse, to the second phase of the return of the Lord Jesus Christ. It is His coming again to this earth. **The purpose** will be to judge ungodly people of their ungodly deeds and hard speeches which they have made against the Lord Jesus Christ.

THE MEANING OF THE GREEK WORD, "EXELENGKO"

The Greek Word used for *"convict"* is EXELENGKO. Some of the meanings of that Greek Word are:

"*1) to prove to be in the wrong, convict*"

Again, the purpose of the second phase of the second coming, is to pour out His judgments upon all the ungodly on the earth for their sins. This phase of the coming of the Lord Jesus Christ will be at the Battle of Armageddon.

- Revelation 19:11-15

"And I saw heaven opened, and behold a white horse; and he that sat upon him *was* called Faithful and True, and in righteousness he doth judge and make war. His eyes *were* as a flame of fire, and on his head *were* many crowns; and he had a name written, that no man knew, but he himself. And he *was* clothed with a vesture dipped in blood: and his name is called The Word of God. And the armies *which were* in heaven followed him upon white horses, clothed in fine linen, white and clean. And out of his mouth goeth a sharp sword, that with it he should smite the nations: and he shall rule

them with a rod of iron: and he treadeth the winepress of the fierceness and wrath of Almighty God."
Because of Christ's judgment, there will be many who will be slain in that battle.
- Revelation 19:17
"And I saw an angel standing in the sun; and he cried with a loud voice, saying to all the fowls that fly in the midst of heaven, Come and gather yourselves together unto the supper of the great God;"

ARMAGEDDON'S FEAST BY FOWLS
The fowls of the air will eat the flesh of kings, captains, mighty men, horses, and men—both bond and free, small and great. You wouldn't want to be that supper. Thousands of ungodly, anti-Christians who hate the Lord Jesus Christ and the people of Israel will be killed by the Judge of all the world, the Lord Jesus Christ. This is the terrible Battle of Armageddon.

- Revelation 19:20
"And the beast was taken, and with him the false prophet that wrought miracles before him, with which he deceived them that had received the mark of the beast, and them that worshipped his image. These both were cast alive into a lake of fire burning with brimstone."
Both the political beast and the religious beast will be cast into Hell's Lake of Fire which was prepared for the Devil and his angels (Matthew 25:41). This verse makes it clear that those who received the mark of the beast will be cast into the Lake of Fire. Some people are teaching falsely that those who receive this mark will be given a second chance.

- Ezekiel 39:1
"Therefore, thou son of man, prophesy against Gog, and say, Thus saith the Lord GOD; Behold, I *am* against thee, O Gog, the chief prince of Meshech and Tubal:"

BATTLE OF ARMAGEDDON NEAR JERUSALEM
Some have identified Meshech with Moscow and Tubal with Tobolsk. There will be those who come to the Battle of Armageddon from the north, the east, the west, and from the south. They will all converge on Jerusalem to destroy it.

- **Ezekiel 39:4**

"Thou shalt fall upon the mountains of Israel, thou, and all thy bands, and the people that *is* with thee: I will give thee unto the ravenous birds of every sort, and *to* the beasts of the field to be devoured."

<u>Gog and all his armies will fall upon the mountains of Israel. Their dead bodies will be devoured by the beasts of the field.</u>

- **Ezekiel 39:9**

"And they that dwell in the cities of Israel shall go forth, and shall set on fire and burn the weapons, both the shields and the bucklers, the bows and the arrows, and the handstaves, and the spears, and they shall burn them with fire seven years:"

<u>The implements of warfare used in this battle will also be destroyed.</u> Some have speculated that these rudimentary weapons might need to be used because of a future shortage of fuel and modern weapons.

- **Ezekiel 39:11-12**

"And it shall come to pass in that day, *that* I will give unto Gog a place there of graves in Israel, the valley of the passengers on the east of the sea: and it shall stop the *noses* of the passengers: and there shall they bury Gog and all his multitude: and they shall call *it* The valley of Hamongog. And seven months shall the house of Israel be burying of them, that they may cleanse the land."

<u>The death toll will be so great that there will be a horrible stench. It will take seven full months to bury all the dead in this Battle of Armageddon.</u>

- **Revelation 16:15-16**

"Behold, I come as a thief. Blessed *is* he that watcheth, and keepeth his garments, lest he walk naked, and they see his shame. And he gathered them together into a place called in the Hebrew tongue Armageddon."

In this second phase of the return of the Lord Jesus Christ, He will come to judge, as Enoch has prophesied in verse 14, with ten thousands of His saints.

GREAT WHITE THRONE JUDGMENT OF THE LOST

<u>The Lord will be judging the ungodly because of their ungodly deeds.</u> This is called the Great White Throne Judgment. It will take place at the end of the thousand-year millennial reign of the Lord Jesus Christ.

Some people falsely teach that there will be a general judgment consisting of both the genuine Christians and the non-Christians who are unsaved. <u>The Bible is clear that the just and the unjust will take part in completely separate final judgments.</u>

- **Revelation 20:11-15**

"And I saw a great white throne, and him that sat on it, from whose face the earth and the heaven fled away; and there was found no place for them. And I saw the dead, small and great, stand before God; and the books were opened: and another book was opened, which is *the book* of life: and the dead were judged out of those things which were written in the books, **according to their works**. And the sea gave up the dead which were in it; and death and hell delivered up the dead which were in them: and they were judged every man according to their works. And death and hell were cast into the lake of fire. And whosoever was not found written in the book of life was cast into the lake of fire."

ALL UNSAVED AT THE GREAT WHITE THRONE

<u>At the Great White Throne Judgment, all lost, spiritually-dead non-Christians</u> will stand before the Lord Jesus Christ. **There will not be one true Christian in this judgment.** The believers' judgment will take place at a completely different time--at the Judgment Seat of Christ (Romans 14:10; 2 Corinthians 5:10).

UNSAVED CONSIGNED TO HELL'S ETERNAL FIRE

This judgment of the unsaved is called *"the second death"* (Revelation 2:11; 20:6, 14; 21:8). Though they will be judged according to their works, they will all be cast into the Lake of Fire of Hell. Apparently there will be degrees of judgment in Hell; nevertheless, all those at this judgment will end up in the Lake of Fire mentioned in the following four verses: Revelation 19:20; 20:10, 14-15.

<u>Sad to say, at least forty-eight proponents of the so-called New Evangelical philosophy like Evangelist Billy Graham, *Christianity Today*, and many others, believe and teach that there is no "real fire" in the Lake of Fire.</u> They do not take these words in a literal fashion. If there is no fire in Hell, how can you have an entire *"lake"* of it?

I think we should take heed to what has been called *"The Golden Rule Of Bible Interpretation."* Here it is:

2 Peter And Jude–Preaching Verse-by-Verse

BIBLE INTERPRETATION'S GOLDEN RULE

"When the PLAIN SENSE of Scripture makes COMMON SENSE, SEEK NO OTHER SENSE. Therefore, take EVERY WORD at its primary, ordinary, usual, literal meaning, UNLESS the facts of the immediate context, studied in the light of related passages, and axiomatic and fundamental truths, indicate CLEARLY otherwise. God, in revealing His Word, neither intends nor permits the reader to be confused. He wants His children to understand." (Author unknown)

The Lord is gracious to the entire world in that His just judgment has been postponed for so many centuries. Ungodliness has been permeating our nation and our entire world. But that judgment will arrive one day known only to the Lord God of Heaven and earth.

Read carefully God's loving invitation to every person in the entire world in the following verse:

- **2 Peter 3:9**

"The Lord is not slack concerning his promise, as some men count slackness; but is longsuffering to us-ward, not willing that any should perish, but that all should come to repentance."

GOD IS NOT WILLING FOR ANY TO PERISH IN HELL

The God of the Bible is longsuffering to every man, woman, and child. He does not want any of them to perish in Hell's Lake of Fire, but He wants everyone to come to trust in His Son; otherwise, they will go to Hell.

THE MEANING OF THE GREEK WORD, "METANOIA"

The Greek Word for *"repentance"* is METANOIA. It comes from META (a change) and NOIA from NOUS (the mind). God's desire is for everyone to change their mind:

(1) about sin–agreeing that they are lost sinners

(2) about the Saviour–that the Lord Jesus Christ died for their sins and the sins of the entire world

(3) about their need to genuinely place their faith in the Lord Jesus Christ as their personal Saviour. He is *"not willing that any should perish."*

Jude 1:16

"**These are murmurers, complainers, walking after their own lusts; and their mouth speaketh great swelling words, having men's persons in admiration because of advantage.**"

Jude further describes these false teachers in the following five ways: (1) murmurers; (2) complainers; (3) walking after their own lusts; (4) speaking great swelling words; and (5) admiring men's persons because of advantage. These are very clear descriptions of what apostate leaders were like. There are many in our day who follow these five patterns.

> **THE MEANING OF THE GREEK WORD, "GOGGUSTES"**
>
> Let's just take a look at their number one characteristic–murmuring. The Greek Word for "*murmurer*" is GOGGUSTES. Some of the meanings of that Greek Word are:
>
> "*1) a murmurer, one who discontentedly complains (against God)*"
>
> In our English language, the word, "murmurer," is what they call an onomatopoeia. This means that the word sounds like what it means. "Murmurmurmur" sounds just like what it means. It says the same thing over and over again. It's especially complaining against God.

This is what these unsaved, unbelieving, false teachers mentioned by Jude were doing. They were also complainers. For them, nothing is right. They were also walking after their own lusts, living a sinful and sexual lifestyle. Even today, many ministers and preachers are also secretly walking after their own lusts.

With their mouths they speak forth great swelling words. **These liberal apostates can talk at length about many things other than the teachings of the Bible**.

Notice their method and purpose; "*having men's persons in admiration because of advantage*." They have men's persons in admiration because of advantage. They will exalt those in power so that they can get something from them and will do anything in order to get ahead.

Verses On Murmuring

- **Exodus 15:24**

"And the people murmured against Moses, saying, What shall we drink?"

The people of Israel murmured against Moses because there was no water for them.

- **Psalms 106:25**

"But murmured in their tents, *and* hearkened not unto the voice of the LORD."

Israel murmured in their tents and refused to hearken to God's voice.

- **Mark 14:5**

"For it might have been sold for more than three hundred pence, and have been given to the poor. And they murmured against her."

The apostles murmured against the woman who anointed the Lord Jesus Christ with costly ointment.

- **Luke 15:2**

"And the Pharisees and scribes murmured, saying, This man receiveth sinners, and eateth with them."

The Pharisees and scribes murmured against the Lord Jesus Christ because He received and ate with sinners.

- **1 Corinthians 10:10**

"Neither murmur ye, as some of them also murmured, and were destroyed of the destroyer."

Paul warned genuine Christians at Corinth to stop their murmuring.

- **Philippians 2:14-15**

"Do all things without murmurings and disputings: That ye may be blameless and harmless, the sons of God, without rebuke, in the midst of a crooked and perverse nation, among whom ye shine as lights in the world;"

All things should be done without murmurings so that true Christians might be blameless and harmless and should shine as lights in this wicked world.

Jude 1:17

"But, beloved, remember ye the words which were spoken before of the apostles of our Lord Jesus Christ;"

YOU MUST REMEMBER THE WORDS OF THE BIBLE

Jude wanted his readers to remember the Words of the Lord Jesus Christ. To remember His Words accurately, they must follow the verbally and plenarily inspired and preserved Traditional Received Greek Words of the New Testament which underlie the King James Bible.

Verses On The Words Of The Lord Jesus Christ
- Matthew 24:35
"Heaven and earth shall pass away, **but my words shall not pass away**."
- Mark 13:31
"Heaven and earth shall pass away: **but my words shall not pass away**."
- Luke 21:33
"Heaven and earth shall pass away: **but my words shall not pass away**."

THE MEANING OF THE GREEK WORDS, "OU ME"

Notice that the same words are repeated exactly in the three synoptic Gospels (Matthew, Mark, and Luke). It is clear that the Words of the Lord Jesus Christ will not pass away. The Greek Word for "*not*" is OU ME. It is the strongest negative in the Greek language. It means "*never, never, never.*"

The Process Of Inspiration

Let's look exactly at what His Words are. Let's examine John 16:12-14 where the Lord Jesus Christ spoke to His disciples about how the New Testament came about after He went back to Heaven.

"I have yet many things to say unto you, but ye cannot bear them now. Howbeit when he, the Spirit of truth, is come, he will guide you into all truth: for he shall not speak of himself; but whatsoever he shall hear, that shall he speak: and he will shew you things to come.

He shall glorify me: for he shall receive of mine, and shall shew it unto you." (John 16:12-14)
Notice what is said here:

(1) The Lord Jesus Christ has many things to say to the apostles, but they couldn't bear them then.

(2) The Spirit of truth (God the Holy Spirit) would guide them into all truth.

(3) The Holy Spirit would not speak of (EK, "*from*") or from Himself as the source of the Words.

(4) Whatever the Holy Spirit would hear from the Lord Jesus Christ, He would speak, including things to come.

(5) The Holy Spirit would glorify the Lord Jesus Christ because the Holy Spirit would receive the Words from the Lord Jesus Christ and show them unto the apostles.

THE TECHNIQUE OF THE BIBLE'S PRODUCTION

In summary, the Lord Jesus Christ would give His specific Words to God the Holy Spirit; then the Holy Spirit would give Christ's Words to human writers; then they would write them down into the New Testament. Since the Lord Jesus Christ is the Revealer of truth, it is likely that the same method took place in the writings of the Old Testament as well.

Dr. Samuel Schaiter of Bob Jones University and many other Bible-believing leaders have denied that God has verbally and plenarily preserved every Word of the Hebrew, Aramaic, and Greek original Bible manuscripts. They say, instead, that God has only preserved the "message, ideas, concepts and thoughts" but not the actual Words. This position is heresy and a strict denial of the Words of the Lord Jesus Christ in these three verses found in the Gospels of Matthew, Mark, and Luke!

- **Mark 8:38**
"Whosoever therefore shall be ashamed of me and of my words in this adulterous and sinful generation; of him also shall the Son of man be ashamed, when he cometh in the glory of his Father with the holy angels."

NEVER BE ASHAMED OF GOD'S WORDS!

Genuine Christians should never be ashamed of the Words of the Lord Jesus Christ. But how can they be ashamed of His Words if you they don't have His Words? I believe His Words in both the Old and New Testaments are the verbal, plenary, preserved Words found in the

> Traditional Texts of Hebrew and Greek that underlie the King James Bible. True Christians must read, study, and know the Words of the Lord Jesus Christ and ask God to help them keep those Words.

- **John 16:4**
"But these things have I told you, that when the time shall come, ye may remember that I told you of them. And these things I said not unto you at the beginning, because I was with you."

> **BIBLE PRESERVATION EXTREMELY NECESSARY**
> The only way people can "*remember*" what the Lord Jesus Christ told His apostles is for His Words to be preserved. I believe He promised to preserve them as mentioned in the verses below.

- **Matthew 24:35**
"Heaven and earth shall pass away, but **my words shall not pass away**."
- **Mark 13:31**
"Heaven and earth shall pass away: but **my words shall not pass away**."
- **Luke 21:33**
"Heaven and earth shall pass away: but **my words shall not pass away**."

God's promise to preserve His original Hebrew, Aramaic, and Greek Words of the Bible is being denied by many teachers even at once-fundamentalist schools. Here is a short list of some of the schools that have denied God's promise: (1) Maranatha Baptist Bible College; (2) Bob Jones University; (3) Detroit Baptist Seminary; (4) Calvary Baptist Seminary; (5) Central Baptist Seminary, and many others that will not be named. There is a very serious battle within the fundamentalist Christian world over the verbal, plenary preservation of God's Hebrew, Aramaic, and Greek Words.

- **Acts 20:31**
"Therefore watch, and remember, that by the space of three years I ceased not to warn every one night and day with tears."

How did Paul warn the pastors-bishops-elders from Ephesus? He warned them, not only by his own words, but also by the Hebrew and Aramaic Words of the Old Testament that God had preserved for him and others to use.

- Acts 20:35

"I have shewed you all things, how that so labouring ye ought to support the weak, and to remember the words of the Lord Jesus, how he said, It is more blessed to give than to receive."

> **GOD'S ORIGINAL WORDS HAVE BEEN PRESERVED**
> For these pastors-bishops-elders of Ephesus to *"remember"* these Words of the Lord Jesus Christ necessitated the fulfillment of God's promise to preserve His original Words.

Jude 1:18

"How that they told you there should be mockers in the last time, who should walk after their own ungodly lusts."

To my knowledge, as never before in the recorded history of our nation, lusts abound and have increased tenfold. People are walking after their own ungodly lusts, including:

(1) undoing, in the U.S.A. military services, all previous rules against homosexuality

(2) undoing all previous laws in the States against homosexuality

(3) allowing homosexual marriages of a man with another man and a woman with another woman

(4) permitting the murder of an estimated 1.4 million babies each year since 1973

(5) using blatant pornography

6) many more ungodly lusts such as the great increase in hard drug addiction, murders, and many other kinds of sins

- 2 Timothy 3:1-6

"This know also, that in the last days perilous times shall come. For men shall be lovers of their own selves, covetous, boasters, proud, blasphemers, disobedient to parents, unthankful, unholy, Without natural affection, trucebreakers, false accusers, incontinent, fierce, despisers of those that are good, Traitors, heady, highminded, lovers of pleasures more than lovers of God; Having a form of godliness, but denying the power thereof: from such turn away. For of this sort are they which creep into houses, and lead captive silly women laden with sins, led away with divers lusts,"

These verses predicted that, in the last days, perilous times will come. Legions of people today have *"no fear of God before their eyes."* They despise that which is good and exalt that which is evil.
- **2 Peter 3:3**
"Knowing this first, that there shall come in the last days scoffers, walking after their own lusts,"

TODAY THERE ARE MANY WORLDWIDE SCOFFERS

Many are scoffing at the Bible, at God the Father, at the Lord Jesus Christ, at Bible doctrines, and at many other things. Ungodly lusts are prevalent today, not only in our own country, but all over the world as well.

Jude 1:19

"These be they who separate themselves, sensual, having not the Spirit."

Some might think that when people believe in Biblical separation, they are *"sensual"* and do not have the Holy Spirit. This is far from the truth. Look at the clear teaching of Biblical separation from the passage below:

"Be ye not unequally yoked together with unbelievers: for what fellowship hath righteousness with unrighteousness? and what communion hath light with darkness? And what concord hath Christ with Belial? or what part hath he that believeth with an infidel? And what agreement hath the temple of God with idols? for ye are the temple of the living God; as God hath said, I will dwell in them, and walk in them; and I will be their God, and they shall be my people. <u>***Wherefore come out from among them, and be ye separate, saith the Lord, and touch not the unclean thing***</u>*; and I will receive you, And will be a Father unto you, and ye shall be my sons and daughters, saith the Lord Almighty."* (2 Corinthians 6:14-18)

BIBLICAL SEPARATION TO BE PRACTICED TODAY

The proper understanding of the kind of *"separation"* in the preceding verses is Biblical, though not accepted by some true Christians. But the separation spoken by this verse in Jude refers to the ungodly and sensual lost people who separate themselves from the genuine Christians and from Bible truth.

Jude 1:20

"But ye, beloved, building up yourselves on your most holy faith, praying in the Holy Ghost,"

The difference is in the 'ye' which refers to genuine Christians. As believers, God wants us to build ourselves up in the holy faith being led by God, the Holy Spirit. The Scriptures have the holy Faith.

Verses On The Need To Build Properly

God wants every genuine Christian to be built up in the truths of the Bible. He wants them to grow more mature day by day.

- Matthew 16:18

"And I say also unto thee, That thou art Peter, and upon this rock I will build my church; and the gates of hell shall not prevail against it."

MEANING OF THE GREEK WORD, "EPOIKODOMEO"

The Greek Word for *"build"* is EPOIKODOMEO. That Greek Word for *"build"* has three parts: EPI ("upon") OIKOS ("house") and DOMEO ("house top or roof"). Some of the meanings of this Greek Word are:

1) to build upon, build up; to finish the structure of which the foundation has already been laid, to give constant increase in Christian knowledge and in a life conformed thereto."

If people are on the Foundation of the Lord Jesus Christ by genuine faith in Him, God wants them to keep building upon that Foundation following the pattern found in clear teachings of the Bible.

- 1 Corinthians 3:11-12

"For other foundation can no man lay than that is laid, which is Jesus Christ. Now if any man build upon this foundation gold, silver, precious stones, wood, hay, stubble;"

WHAT ARE CHRISTIANS BUILDING ON CHRIST?

True Christians must beware what building materials they use when building upon their Saviour, the

> Lord Jesus Christ. Things that are large and seen easily by people (wood, hay, and stubble) are the wrong kind of materials to build with. They will all be burned up in the fire. However, things that are small, difficult to see, yet valuable (gold, silver, and precious stones) are the proper things to build with upon their Foundation and Saviour. When the fire comes, these will all be purified rather than destroyed.

- **1 Peter 2:2**

"As newborn babes, desire the sincere milk of the word, that ye may grow thereby:"

God commands genuine Christians to grow by means of desiring the Words of God in the Bible and following them as the Lord gives them the courage and power to do it. God wants all of His "*newborn babes*" to grow by means of His Words.

- **2 Peter 3:18**

"But grow in grace, and *in* the knowledge of our Lord and Saviour Jesus Christ. To him *be* glory both now and for ever. Amen."

God wants true Christians to grow in His matchless grace and also in the knowledge of their Lord and Saviour Jesus Christ.

> **FOLLOW YEARLY BIBLE READING--85 VERSES DAILY**
>
> This is why I urge all Christians to read the Bible from Genesis through Revelation at least once each year. This can be done by reading 85 verses per day. I have printed up the schedule to accomplish this: "*YEARLY BIBLE READING SCHEDULE.*" To receive a free copy of it, email BFT@BibleForToday.org Or you could call our office at 856-854-4452 and request your copy.
>
> Reading 85 verses takes from 10 to 15 minutes, depending on a person's reading speed. They can also study these verses if they wish to do so, spending more time in the Words of God each day.

2 Corinthians 10:15

"Not boasting of things without *our* measure, *that is*, of other men's labours; but having hope, when your faith is increased, that we shall be enlarged by you according to our rule abundantly,"

All genuine Christians should have their faith growing and increasing day by day. This is what God wishes for all of them.

- Colossians 1:10

"That ye might walk worthy of the Lord unto all pleasing, being fruitful in every good work, and increasing in the knowledge of God;"

INCREASE IN THE KNOWLEDGE OF GOD'S WORDS

God wants all true Christians to walk worthy of Him and increase in the knowledge of God. This increase is done by the study of God's Words. In English, this study should be in the King James Bible for two reasons:

(1) Its foundation is on the only true verbal, plenary, inspired and preserved Hebrew, Aramaic, and Greek Words;

(2) It has been translated from superior texts based on the preserved original Words by superior translators who used superior translation techniques resulting in superior theology.

- 1 Thessalonians 3:12

"And the Lord make you to increase and abound in love one toward another, and toward all *men*, even as we *do* toward you:"

God wants all genuine Christians to grow, increase, and abound in love for one another as well as for other people.

Jude 1:21

"Keep yourselves in the love of God, looking for the mercy of our Lord Jesus Christ unto eternal life."

Jude commands his readers to keep themselves in God's love while looking for the mercy of the Lord Jesus Christ to eternal life.

THE MEANING OF THE GREEK WORD, "ELEOS"

The Lord Jesus Christ is a merciful Saviour. The Greek Word for *"mercy"* is ELEOS. Some of the meanings of that Greek Word are:

"1) mercy: kindness or good will towards the miserable and the afflicted, joined with a desire to help them; 1a) of men towards men: to exercise the virtue of mercy, show one's self merciful"

Verses On The Love Of God

In order for genuine Christians to keep themselves in the love of God, they must know what that love is. Here are a few verses about God's love.

- **John 5:42**

"But I know you, that ye have not the love of God in you."

The Apostle John told his readers that they did not have God's love in them. He was referring to those who would not receive or believe Him.

- **Romans 5:5**

"And hope maketh not ashamed; because the love of God is shed abroad in our hearts by the Holy Ghost which is given unto us."

The love of God is shed abroad in the hearts of true Christians by the power of God the Holy Spirit Who indwells them. *"Love"* is one of the fruits of the Holy Spirit (Galatians 5:22-23).

- **Romans 8:39**

"Nor height, nor depth, nor any other creature, shall be able to separate us from the love of God, which is in Christ Jesus our Lord."

TRUE CHRISTIANS–NEVER SEPARATED FROM GOD

Though much evil can be perpetrated upon genuine Christians, one thing is true . . . they can never be separated from God's love which is found in the Lord Jesus Christ.

- **2 Thessalonians 3:5**

"And the Lord direct your hearts into the love of God, and into the patient waiting for Christ."

Paul's prayer for Christians is that the Lord might direct their hearts in two areas:
   (1) in the love of God
   (2) in the patient waiting for the return of the Lord Jesus Christ

- **1 John 3:16**

"Hereby perceive we the love *of God*, because he laid down his life for us: and we ought to lay down *our* lives for the brethren."

The proof of God's love for all mankind is that the Lord Jesus Christ laid down His life for them. Because of this, genuine Christians should be willing to lay down their lives for their fellow brethren.

- 1 John 4:9

"In this was manifested the love of God toward us, because that God sent his only begotten Son into the world, that we might live through him."

- 1 John 5:3

"For this is the love of God, that we keep his commandments: and his commandments are not grievous."

The proof that true Christians sincerely love God is if they keep and obey His commandments. If they do not keep His Words, their love for Him is not genuine.

Jude 1:22

"And of some have compassion, making a difference:"

Jude wants his readers to have compassion on some, showing them that there is a difference between unsaved people and genuine Christians. These Christians should exercise compassion on those who need it.

THE MEANING OF THE GREEK WORD, "ELEEO"

The Greek Word for *"compassion"* is ELEEO. Some of the meanings of that Greek Word are:

"1) to have mercy on; 2) to help one afflicted or seeking aid; 3) to help the afflicted, to bring help to the wretched; 4) to experience mercy."

Verses On Compassion

- Exodus 2:6

"And when she had opened *it*, she saw the child: and, behold, the babe wept. And she had compassion on him, and said, This *is one* of the Hebrews' children."

Pharaoh's daughter opened up this little basket where baby Moses was. When he wept, she had compassion on him.

- Psalms 86:15

"But thou, O Lord, *art* a God full of compassion, and gracious, longsuffering, and plenteous in mercy and truth."

One of the attributes of the God of the Bible is that He is full of compassion. Because of this, He wants *"to help the afflicted"* and *"to bring help to the wretched."*

- **Lamentations 3:22-23**
"*It is of* the LORD'S mercies that we are not consumed, because his compassions fail not. *They are* new every morning: great *is* thy faithfulness."

God's mercies, compassions, and faithfulness never fail. They are renewed daily. It is sad that many people do not take advantage of these Divine attributes and trust Him and His Son fully.

- **Matthew 9:36**
"But when he saw the multitudes, he was moved with compassion on them, because they fainted, and were scattered abroad, as sheep having no shepherd."

The Lord Jesus Christ was moved with compassion as He beheld the many forgotten people of His day. They were as sheep without any Shepherd. Such is the case today all around the world. May true Christians show them the same compassion as their Lord showed.

- **Luke 15:20**
"And he arose, and came to his father. But when he was yet a great way off, his father saw him, and had compassion, and ran, and fell on his neck, and kissed him."

This is the reaction of a loving and compassionate father for his prodigal son who returned to him after a life of sin. The Heavenly Father exercises compassion and understanding to sinners who come to Him and trust His Son as their Saviour.

- **1 Peter 3:8**
"Finally, *be ye* all of one mind, having compassion one of another, love as brethren, *be* pitiful, *be* courteous:"

PETER WANTED UNITY, COURTESY & COMPASSION
Peter wanted his readers not only to have unity, pity, and courtesy, but also compassion with one another. That is not always easy to do.

Jude 1:23

"And others save with fear, pulling them out of the fire; hating even the garment spotted by the flesh."

BE CAREFUL WHEN DEALING WITH EVIL PEOPLE
Genuine Christians can exercise compassion without any problems on some people. However, when dealing

with others, they must be afraid of what might happen to them. They must be careful.

As a Red Cross Water Safety Instructor (WSI) for many years, I am familiar with the instructions of the American Red Cross regarding life-saving techniques. I would relay these instructions to those who were in my classes either for junior or senior life-saving.

When a person was about to drown in a river, lake, or ocean, there were four things that lifeguards should do in this order:

(1) The first thing to do is to **row** if a boat is available; row out to the person and rescue them.

(2) The second thing to do is to **throw** out a ring buoy (if available) to the person in trouble.

(3) The third thing to do is to tow. Extend a board or a paddle to the drowning person for them to take hold of and tow them to safety.

(4) The fourth thing to do, when the first three things were not possible, was to **go**.

That is, the lifeguard was to swim out to the drowning person, take hold of them with the proper approach and manner, and safely swim back with them in tow to shore.

True Christians who want to win people to saving faith in the Lord Jesus Christ must often be very careful. This is especially true when seeking to win hardened sinners or others who might harm the soul winner in some way.

THE MEANING OF THE GREEK WORD, "XITON"

"The garment spotted by the flesh" is used here. The Greek Word for *"garment"* is XITON. Some of the meanings of this Greek Word are:

> *"1) a tunic, an undergarment, usually worn next to the skin, a garment, a vestment"*

This is not the outer garment of a person, but it a garment that is next to the skin.

These are the garments that can have much pollution and disease. We must be careful and stay away from such spotted garments. When EMT's, paramedics, and firemen go out to render help to accident victims, there is oftentimes blood on them. These workers wear gloves because of the possibilities of HIV/AIDS or other contagious diseases they might encounter.

THE MEANING OF THE GREEK WORD, "HARPAZO"

These are the kind that genuine Christians must pull out of the fire. The Greek Word for *"pull"* is HARPAZO. Some of the meanings of this Greek Word are:

"1) to seize, carry off by force; 2) to seize on, claim for one's self eagerly; 3) to snatch out or away"

This is the same Greek Word for *"caught up"* in 1 Thessalonians 4:17 which speaks of the Rapture of true Christians to meet the Lord Jesus Christ in the air.

This will be a wonderful day for every born-again child of God. It might occur at any time. There is no prophecy that must be fulfilled before this event takes place when Christians will be taken out of this earth and brought to their eternal Home in Heaven.

Jude 1:24

"Now unto him that is able to keep you from falling, and to present you faultless before the presence of his glory with exceeding joy,"

ONLY GOD CAN KEEP CHRISTIANS FROM FALLING

God is the only One Who is able to keep genuine Christians from falling and losing their eternal life. This is a continuous action of His ability. He never surrenders that ability.

Verses On Eternal Salvation

- John 3:15-16

"That whosoever believeth in him should not perish, but have eternal life. For God so loved the world, that he gave his only begotten Son, that whosoever believeth in him should not perish, but have everlasting life."

Those who genuinely believe in Him will never perish or fall from that salvation.

- John 5:24

"Verily, verily, I say unto you, He that heareth my word, and believeth on him that sent me, hath everlasting life, and shall not come into condemnation; but is passed from death unto life."

> **TRUE CHRISTIANS CAN NEVER LOSE SALVATION**
> The Lord Jesus Christ said in this verse that once true Christians have passed from death unto life, by exercising genuine faith in the Lord Jesus Christ as their Saviour, they will never be lost. They will never lose that everlasting life.

- **John 10:27-30**

"My sheep hear my voice, and I know them, and they follow me: And I give unto them eternal life; and they shall never perish, neither shall any *man* pluck them out of my hand. My Father, which gave *them* me, is greater than all; and no *man* is able to pluck *them* out of my Father's hand. I and *my* Father are one."

Again, the Lord Jesus Christ said that those who have genuinely trusted in Him "*shall never perish*." They have eternal and everlasting life.

Verses On The Uses Of The Word, Falling

There are a number of verses that use the word, "*fall*" or "*falling*." However, the word never means losing one's salvation.

- **Psalms 116:8**

"For thou hast delivered my soul from death, mine eyes from tears, *and* my feet from falling."

> **GOD CAN KEEP TRUE CHRISTIANS FROM FALLING**
> The God Who delivered the souls of genuine Christians from eternal death is also able to keep their feet from falling into any kind of difficulty if they only truly trust Him moment by moment.

- **Psalms 145:14**

"The LORD upholdeth all that fall, and raiseth up all *those that be* bowed down."

True Christians might fall into sin, but they can never fall into eternal damnation.

- **Proverbs 16:18**

"Pride *goeth* before destruction, and an haughty spirit before a fall."

Pride often causes people to fall into very sad and difficult circumstances.

- **Romans 14:13**

"Let us not therefore judge one another any more: but judge this rather, that no man put a stumbling block or an occasion to fall in *his* brother's way."

> **DON'T BE A STUMBLING BLOCK TO OTHERS**
> Genuine Christians should be concerned for other Christians lest they become a stumbling block. They should not think only of themselves.

- 1 Corinthians 10:12

"Wherefore let him that thinketh he standeth take heed lest he fall."

Cockiness and self-assuredness is dangerous. It is those people who should take heed lest they fall.

- 1 Timothy 3:6-7

"Not a novice, lest being lifted up with pride he fall into the condemnation of the devil. Moreover he must have a good report of them which are without; lest he fall into reproach and the snare of the devil."

> **PASTORS SHOULD NOT BE NOVICES**
> This is one of the requirements for the office of a pastor-bishop-elder. They should not be novices in the Christian Faith, lest they be lifted up with pride and fall into condemnation.

- 1 Corinthians 10:13

"There hath no temptation taken you but such as is common to man: but God *is* faithful, who will not suffer you to be tempted above that ye are able; but will with the temptation also make a way to escape, that ye may be able to bear *it*."

God is faithful and powerful. He will make a way of escape for any temptations or tests brought upon genuine Christians. He can make a way to escape so that they can put up with whatever trial they are facing if they sincerely seek it.

> **TRUE CHRISTIANS WILL BECOME FAULTLESS**
> Jude reminds his Christian readers that God is able to present them faultless before His Presence with exceeding joy. One day, He has promised to take those who have been saved--that is, redeemed by genuine faith in the Lord Jesus Christ--into Heaven. They will be spotless and faultless before Him with their glorified bodies like unto that of their Saviour's glorified body.

Jude 1:25

"To the only wise God our Saviour, be glory and majesty, dominion and power, both now and ever. Amen."

> **THE BIBLE'S GOD IS "THE ONLY WISE GOD "**
> This benediction talks about *"the only wise God."* The fathers of modern versions, Westcott and Hort, remove the word *"wise"* in the various translations we have today. Apostate leaders who use these corrupt versions don't want to teach that God is wise.

The term, "open theism" was introduced in 1980 and teaches that God doesn't know everything. Such false teaching has grown in popularity among evangelical circles and promotes that *"God does not know every detail about what will come to pass."* Sadly, evangelicals did not throw those who taught such blasphemy out of their churches. They kept them right in the fold and accepted such false teaching. But, in the end, we know that God is all wise and will judge accordingly!

Verses On The Wisdom Of God
- **Psalms 104:24**

"O LORD, how manifold are thy works! in wisdom hast thou made them all: the earth is full of thy riches."

God's wisdom is seen in His creation and all of His works.
- **Psalms 136:5**

"To him that by wisdom made the heavens: for his mercy *endureth* for ever."

By His wisdom, God made the vast heavens with their planets and millions of stars.
- **Luke 11:49**

"Therefore also said the wisdom of God, I will send them prophets and apostles, and *some* of them they shall slay and persecute:"

> **GOD'S PROPHETS WERE PERSECUTED AND SLAIN**
> God's wisdom predicted what people would do to His prophets and apostles. They would persecute them and slay some of them as well.

- **Romans 11:33**

"O the depth of the riches both of the wisdom and knowledge of God! how unsearchable *are* his judgments, and his ways past finding out!"

God does not have shallow riches. He has a depth of riches in the areas of wisdom, knowledge, judgments, and all His ways.

- **1 Corinthians 1:24**

"But unto them which are called, both Jews and Greeks, Christ the power of God, and the wisdom of God."

The Lord Jesus Christ is not only called the *"power of God,"* but also the *"wisdom of God."* True Christians have a wise and powerful Saviour!

- **1 Corinthians 2:7**

"But we speak the wisdom of God in a mystery, *even* the hidden *wisdom*, which God ordained before the world unto our glory:"

- **Ephesians 3:10**

"To the intent that now unto the principalities and powers in heavenly *places* might be known by the church the manifold wisdom of God,"

One day principalities and powers will understand God's manifold wisdom. This will be communicated by true Christians who make up the church which is the body of Christ.

- **Colossians 2:2-3**

"That their hearts might be comforted, being knit together in love, and unto all riches of the full assurance of understanding, to the acknowledgment of the mystery of God, and of the Father, and of Christ; In whom are hid all the treasures of wisdom and knowledge."

All the treasures of wisdom and knowledge are hidden and found in the Lord Jesus Christ.

- **1 Timothy 1:17**

"Now unto the King eternal, immortal, invisible, the only wise God, *be* honour and glory for ever and ever. Amen."

The God of the Bible is called here the *"only wise God."* None other in the world is as wise as He.

- **James 1:5**

"If any of you lack wisdom, let him ask of God, that giveth to all *men* liberally, and upbraideth not; and it shall be given him."

GOD IS THE ONLY SOURCE OF TRUE WISDOM

The only source of wisdom for genuine Christians is God Himself as He has revealed much of it in His Words. They must ask for this wisdom from God. If they ask sincerely, He has promised to give it to them liberally without upbraiding them. May this be practiced by all true Christians on a daily basis.

MANY IMPORTANT TRUTHS IN THIS BOOK OF JUDE

Though Jude is only a one-chapter book, there are many important and needful truths contained therein. We should thank the Lord for including it in His Bible. May Jude be used and followed by all for God's glory.

Index Of Words And Phrases

1 Corinthians 11:15. 55
1. God's Judgment On The Egyptians.. 150
1. Peter's Call. 1
10. Peter's Lying Boast. 5
11. Peter Falling Asleep During Prayer. 6
12. Peter's Swordsmanship. 6
13. Peter Following Afar Off. 7
15. Peter Going To The Tomb. 8
16. Peter's Return To Fishing. 9
17. Peter Throwing Himself Into The Water. 9
18. Peter's Restoration. 10
1881 Greek text.. 105
19 years. 61
19. Peter's Sermon To The 120 Disciples. 10
1978. 84
2 Peter & Jude. 1
2 Peter Chapter One. iv
2 Peter Chapter Three. iv
2 Peter Chapter Two. iv
2. Peter And The Other Apostles.. 2
3. God's Judgment On Sodom And Gomorrah. 154
3. Peter Walking On Water. 2
356 DOCTRINAL ERRORS. 24
356 doctrinal passages. 98, 147, 148
356 false doctrinal passages. 24, 96, 147
356 FALSE DOCTRINAL PASSAGES IN GREEK TEXTS. 96
356 FALSE DOCTRINAL PASSAGES IN NEW BIBLES. 147
4. God's Judgment On Cain, Balaam, And Korah. 160
4. Peter's Confession Of Faith. 3
5. Peter's Contradiction And Rebuke. 3
6. Peter On The Mount Of Transfiguration. 4
7. Peter And The Question Of Tribute. 4
8. Peter And Forgiveness. 5
8,000 DIFFERENCES IN N.T. GREEK TEXTS.. 96
85 Verses. 182
9. Peter And What Reward Do I Get?. 5
99% of the other English Bibles. 36
A CHRISTIAN'S DEATH IS PRECIOUS IN GOD'S SIGHT. 31
A HEAVENLY CALLING IS A SUMMONS TO HEAVEN. 30
About the Author. iv

Abraham.. 14, 59, 81
absent from the body............................... 31, 32
Acknowledgments.................................. ii, iv
ADULTERERS IN THE O.T. WERE TO BE KILLED.......... 75
adultery...................... 50, 74, 75, 111, 149, 154, 156
adultery in the heart.................................. 75
AFTER DEATH A PERSON GOES TO HEAVEN OR HELL.... 32
AGAPE... 23
AGRIOS... 166
AKARPOS.. 25
ALL PROPHECY HAS BEEN PRESERVED BY GOD.......... 42
ALL UNSAVED AT THE GREAT WHITE THRONE......... 172
ALOGOS.. 70, 159
Amen.................. 18, 20, 65, 134, 136, 137, 182, 191, 192
AMOMETOS.. 127
angels............. 53-58, 60, 62, 66, 68, 76, 78, 106, 108, 136,
                                          151-154, 158, 170, 177
ANGELS–SUPERHUMAN, BUT NOT OMNIPOTENT........ 68
Anglican leaders, Bishop Westcott and Professor Hort....... 105
Anti-Christians..................................... 170
aorist tense....................................... 108
Apocrypha... 39
APOLEIA... 51
apostate.............. 38, 47, 52, 68, 70, 97, 100, 102, 105, 146,
                                  149, 159-162, 165-167, 174, 191
APOSTATE DOCTRINES IN ALL KINDS OF CHURCHES..... 52
apostates............... 47, 67, 102, 155, 158, 159, 161, 165, 174
APOSTATES CAN'T UNDERSTAND THE BIBLE........... 158
apostolic times..................................... 148
ARETEN.. 21
ARGOS... 25
Armageddon.................... 106, 119, 120, 169-171
ARMAGEDDON'S FEAST BY FOWLS..................... 170
ASELGEIA..................................... 62, 85, 149
ASPILOS... 128
AUXANO... 134
babes in Christ.................................... 18, 22
Balaam........................... 78-80, 154, 160-163
BALAAM WAS A FALSE PROPHET FOR HIRE............. 162
BALAAM WAS REBUKED BY AN UNCLEAN ANIMAL....... 80
BALAAM'S ASS WAS WISER THAN BALAAM.............. 79
Barjesus... 49
barren... 24-26

BASANIZO. 63
Battle of Armageddon. 106, 119, 120, 169-171
BATTLE OF ARMAGEDDON NEAR JERUSALEM. 170
BE CAREFUL WHEN DEALING WITH EVIL PEOPLE.. 186
BE MINDFUL OF GOD'S PRESERVED WORDS. 98
BEFORE CHRIST'S RETURN–VERY GREAT EVIL.. 58
beguile. 76, 85
beguiling. 74, 76, 77
BELIEF IN CHRIST FROM THE HEART NEEDED.. 129
bestiality. 155, 156
beware. 48, 133, 134, 181
BFT #2548-T. 13, 161
BFT #2548-T @ 10/$2.00 + S&H. 161
BFT #2945 @ $12.00+ $7.00 S&H. 38
BFT #3230. 24
BFT #3230 @ $20.00 + $8.00 S&H. 24
BFT #4147.. i
BFT Phone: 856-854-4452. i
BFT@BibleForToday.org. .... i, 182
Bible Christology. 47
Bible colleges and seminaries.. 38
Bible Doctrine.. .... 44, 145
Bible For Today Baptist Church. .... i, iii, 167
Bible For Today Baptist Church earnestly contends. 167
BIBLE FOR TODAY PRESS. i
BIBLE INTERPRETATION'S GOLDEN RULE. 172
Bible preservation. 44, 46, 178
BIBLE PRESERVATION EXTREMELY NECESSARY. 178
Bible translation.. .... 147, 168
Bible versions. 146-148
Bible-believing. 16, 33, 39, 57, 74, 107, 147, 161, 166,
177
Bible's doctrines. 144
Bible's Heaven. 31
BIBLE'S ORIGINAL WORDS WILL NEVER PASS AWAY. 45
BIBLE'S VERBAL, PLENARY PRESERVATION NEEDED..... 33
Biblical morality. 64, 84, 160
BIBLICAL MORALITY SCOFFED AT BY THE LOST. 160
BIBLICAL QUALITIES NEEDED FOR PASTORS. 103
Biblical salvation. 128
Biblical truth.. 51
Billy Graham.. 172
blameless.. .... 68, 71, 73, 101, 126, 127, 175

blaspheme.. 68, 156, 157
BLASPHEMEO. 156
blemishes. 71-74
blind. 27, 28, 118
blindness... 27, 28, 104
blood............ 3, 13, 20, 29, 34, 48, 50, 65, 72, 74, 90, 91, 117-
120, 150, 161, 169, 187
Bob Jones University. 24, 38, 44, 45, 98, 177, 178
bodily resurrection. 19, 47
bodily resurrection of the Lord Jesus Christ. 19
bondage... 34, 65, 86, 87
born-again. 66, 68, 73, 112, 119, 124, 129, 147, 188
BOTH FLESH AND SPIRIT SHOULD BE CLEANSED....... 123
BRADUNO. 109
brothers in Christ.. 23
BY LOOKING BACK, LOT'S WIFE WAS DESTROYED........ 60
Cain.................................... 154, 160, 161, 167
calling. 9, 29, 30, 159
Calvary. 6, 7, 12, 28, 33, 38, 45, 47, 65, 98, 114, 166,
178
Calvary Baptist Seminary............................ 38, 178
Calvinism. 113
Canter, Mrs. Patty. iii
carnal Christian.. 149
Catholic Church......................... 30, 34, 38, 52, 148
Central Baptist Seminary............................ 38, 178
certain of their salvation................................ 29
CHARIS.. 15, 135
Christ............. 1-19, 21-35, 37-42, 44-48, 50, 52, 55, 58, 60,
64, 65, 67, 68, 70-76, 78, 81, 82, 87-91, 94, 95,
97, 100-107, 112-115, 118, 119, 122-130, 132,
134-136, 139-143, 145-148, 151-153, 159-161,
168-173, 175-184, 186-190, 192
CHRIST BORE THE WORLD'S SINS ON THE CROSS........ 114
CHRIST CALLED HEROD A FOX. 159
CHRIST CAN DELIVER FROM SATAN'S BONDAGE......... 65
CHRIST CAN KEEP CHRISTIANS FROM FALLING. 30
CHRIST DESERVES ALL MAJESTY AND GLORY. 136
CHRIST DESTROYED SATAN AT THE CROSS.............. 65
CHRIST LOVES EVERYONE & WANTS THEM SAVED....... 91
CHRIST QUESTIONED PETER'S TRUE LOVE. 10
CHRIST WAS IMPECCABLE–WITHOUT ANY SIN. 72
Christianity Today. 172

CHRISTIANS MUST AVOID EVIL ASSOCIATIONS. 64
CHRISTIANS MUST BE ESTABLISHED IN THE BIBLE. 146
Christian evolutionists. 109
CHRIST'S BLOOD IS PRECIOUS TO GOD THE FATHER. 13
Christ's coming with His saints. 168
Christ's finished work at Calvary. 166
CHRIST'S PROPITIATION FOR EVERYONE'S SINS. 115
CHRIST'S RESURRECTION WITNESSED CLEARLY. 9
CHRIST'S SINLESS BLOOD. 29
Christ's Words. 46, 177
CHRIST–THE SIN OFFERING FOR EVERY PERSON. 15
Church Phone: 856-854-4747. i
colleges. 15, 38, 51, 149
Collingswood, New Jersey. . . . . i, iii
Colossians. 17, 19, 67, 76, 112, 134, 146, 182, 192
compassion. 111, 185, 186
Congregation. . . . . ii, 52, 69, 157, 163, 164
Congregationalists. 52
consubstantiation. 34
contend. 143-145, 147, 148, 167
contend for this Faith. 148
CONTINUE IN THE DOCTRINES OF THE BIBLE. 145
covetous.. . . . . 74, 77, 78, 97, 99, 179
covetousness.. . . . . 20, 52, 53, 67, 77, 78, 89
creation. 99, 100, 102-104, 109, 122, 124, 125, 153,
191
Critical Greek Text. 24
cross. 6, 7, 18, 28, 34, 38, 47, 48, 50, 65, 72, 95, 114,
115, 128, 134, 186
crucifixion. 6, 37
D. A. Waite. . . . . 1, i, iii
day. 3, 8, 16, 17, 30, 32, 33, 35, 37, 42, 47, 51, 54-58,
60, 63, 64, 66, 67, 71-73, 78, 80, 84, 85, 87, 89,
90, 93-95, 98, 102, 103, 105-109, 114, 116-121,
124, 129, 130, 133, 140, 144, 150, 151, 153, 157,
160-162, 165-167, 171, 173, 174, 178, 181, 182,
186, 188, 190, 192
DAY OF OUR DEATH. 37
Day of the Lord.. 116-120
Dean Burgon Society. . . . . ii, 84
death. 1, 6, 11, 12, 19, 31-34, 37, 38, 40, 47, 48, 57, 65,
67, 69, 72, 74, 75, 81, 88, 115, 128, 164, 168, 171,
172, 188, 189

death of Moses. 69
Defined King James Bible Orders. iv
Deity. 47, 68, 136
DELEAZO. 76, 85
DELIVERANCE OF ISRAEL. 34
denied God's promise. 39, 178
departure from the Faith. 146
despise government. 66
destroyed them all. 58, 60, 105
Devil. 55, 65, 68, 70, 78, 107, 108, 151, 152, 157, 158,
170, 190
Devil's place of everlasting fire. 55
doctrinal errors. 24
doctrinal, historical, and grammatical errors. 147
doctrine. 21, 34, 38, 44, 45, 48, 79, 96, 112, 113, 132,
134, 144, 145, 161, 163, 166
doctrines. 12, 13, 16, 20, 21, 24, 34-36, 44, 47, 51, 52,
83, 97, 98, 105, 143-147, 156, 160, 162, 180
doctrines of the Bible. 12, 145-147, 160
doctrines of the faith. 16, 35, 143-147
DON'T BE A STUMBLING BLOCK TO OTHERS. 189
DON'T STAY BABES IN CHRIST, BUT MATURE. 22
double minded man. 77
DOULOO. 86
DOXA. 135
Dr. Jack Moorman. 24
Dr. Mark Minnick. 24
Dr. Samuel Schnaiter. 24
dragon. 49, 152, 158
drift. 35
drug addiction. 179
*Early Manuscripts, Church Fathers, and the King James Bible.*24
earth does not move. 35
earthly house. 36
EGYPT. 34, 59, 150, 151
Egyptian armies. 34
Egyptian bondage. 34
EIGHT THINGS PREVENT UNFRUITFULNESS. 24
EIRENE. 142
elect. 13, 29, 48, 112-115
election. 29
ELEEO. 185
elements. 23, 52, 107, 113, 116, 120, 121, 124, 125

ELENCHO	26
ELEOS	142, 183
Elymas the sorcerer	28
EMPAIKTES	99
ENDURE TEMPTATIONS	66
ENEMIES AT ARMAGEDDON--DESTROYED BY FIRE	106
ENKRATEIA	22
Enoch	167, 168, 171
ENUPNEAZOMAI	155
Ephesians 1:22-23	73
EPIAGONIZOMAI	144
EPITHUMIA	67, 85, 100
EPOIKODOMEO	181
ERROR AND FALSE DOCTRINE SHOULD BE EXPOSED	134
errors	24, 51, 83, 132, 134, 147
establish	95, 103
established	33-36, 95, 103, 145, 146
established firmly	146
established in the faith	35, 145
ESV, English Standard Version	148
EUSEBEIA	22
Evangelicals	161, 191
Evangelist Billy Graham	172
evening and the morning were the first day	109
everlasting fire	55, 78, 107, 108, 151
EVERLASTING FIRE FOR ALL NON-CHRISTIANS	78
EVERY HUMAN BEING IS TRIPARTITE	127
evil associations	64
evolutionists	99, 109
EXELENGKO	169
expose	71, 134
e-mail: BFT@BibleForToday.org	i
fables	39, 40
FABLES TURN PEOPLE AWAY FROM TRUTH	40
fairy tales	40
faith	1-3, 11, 12, 14-16, 21, 22, 24, 29, 31, 32, 34, 35, 40, 47, 50, 72, 83, 88, 90, 94, 98, 111, 112, 115, 119, 128, 129, 132, 135, 141, 143-148, 160, 161, 165, 167, 168, 173, 181, 182, 187, 188, 190
FAKE & PHONY PEOPLE ABOUND IN OUR WORLD	89
fallen angels	55
fallen ones	54
falling	6, 30, 188, 189

false Hebrew, Aramaic, and Greek Words.................. 36
FALSE LEADERS UNDEPENDABLE FOR GUIDANCE...... 167
false prophet......................... 49, 78, 107, 161, 162, 170
false prophet, Barjesus.................................. 49
false prophets............................. 47-49, 51, 52, 75
false teachers............ 47, 51-53, 68, 70, 71, 73, 74, 76-78, 80-87, 100, 102-105, 133, 148, 149, 155, 156, 161, 166-168, 174
FALSE TEACHERS ARE AS WELLS AND CLOUDS.......... 81
FALSE TEACHERS ARE LIKE WAVES AND STARS. 166
FALSE TEACHERS BRING PEOPLE INTO BONDAGE. 87
FALSE TEACHERS CALLED "WILLINGLY IGNORANT". ... 102
FALSE TEACHERS HAVE BEEN PREDICTED. 47
FALSE TEACHERS HAVE MANY BLEMISHES & SPOTS..... 73
FALSE TEACHERS MIXING WITH TRUE CHRISTIANS. 71
FALSE TEACHERS SPEAK EMPTY & VAIN WORDS......... 83
FALSE TEACHERS TEACH MANY FALSE DOCTRINES..... 105
FALSE TEACHERS--TREES WITH WITHERED FRUIT. 166
FALSE TEXTS & VERSIONS=356 DOCTRINAL ERRORS..... 24
Father's house.. 21, 31
favorable to homosexuals and homosexuality................ 61
FAX: 856-854-2464. i
fellowship.................. 10, 11, 19, 26, 29, 73, 107, 165, 180
fight.................................. 32, 119, 144, 147, 167
fire.............. 10-12, 49, 55, 59, 60, 64, 70, 78, 90, 106-108, 115-117, 119, 120, 124, 125, 150, 151, 154, 164, 169-173, 181, 182, 186, 187
fire and brimstone........................... 49, 60, 107, 150
first phase of His second coming......................... 100
fishers of men.. 1
Five Promises Of God..................................... 20
FIVE SINS OF THOSE WALKING AFTER THE FLESH....... 66
FOLLOW YEARLY BIBLE READING--85 VERSES DAILY. .. 182
FOLLOWING AFAR OFF FOR FEAR....................... 7
FOR TRUE CHRISTIANS, DEATH IS PRECIOUS............. 11
foreign language Bibles.................................. 36
Foreword... iii, iv
FORGIVING FOUR HUNDRED AND NINETY TIMES.......... 5
fornication............... 50, 67, 75, 79, 111, 149, 154, 156, 163
four things that lifeguards should do..................... 187
fundamental doctrines................................... 47
fundamental schools..................................... 39
Fundamentalist............................... 38, 98, 146, 178

fundamentalist world. 146
Gail Riplinger. 84, 130, 132
Genesis 19:1-7. 61
Genesis 6. .... 54-57, 105, 152, 153
GENESIS 6 "SONS OF GOD" WERE EVIL ANGELS. 152
genuine Christians. .... iii, 3, 6, 7, 10, 11, 13, 16-19, 21-23,
      25-27, 30, 31, 33-37, 42, 43, 50, 56, 59, 63-66,
      68, 70-73, 75, 81, 83, 87, 90, 93, 95, 104, 108,
      111, 112, 123, 126, 134, 140, 146, 147, 149, 159,
      165, 168, 171, 175, 177, 180-190, 193
GENUINE CHRISTIANS ARE CALLED TO HOLINESS. 68
GENUINE CHRISTIANS HAVE BEEN WASHED BY GOD. ... 90
GEOCENTRICITY. 35
GEOCENTRICITY IS CLEARLY TAUGHT IN THE BIBLE. 35
Gertrude Grace Sanborn. 162
giants. 54, 152
given by inspiration of God, the Hebrew, Aramaic, and Greek. 132
GLORIFIED CHRISTIANS RETURN WITH CHRIST. 168
glory. 4, 5, 11, 12, 16, 18, 19, 28, 30-32, 38, 41, 42, 46,
     55, 65, 77, 108, 134-136, 151, 157, 177, 182, 188,
     191-193
GNOSIS. 21
Gnostic Critical Greek Text, the foundation of modern Bibles. . 24
God and His Bible doctrines.. 146
God and His Words. 16
GOD CALLED LOT "JUST" THOUGH VERY SINFUL.. 61
GOD CAN DELIVER THE JUST & PUNISH THE EVIL. 64
GOD CAN KEEP TRUE CHRISTIANS FROM FALLING. 189
GOD DID NOT DESTROY FAITHFUL ISRAELITES. 150
GOD IS NOT WILLING FOR ANY TO PERISH IN HELL. 173
GOD IS THE ONLY SOURCE OF TRUE WISDOM. 192
GOD SLEW OVER 15,000 JEWS DUE TO THEIR SINS. 165
God spared only eight people. 54, 56
God the Father. 3, 7, 13, 15, 30, 41, 109, 114, 136, 139,
     180
GOD THE FATHER IS WELL-PLEASED WITH HIS SON. 41
God The Father's Being Well Pleased With His Son. 41
God the Holy Spirit. 19, 30, 33, 43, 94, 109, 112, 135,
     143, 177, 184
God the Son. 15, 109
GOD WANTS TO USE CHRISTIANS' BODIES. 123
GOD WILL CREATE A NEW HEAVEN AND NEW EARTH. .. 121
God-Breathed, meaning "inspired". 130

GOD'S DELIVERANCE OF ISRAEL OUT OF EGYPT. 34
GOD'S FIRE POURED OUT ON THE SODOMITES. 59
GOD'S GRACE AND PEACE. 15
GOD'S LONGSUFFERING IS VERY IMPORTANT. 111
GOD'S LOVE SUMMED UP IN JOHN 3:16. 143
God's original Words in Hebrew, Aramaic, and Greek. 179
GOD'S ORIGINAL WORDS HAVE BEEN PRESERVED. 179
God's power. 18, 19
God's preserved Words. 98
God's promise to preserve. 39, 44, 178, 179
GOD'S PROPHETS WERE PERSECUTED AND SLAIN. 191
GOD'S WAY TO ESCAPE WHEN FACING TEMPTATION. 66
God's will. 17
GOD'S WILL FOUND IN GOD'S WORDS. 17
God's Words. . . . . iii, 13, 17, 18, 26, 35, 42, 44, 46, 94, 97,
                                99, 103, 106, 129, 133, 141, 177, 183
God's Words will be both kept. 44
GOGGUSTES. 174
gold, silver, and precious stones. 106, 181
Golden Rule Of Bible Interpretation. 172
gospel of Christ. 18, 28, 128
Gospel of Luke. 41
Gospel of Mark. 41
gospel preaching. 46
grace. 15, 16, 18-20, 29, 34, 44, 56, 57, 87, 97, 134-
                                        136, 141, 148, 149, 162, 182
gradually abandoned. 51
Graham, Billy. 172
GRAPHE. 130
Great White Throne Judgment. 116, 124, 125, 171, 172
GREAT WHITE THRONE JUDGMENT OF THE LOST. . . 125, 171
Greek and Hebrew original Words. 23
Greek present tense. 42, 43, 108, 144, 150, 155
Greek Word. 12, 21-23, 25-27, 35, 39, 43, 50-53, 62,
                                63, 67, 70, 74, 76, 82, 84-86, 93, 97, 99, 100,
                                109, 110, 115, 120-122, 124-128, 130, 132-136,
                                140, 142, 143, 149, 154-156, 159, 166, 167, 169,
                                173, 174, 176, 181, 183, 185, 187, 188
Greenville, South Carolina. 23, 24
grievous words. 37
HAGIAZO. 140
hair is given her for a covering, a woman. 55
HARPAZO. 187

HAVING ONLY A FORM OF GODLINESS. 20
he shall take of mine, and shall shew it unto you. 45
Heaven.. . . . . 3, 21, 30-32, 36, 41, 42, 44, 45, 57, 59, 60,
65, 72, 82, 88, 104-106, 116, 118-122, 124-127,
136, 141, 142, 146, 151, 152, 157, 158, 167-170,
172, 173, 176, 188, 190
Hebrew Word YODH.. 44
HEBREW, ARAMAIC, & GREEK WORDS PRESERVED. 133
Hebrew, Aramaic, and Greek Words. 12, 33, 36, 38,
39, 42, 44-46, 132, 147, 168, 178, 183
HEILIKRINES. 93
heliocentricity. 35
hell. 32, 49, 51-53, 55, 64, 78, 81, 86, 90, 107, 115,
124, 125, 128, 151, 152, 167, 172, 173, 181
HELL IS GENUINE, REAL, AND EVERLASTING FIRE. 107
heresies. 47-51, 71, 111, 149
heresy. 13, 49-51, 84, 113-115, 132, 161, 177
heretical.. . . . . 44, 45, 114, 149
heretical position. 45
HETEROS. 155
HILASMOS.. 115
His bodily resurrection. 47
His Deity. 47
His virgin birth. 47
His Words. 16, 34, 38, 39, 46, 77, 78, 97, 100, 130,
157, 176-178, 182, 185, 193
HOLINESS. 67, 68, 101, 123, 124
holy men of God. 43
homosexual marriages. 61, 100, 156, 179
homosexual sodomites. 60
homosexual sodomy. 58, 61
homosexualism. 61
homosexuality. 60, 61, 83, 154, 156, 179
HUPOMONE. 22
Hyper-Calvinism. 113
hyper-Calvinist. 114
hypocrites. 67, 71, 89
I am well pleased. 4, 41
IDIOS.. 43
if a woman have long hair. 55
impeccable. 72
IMPORTANCE OF THE DOCTRINES OF THE FAITH. 145
in no wise. 44

INCREASE IN THE KNOWLEDGE OF GOD'S WORDS...... 183
INCREASING IN THE KNOWLEDGE OF GOD.............. 17, 182
Index of Words and Phrases....................... iv, 195
inspiration...................... 33, 42, 45, 96, 130, 132, 176
inspired, and preserved Hebrew, Aramaic, & Greek Words. 36, 168
ISBN #978-1-56848–108-1................................ i
Israel............ 2, 5, 34, 69, 78-80, 102, 104, 106, 110, 117, 118, 151, 157, 158, 162-165, 170, 171, 175
John 16:12-14... 176
John 16:12-15.. 45
John 3:16.......................... 20, 48, 113, 114, 143, 184
JOHN MACARTHUR–A HERETIC ON CHRIST'S BLOOD!.... 13
John MacArthur's Heresy On The Blood................... 13
JOHN WAS PATIENT AT CHRIST'S TOMB................. 8
jot... 44
Judas....................................... 4, 10, 12, 139-141
Jude.............. 1-iv, 30, 34, 55, 68, 70, 71, 73, 108, 139-144, 147, 148, 150, 151, 154, 155, 157-160, 163, 165-169, 173-176, 179, 180, 183, 185, 186, 188, 190, 193
Jude Chapter One.. iv
judgment of angels..................................... 53
judgment of Sodom and Gomorrha....................... 53
Judgment of The Flood.................................. 56
judgment of the old world........................... 53, 56
judgment of the universal flood......................... 56
judgment seat of Christ............................ 106, 172
KAINOS... 126
KATAKAIO... 122
KATAPONEO... 62
KAUSAOO... 125
King James Bible.............. i, iv, 11, 25, 33, 36, 39, 42, 46, 84, 94, 96, 116, 130, 132, 133, 144, 146-148, 168, 176, 177, 183
KING JAMES BIBLE FAITHFUL TO PETER'S WORDS....... 39
King James Bible translators did in 1604 to 1611............. 94
KNOWLEDGEABLE LIPS ARE PRECIOUS JEWELS........ 12
Korah...................................... 154, 160, 163-165
KURIOTES... 156
LAILAPS... 82
Lake of Fire........... 49, 70, 78, 90, 107, 115, 116, 124, 125, 170, 172, 173

Lake of Fire of Hell.	124, 172

Lake of Fire of Hell. 124, 172
Lake that burns with fire and brimstone. 150
last days.. .... 71, 97-99, 146, 179, 180
LEAVE & REPROVE DARK & UNFRUITFUL WORKS. 26
leaven.. 29
lesbian. 60
LESBIAN MOLLENKOTT'S FALSE VIEW OF SODOM. 60
lesbianism. 60, 61, 154
liberal-apostate teachers and ministers. 38
LIES. 40, 75, 88, 98, 136
light shining in dark places. 42
literal hell. 107
Living Water. 81, 82
long hair. 55
longsuffering.. .... 19, 109-113, 128, 173, 185
LONGSUFFERING–A FRUIT OF THE HOLY SPIRIT. 112
LONGSUFFERING--PUT ON LIKE A GARMENT. 112
Lord Jesus Christ. 1-17, 19, 22-35, 37-42, 44-48, 50,
52, 55, 58, 60, 64, 65, 67, 68, 70-75, 78, 81, 82,
87-91, 94, 95, 97, 100-107, 113-115, 119, 122-
130, 134-136, 139-142, 145, 147, 148, 151-153,
159-161, 168-173, 175-181, 183, 184, 186-190,
192
Lord's Supper. 33, 34, 165
Lord's Table. 71
loss. 17, 106
Lot. 58-64, 143
Lot chose to go into the land of Sodom.. 59
Lot was adversely affected. 62
LOT'S WIFE. 60
love of God. 183-185
love of the brethren. 24, 94
LOVE WITH KNOWLEDGE AND DISCERNMENT.. 17
Lucifer. 151
LUO. 121, 124
lust. 14, 20, 21, 62, 66, 67, 74, 75, 83, 85, 149
lust of uncleanness.. .... 66, 67
lusts. 67, 83, 84, 94, 98-100, 173, 174, 179, 180
Lutherans. 52
Lystra.. 32
MacArthur, John. 13, 161
MacArthur's heresy on the blood. 13, 161
MAJESTY AND GLORY. 136

MAKROTHUMIA.	110
male and female sodomites.	155
MALE AND FEMALE SODOMITES ARE INCREASING.	155
MANY EVIL ANGELS FOLLOWED SATAN.	151
MANY IMPORTANT TRUTHS IN THIS BOOK OF JUDE.	193
many things to say.	45, 176, 177
MANY TRUE CHRISTIANS DENY THE LITERAL HELL.	107
mark of the beast.	49, 170
mass.	30, 34
MATAIOTES.	84
Matthew's Gospel.	41
MEANING OF PROHIBITIONS IN THE AORIST TENSE.	108
MEANING OF THE GREEK WORD, "ANASTROPHE".	124
MEANING OF THE GREEK WORD, "BLASPHEMEO".	156
MEANING OF THE GREEK WORD, "ENUPNEAZOMAI".	155
MEANING OF THE GREEK WORD, "EPOIKODOMEO".	181
Messiah.	54, 114, 136
Messiah, the Lord Jesus Christ.	114
METANOIA.	173
Methodists.	52
MIANO.	156
MIASMOS.	67
Michael.	68-70, 152, 157, 158
Michael the archangel.	68, 157, 158
Millennial reign.	122, 124, 125, 171
Millennial Reign of the Lord Jesus Christ.	122, 124, 125, 171
Millennium.	100, 107, 116
mindful.	96-98
MINDS EVILLY AFFECTED AGAINST CHRISTIANS.	95
Minnick, Mark, teacher at Bob Jones University.	24
modern Bible versions.	147, 148
modern perversions.	148
Modern Versions.	24, 148, 191
modernist-liberal-apostate teachers and ministers.	38
Mollenkott, Virginia, an admitted lesbian homosexual.	60
Moorman, Dr. Jack.	24
Moses.	29, 38, 40, 52, 68-70, 87, 131, 145, 151, 157, 158, 163-165, 174, 175, 185
MOSES KEPT OUT OF CANAAN BECAUSE OF HIS SIN.	157
Mount Of Transfiguration.	4, 40, 42
moved.	43, 57, 186
Mrs. Waite.	ii, 120

MULTITUDES TODAY ARE SPIRITUALLY BLIND. 27
MUOPAZO. 27
murder of an estimated 1.4 million babies. 179
murmurers. 173, 174
MUTHOS. 39
my words shall not pass away. 45, 176, 178
myopia.. 27
myth and a falsehood. 39
NASV, New American Standard Version. 148
natural brute beasts..................................... 70
NEED FOR A PROPER HEART, CONSCIENCE, & FAITH..... 94
NEOS.. 126
NEPHALIM. 54, 153
nephew of Abraham..................................... 59
NEVER BE ASHAMED OF GOD'S WORDS!................. 177
never, never, never.................................. 45, 46
New Evangelical philosophy............................. 172
New Evangelicalism................................... 146
new heaven and a new earth..................... 122, 124, 125
NIV, New International Version. 148
no doctrinal changes................................... 24
Noah. 54, 56, 57, 105, 113, 152
NOAH WAS A PREACHER OF RIGHTEOUSNESS........... 56
Noah's flood. 57, 58, 105
NOAH'S FLOOD WAS NOT LOCAL, BUT UNIVERSAL....... 58
NOAH'S FLOOD WAS UNIVERSAL, NOT LOCAL. 105
NRSV.. 148
O.T. FALSE PROPHETS PRACTICED ADULTERY........... 75
O.T. "SONS OF GOD" WERE ANGELS. 55
Obama... 61, 83
OLD TESTAMENT AND NEW TESTAMENT WRITINGS. 96
OLDER PEOPLE MUST ALSO AVOID YOUTHFUL LUSTS.... 84
omnipotent.. 68, 104
once delivered unto the saints. 143
ONCE DELIVERED WORDS--NOT IN NEW BIBLES........ 148
ONLY CHRIST'S SINLESS BLOOD CAN PURGE SINS........ 29
ONLY GOD CAN KEEP CHRISTIANS FROM FALLING...... 188
ONLY NOAH FOUND GRACE IN GOD'S EYES. 57
Order Blank Pages..................................... iv
Orders: 1-800-John 10:9. i
original inspired Hebrew, Aramaic, and Greek Words......... 38
OU ME... 45, 176
PAREISDUNO. 149

Passover. 29, 73
Pastor D. A. Waite, ThD, PhD. .... i, iii, 1
Pastor Timothy.. .... 34, 37, 40, 94, 98, 99, 112
pastors............ 34, 52, 58, 68, 71, 78, 103, 109, 130, 146, 149,
165, 178, 179, 190
PASTORS SHOULD NOT BE NOVICES. 190
pastors-bishops-elders. 68, 71, 178, 179
PASTORS-BISHOPS-ELDERS–NOT COVETOUSNESS....... 78
PASTORS-BISHOPS-ELDERS–NOT TO BE SELFWILLED.... 68
Patricia Canter.. iii
Paul. 17, 19, 28, 31, 32, 34, 36, 37, 40, 49, 50, 65, 76,
95, 97-99, 103, 104, 112, 128, 129, 131, 145-147,
175, 178
PAUL & OTHERS FALSELY ACCUSED OF HERESY. 50
PAUL GUARDED BIBLE DOCTRINES–SO SHOULD WE.... 147
Paul had fame.. 17
PAUL TO BE A PATTERN OF LONGSUFFERING.. 112
PAUL WANTED TO VISIT THE CHRISTIANS IN ROME. ... 103
Paul was beheaded. 65
PAUL WAS STONED TO DEATH AT LYSTRA............... 32
Paul was transformed.................................... 19
Paul's departure to Heaven. 32
Paul's last letter. 65
PAUL'S PRAYER FOR THE EPHESIAN CHRISTIANS........ 16
pernicious ways.. 51, 84
PERNICIOUS WAYS ABOUND IN OUR DAY AS WELL.. 51
perversion... 60
PERVERTED LOT WAS ALLOWED TO FLEE SODOM. 59
Peter. 1-iv, 1-15, 18, 20-25, 27-30, 33, 36-43, 46-48,
51-53, 56, 58, 61, 63-66, 68, 70-74, 76-79, 81,
83-88, 90, 93-100, 102, 105-109, 113, 114, 116,
120, 122-130, 132-134, 136, 141, 147, 152, 162,
173, 180-182, 186
PETER CALLED JESUS A LIAR A SECOND TIME............ 6
Peter called the Lord Jesus a liar.......................... 3
PETER FORSOOK HIS DIVINE CALLING.................. 9
Peter lied.. 5, 8
PETER LIED THREE TIMES AT CHRIST'S TRIAL........... 8
PETER LOOKED FOR A SELFISH REWARD................ 5
PETER LOST HIS FAITH AND WAS SINKING............... 2
PETER RESTORED TO FELLOWSHIP WITH THE LORD. ... 10
Peter Ruckman, held a false view of the KJB........ 84, 130, 132
PETER TOOK MATTERS INTO HIS OWN HANDS. 7

PETER WANTED HIS WORDS REMEMBERED............ 38
PETER WANTED TO STIR UP PURE MINDS............... 93
PETER WANTED UNITY, COURTESY & COMPASSION..... 186
PETER WAS CALLED BY THE LORD...................... 1
PETER WAS INFLUENCED BY THE SATAN................ 4
PETER'S EAGER SWIM TO SHORE....................... 9
PETER'S FIRST CALL WAS TO THE JEWS................. 2
PHARAOH WANTED TO ENSLAVE ISRAEL AGAIN........ 151
Pharisees......................... 27, 28, 67, 77, 89, 160, 175
PHILADELPHIA............................... 23, 51, 61
phony... 70, 88-90
PHTHORA.. 86
PHULASSO.. 133
PHUSIKOS... 70
physical death................................ 31, 69, 88
Pillsbury Baptist Bible College..................... 38, 45, 98
PLAIN SENSE of Scripture............................ 172
PLANE.. 85
PLANETES.. 167
plastic... 53
PLASTOS.. 53
plenary............. 33, 38, 39, 42-46, 94, 96, 130, 177, 178, 183
PLEONAZO.. 25
PLEONEXIA.. 52
PNEO.. 132
political beast..................................... 170
PORNEIA... 154
pornography....................................... 179
preaching of the cross............................... 18
Preaching Verse-by-Verse............................ 1
Presbyterian.. 34
Presbyterian Churches............................... 34
Presbyterians....................................... 52
present with the Lord............................... 31
preservation.............. 33, 38, 42-46, 96, 130, 178
preserved verbally and plenarily..................... 39
preserved Words................... 33, 46, 94, 96, 98, 177
presumptuous....................................... 66
priest... 7, 30, 163
Princeton Seminary................................. 51
prohibitions....................................... 108
Promise of An Eternal Home In Heaven................ 21
Promise of Everlasting Life.......................... 20

Promise of Our Saviour's Presence With Us. 20
Promise of Redemption and Forgiveness. 20
Promise of The Indwelling Holy Spirit. 20
promises of God. 14, 20
proper and preserved Hebrew, Aramaic, and Greek Words. ... 12
prophet for hire. 78, 162
propitiation.. 115
PROSDOKAO. 127
Protestant churches.. .... 146, 166
Protestant groups. 52
PRO-SODOMITE AMERICA. 61
PSUCHIKOS.. 159
Publisher's Data.. iv
qualifications. 68, 78
Rapture of true Christians, before the Tribulation. 61, 188
read God's Words. 18
rebellious people. 163
rebuked sharply. 147
RECEIVING RIGHTEOUSNESS BEFORE GOD. 103
Red Cross Water Safety Instructor. 186
Reformed. 34
Reformed and Presbyterian Churches. 34
religious beast. 170
remembrance. 33, 34, 36-38, 93, 95, 96, 150
repent. 8, 89, 109, 113, 173
repentance. 89, 109, 113, 173
righteousness. 1, 11, 14, 15, 56, 83, 84, 88, 94, 103,
                          114, 122, 123, 125, 129, 132, 168, 169, 180
RIGHTEOUSNESS ONLY BY GENUINE FAITH. 14
Rioting.. .... 71, 72
Riplinger, Gail, holds a false view of the KJB.. .... 84, 130, 132
Roman Catholic. 30, 34, 38, 39, 52, 146, 148, 166
Roman Catholic Mass. 30
Rome. 16, 36, 103, 104
RSV, Revised Standard Version. 148
salvation. 1, 14, 15, 17, 18, 28, 29, 48, 50, 87, 90, 114,
                      115, 128, 129, 132, 140, 142, 143, 165, 188, 189
Salvation is not of works.. 14
SALVATION THROUGH GENUINE FAITH IN CHRIST. 128
Sanborn.. .... ii, 162
SANCTIFIED BY GOD'S WORDS. 141
Satan. 3, 4, 28, 54, 65, 76, 104, 147, 151-153, 157
Satan who must be resisted. 147

Satanic giants.	54
satanic trinity.	49, 107
Saviour.	1, 6, 7, 9, 11, 14-18, 20, 26-31, 47, 48, 50, 54, 55, 64, 65, 70-72, 87, 89-91, 94-96, 103, 107, 114, 115, 128, 129, 134, 135, 142, 143, 152, 168, 169, 173, 181-183, 186, 189, 191, 192
Schnaiter, Samuel, Professor at Bob Jones University.	24
School District of Philadelphia.	61
SCOFFERS ARE MANY IN THESE LAST DAYS.	99
scribes.	3, 67, 160, 175
Scripture.	iii, 13, 14, 18, 43, 129, 132, 158, 172
Scriptures as the Hebrew and Aramaic Words.	130
second phase of His coming.	100, 168
self-willed.	66, 68
seminaries.	15, 38, 51, 98, 130, 149
separate from evil influences.	63
separation.	73, 180
serious heresy.	115, 132, 161
Sermons.	ii, iii, 71, 162
SEVERE PUNISHMENT DURING THE TRIBULATION.	119
SHALOM.	15
Shem, Ham, and Japheth.	54, 105
Simon Peter.	1-3, 6, 8-10, 97
sin of homosexual sodomy.	61
sins.	7, 12, 14, 15, 20, 27-29, 56, 60, 61, 63, 64, 66, 69, 72, 73, 78, 90, 91, 99, 110, 111, 113-115, 117, 128, 142, 154, 155, 160, 161, 164, 165, 169, 173, 179
sins unto physical death.	69
slackness.	109, 110, 173
SLEEPING INSTEAD OF WATCHING.	6
smallest Hebrew letter, the yodh.	44
Sodom.	53, 58-63, 67, 75, 154, 155
Sodom and Gomorrah.	58-61, 67, 75, 154, 155
sodomites.	59, 60, 62, 155
sodomy.	58, 60, 61
sodomy and lesbianism are being pushed on school children.	61
Sodom's sinful lifestyle.	62
SOME HYPER-CALVINISTS ADD TO JOHN 3:16.	114
SOME OF THE PEOPLE NAMED "JUDE" OR "JUDAS".	139
SOME TRUE CHRISTIANS WALK AFTER THEIR FLESH.	75
sons of God, as fallen angels.	54, 55, 123, 127, 152, 153, 169, 175
SOPHIZO.	39
so-called Bible-believing.	39

spake unadvisedly with his lips. 69, 157
speak evil.. .... 66, 68, 70, 155, 157, 158
speak evil of dignities. 66, 68, 155
special grace. 34
SPECIFIC HERESIES ABOUND TODAY WORLDWIDE. 47
spiritually blind. 27
spotless. 29, 73, 128, 190
spotless, perfect, and without blemish. 73
SPOUDE. 143
STERIZO.. 35
STOICHEION.. .... 120, 124
stoned. 32
STREBLOO.. 130
substitutionary death on the cross. 128
SUNEUOCHEO. 74
superior texts. 183
superior theology. 183
superior translators. 183
tabernacle. 36, 37, 163, 164
Table of Contents. iv
teacher.. 61
TEI PISTEI. 143, 145
TEKO. 125
temperance. 22, 25
Temple University. 51
temporary tent. 36
temptation. 6, 65, 66, 190
TEV, Today's English Version. 148
THE ACCEPTED TIME FOR SALVATION IS "NOW". 129
The Background Of 2 Peter. 1
THE BEAST AND FALSE PROPHET CAST INTO HELL. 49
THE BEGINNING OF THE DAY OF THE LORD. 116
THE BIBLE SHINES AS A LIGHT IN DARK PLACES.. 42
THE BIBLE'S GOD IS "THE ONLY WISE GOD ". 191
THE BIBLE'S VERBAL, PLENARY INSPIRATION. 33
THE BIBLICAL VIEW OF THE LORD'S SUPPER. 33
The Covetousness Of False Teachers. 52
THE CREATION OF THE NEW HEAVENS AND EARTH. ... 125
the cross. 6, 7, 18, 28, 34, 38, 47, 48, 50, 65, 72, 95,
114, 115, 128
The Damnation Of False Teachers. 53
THE DAY OF THE LORD BRINGS PUNISHMENT. 117
THE DESTINY OF THE DEVIL–EVERLASTING HELL. 55

THE FALSE UNIFORMITARIAN VIEW OF CREATION. 100
The Feigned Words Of False Teachers. 53
The Heresy Of Hyper-Calvinism. 113
The Judgment Of Sodom And Gomorrah. 58
The Judgment Of The Old World. 53, 56
THE KING JAMES BIBLE ACCURATELY TRANSLATES. 46
THE KING JAMES BIBLE, NOT "GOD-BREATHED". 132
the Lord Jesus Christ. 1-17, 19, 22, 23, 25-35, 37, 38,
    40-42, 44-48, 50, 52, 55, 58, 60, 65, 67, 68, 70-
    75, 78, 81, 82, 87-91, 94, 95, 97, 100, 103-107,
    113-115, 119, 122-130, 134-136, 139-142, 145,
    147, 148, 151-153, 159-161, 168-173, 175-181,
    183, 184, 186-190, 192
THE MEANING OF THE GREEK WORD FOR "HERESY". 50
THE MEANING OF THE GREEK WORD, " KATAPONEO". ... 62
THE MEANING OF THE GREEK WORD, "AGAPE". 23
THE MEANING OF THE GREEK WORD, "AGRIOS". 166
THE MEANING OF THE GREEK WORD, "AKARPOS". 25
THE MEANING OF THE GREEK WORD, "ALOGOS". 70, 159
THE MEANING OF THE GREEK WORD, "AMEN". 136
THE MEANING OF THE GREEK WORD, "AMOMETOS". ... 127
THE MEANING OF THE GREEK WORD, "APOLEIA". 51
THE MEANING OF THE GREEK WORD, "ARETEN". 21
THE MEANING OF THE GREEK WORD, "ARGOS". 25
THE MEANING OF THE GREEK WORD, "ASELGEIA". .. 62, 149
THE MEANING OF THE GREEK WORD, "ASPILOS". 128
THE MEANING OF THE GREEK WORD, "AUXANO". 134
THE MEANING OF THE GREEK WORD, "BASANIZO". 63
THE MEANING OF THE GREEK WORD, "CHARIS". 135
THE MEANING OF THE GREEK WORD, "DELEAZO". 85
THE MEANING OF THE GREEK WORD, "DOXA". 135
THE MEANING OF THE GREEK WORD, "EIRENE". 142
THE MEANING OF THE GREEK WORD, "ELEEO". 185
THE MEANING OF THE GREEK WORD, "ELEOS". 142, 183
THE MEANING OF THE GREEK WORD, "ENKRATEIA". 22
THE MEANING OF THE GREEK WORD, "EPITHUMIA". 67
THE MEANING OF THE GREEK WORD, "EUSEBEIA". 22
THE MEANING OF THE GREEK WORD, "EXELENGKO". ... 169
THE MEANING OF THE GREEK WORD, "GOGGUSTES". ... 174
THE MEANING OF THE GREEK WORD, "HAGIAZO". 140
THE MEANING OF THE GREEK WORD, "HARPAZO". 187
THE MEANING OF THE GREEK WORD, "HETEROS". 155
THE MEANING OF THE GREEK WORD, "IDIOS". 43

THE MEANING OF THE GREEK WORD, "KAINOS"........ 125
THE MEANING OF THE GREEK WORD, "KATAKAIO"..... 122
THE MEANING OF THE GREEK WORD, "KAUSAOO"...... 125
THE MEANING OF THE GREEK WORD, "KURIOTES"..... 156
THE MEANING OF THE GREEK WORD, "LUO".......... 124
THE MEANING OF THE GREEK WORD, "METANOIA"..... 173
THE MEANING OF THE GREEK WORD, "MIANO"........ 156
THE MEANING OF THE GREEK WORD, "MIASMOS"....... 67
THE MEANING OF THE GREEK WORD, "MUOPAZO"...... 27
THE MEANING OF THE GREEK WORD, "MUTHOS"........ 39
THE MEANING OF THE GREEK WORD, "NEOS".......... 126
THE MEANING OF THE GREEK WORD, "PHILADELPHIA". 23
THE MEANING OF THE GREEK WORD, "PHULASSO"..... 133
THE MEANING OF THE GREEK WORD, "PHUSIKOS"...... 70
THE MEANING OF THE GREEK WORD, "PLANETES"..... 167
THE MEANING OF THE GREEK WORD, "PLASTOS"........ 53
THE MEANING OF THE GREEK WORD, "PLEONAZO"...... 25
THE MEANING OF THE GREEK WORD, "PLEONEXIA"..... 52
THE MEANING OF THE GREEK WORD, "PORNEIA"...... 154
THE MEANING OF THE GREEK WORD, "PROSDOKAO"... 126
THE MEANING OF THE GREEK WORD, "PSUCHIKOS".... 159
THE MEANING OF THE GREEK WORD, "SOPHIZO"........ 39
THE MEANING OF THE GREEK WORD, "SPOUDE"....... 143
THE MEANING OF THE GREEK WORD, "STERIZO"........ 35
THE MEANING OF THE GREEK WORD, "STREBLOO"..... 130
THE MEANING OF THE GREEK WORD, "TEKO".......... 125
THE MEANING OF THE GREEK WORD, "XITON"......... 187
THE MEANING OF THE GREEK WORD,"PAREISDUNO"... 149
THE MEANING OF THE GREEK WORDS, "OU ME"........ 176
THE METHOD OF THE BIBLE'S ORIGINATION............ 45
The Mount Of Transfiguration....................... 4, 40, 42
THE ORIGINATION OF THE BIBLE'S WORDS............. 43
THE PERDITION OF UNGODLY MEN WILL BE BY FIRE... 106
THE POWER OF CHRIST NEEDED....................... 19
THE PRECIOUSNESS OF CHRIST....................... 13
THE PRE-FLOOD WORLD WAS CONTINUALLY EVIL....... 56
THE SATANIC TRINITY IS NAMED....................... 49
THE SATANIC TRINITY WILL BE SENT TO HELL......... 107
THE SIN OF HOMOSEXUALITY IS ON THE INCREASE.... 156
The sin of Sodom and Gomorrah........................ 59
THE SIXTH THING TO BE ADDED TO CHRISTIANS....... 23
THE TECHNIQUE OF THE BIBLE'S PRODUCTION......... 177
THE UNCERTAINTY OF THE DAY OF OUR DEATH........ 37

THE USE OF "AMEN" AROUND THE WORLD............ 137
THE VIRTUOUS WOMAN WORKS WILLINGLY.......... 102
theological errors..................................... 132
theological modernists................................ 47
THEOPNEUSTOS....................................... 132
THEOS... 132
THINGS PERTAINING TO LIFE AND GODLINESS.......... 18
Till heaven and earth pass............................... 44
Timothy.............. 1, 19, 29, 32, 34, 37, 40, 65, 72, 77, 83, 94,
            95, 97-99, 112, 113, 130, 132, 133, 144, 146, 147,
                                                179, 190, 192
tittle.. 44
TODAY THERE ARE MANY WORLDWIDE SCOFFERS..... 180
Traditional Received New Testament Greek Text............ 105
Transcription... iii
translation...................... 33, 39, 42, 46, 147, 168, 183
TRANSLATION–OF ENOCH AND OF THE BIBLE.......... 168
transubstantiation...................................... 34
Tribulation................... 49, 61, 106, 116-119, 124, 145
Tribulation Period......................... 61, 116-119, 124
tripartite.. 127
TRUE BIBLE TEXTS & TRANSLATIONS NEEDED.......... 36
true Christian pastors................................... 34
true Christians.............. 3, 6, 10, 11, 13-17, 19, 20, 22, 25-27,
            29, 30, 32, 35, 36, 42, 44, 50, 61, 64, 66, 67, 71,
            72, 75-77, 84, 87, 88, 90, 95, 100, 103, 107, 112,
            115, 123, 124, 127, 128, 134, 136, 142, 146, 148,
                            168, 175, 177, 180-190, 192, 193
TRUE CHRISTIANS CAN NEVER LOSE SALVATION....... 188
TRUE CHRISTIANS HAVE CHANGED THEIR ACTIONS..... 72
TRUE CHRISTIANS HAVE THEIR SPOTS REMOVED....... 72
TRUE CHRISTIANS MUST ENDURE TEMPTATIONS....... 66
TRUE CHRISTIANS SHOULD NOT WORSHIP ANGELS..... 76
TRUE CHRISTIANS WILL BECOME FAULTLESS.......... 190
TRUE CHRISTIANS–NEVER SEPARATED FROM GOD..... 184
true faith..................... 14, 15, 22, 29, 31, 72, 129, 141
true gospel preaching................................... 46
TURNING AWAY FROM TRUTH LEADS TO LIES........... 40
TWO ANIMALS IN THE O.T. WERE ABLE TO TALK......... 80
unbelievers.................. 99, 102, 155, 158, 159, 165, 180
UNBELIEVERS--LIKE SPOTS, CLOUDS AND TREES....... 165
unbelieving apostate ministers.......................... 165
unBiblical morality..................................... 84

unfruitful. 24-26
ungodly lusts. 179, 180
UNGODLY MEN CREPT INTO CHURCHES SECRETLY..... 149
uniformitarian. 100
universal salvation.. 48
universalism. 115
UNIVERSALISM HELD BY MANY IS SERIOUS HERESY..... 115
unlimited atonement.. .... 48, 109, 115
UNLIMITED ATONEMENT IS CLEARLY TAUGHT.......... 48
UNSAVED CONSIGNED TO HELL'S ETERNAL FIRE....... 172
vacuum cleaner. 17
verbal. 33, 38, 39, 42-46, 94, 96, 130, 177, 178, 183
VERBAL, PLENARY INSPIRATION.. .... 33, 42, 96, 130
VERBAL, PLENARY PRESERVATION. 33, 38, 42,
44-46, 96, 130, 178
VERBAL, PLENARY PRESERVATION NEEDED.. 33,
38
VERBAL, PLENARY PRESERVATION TAUGHT HERE.. 44
VERBAL, PLENARY PRESERVED WORDS NEEDED. 94
verbal, plenary, inspired Words.. 94
verbal, plenary, preserved Words. 177
Verses About Barren. 25
Verses About Blindness. 27
Verses About Heaven. 31
Verses About Michael. 158
Verses About The Burial Of Moses. 157
Verses Against Hyper-Calvinism.. 113
Verses From Paul On Salvation. 128
Verses Of Personal Words From One Of The Apostles......... 97
Verses On Adultery. 74
Verses On Balaam's Judgment. 161
Verses On Beasts. 70
Verses On Beguiling. 76
Verses On Being Bought. 50
Verses On Being Established. 34
Verses On Bible Preservation. 44
Verses On Blameless. 127
Verses On Blemishes. 73
Verses On Bondage. 87
Verses On Cain's Judgment. 160
Verses On Calling.. 29
Verses On Christ's Coming With His Saints. 168
Verses On Christ's Second Coming--In Two Phases. 101

Verses On Clouds. 82
Verses On Compassion. 185
Verses On Contending.. 144
Verses On Covetousness. 52, 77
Verses On Creation. 104
Verses On Cursed. 78
Verses On Deliverance.. 64
Verses On Eternal Salvation. 188
Verses On Fables. 40
Verses On Falling. 30
Verses On False Prophets In The New Testament. 48
Verses On Fire. 106
Verses On Heresies. 49
Verses On Ignorant. 103
Verses On Knowledge. 15
Verses On Korah's Judgment. 163
Verses On Last Days. 99
Verses On Longsuffering.. .... 111, 128
Verses On Lusts. 83
Verses On Murmuring.. 174
Verses On Power. 18
Verses On Purging. 28
Verses On Purity. 94, 123
Verses On Purity And Holiness. 123
Verses On Remembering. 95
Verses on Remembrance.. 33
Verses On Repentance.. 89
Verses On Righteousness. 14
Verses On Riot. 71
Verses On Sanctify. 141
Verses On Sinning Angels. 54
Verses On Slackness. 110
Verses On Spots. 72
Verses On Stir Up.. 37
Verses On The Body As A Tabernacle. 36
Verses On The Destruction Of Sodom And Gomorrah. 58
Verses On The Faith As Bible Doctrine. 145
Verses On The Judgment Of The Flood. 56
Verses On The Love Of God. 183
Verses On The Mind. 95
Verses On The Mouth Related To The Heart. 88
Verses On The Need To Build Properly.. 181
Verses On The Scriptures. 130

Verses On The Second Coming Of Christ To Earth.......... 169
Verses On The Uses Of The Word, Falling................. 189
Verses On The Wisdom Of God............................ 191
Verses On The Words Of The Lord Jesus Christ............ 176
Verses On The "Day Of The LORD"........................ 116
Verses On True Divine Washing........................... 90
Verses On Uncleanness.................................. 67
Verses On Unstable..................................... 77
Verses On Wells.. 81
Verses On Willingly.................................... 102
Verses On "Precious" Things............................. 11
Verses With The Name, Jude Or Judas.................... 140
verse-by-verse book on 1 Peter.......................... 38
vexed... 61, 63
vicarious death on the cross............................ 34
vipers.. 160
virgin birth... 47
Waite, Dr. D. A., or Yvonne, or Tamie............. 1, i-iii, 120
WALKING AFTER THE FLESH........................... 66
WARNINGS OF THINGS IN THE LAST DAYS............. 98
washed... 90, 91, 141
wavering... 146
WE MUST CONTEND FOR THE BIBLE'S DOCTRINES..... 144
Website: www.BibleForToday.org........................... i
Westcott and Hort, editors of a false Greek Text...... 96, 105, 191
WHAT ARE CHRISTIANS BUILDING ON CHRIST?........ 181
WHEN WILL GOD JUDGE PRO-SODOMITE AMERICA?..... 61
whosoever believeth.............. 20, 48, 113, 114, 143, 188
wicked, corrupt, and sinful father...................... 62
wise............................... 9, 39, 44, 104, 132, 191, 192
with Christ..................................... 21, 31, 168
without wavering..................................... 146
WOE TO THOSE WHO PRACTICE COVETOUSNESS....... 53
wood, hay, and stubble................................ 181
Word of the Lord endureth for ever..................... 46
Words............... ii-iv, 3, 6, 11-13, 16-18, 23, 26, 27, 32-39, 42-46, 48, 51-53, 63-65, 76-78, 83-85, 89, 94, 96-100, 102, 103, 106, 108, 109, 113, 114, 128-133, 141, 144, 147, 148, 157, 162, 168, 172, 174, 176-179, 182, 183, 185, 193, 195
Words of God............ iii, 11, 12, 17, 34, 42, 43, 51, 52, 64, 94, 102, 113, 130, 182
words of the Bible...................... 38, 42, 44, 45, 176, 178

Words of the Lord Jesus Christ. 46, 176-179
XITON. 187
YOU MUST REMEMBER THE WORDS OF THE BIBLE. 176
zeal. 15
zealous. 15
"GIVEN BY INSPIRATION OF GOD"=THEOPNEUSTOS. . . . 132
"PROFESSING-ONLY CHRISTIANS" ARE PHONY. 88
"scribal errors" in God's Hebrew, Aramaic, and Greek Words. . 39
"the Faith" the doctrines of the Bible. 12, 143, 145
"THE FAITH" REFERS TO BIBLE DOCTRINES. 143
"THE FAITH" REFERS TO THE DOCTRINES. 12

About The Author

The author of this book, Dr. D. A. Waite, received a BA (Bachelor of Arts) in classical Greek and Latin from the University of Michigan in 1948, a ThM (Master of Theology), with high honors, in New Testament Greek Literature and Exegesis from Dallas Theological Seminary in 1952, an MA (Master of Arts) in Speech from Southern Methodist University in 1953, a ThD (Doctor of Theology), with honors, in Bible Exposition from Dallas Theological Seminary in 1955, and a PhD in Speech from Purdue University in 1961. He held both New Jersey and Pennsylvania teacher certificates in Greek and Language Arts.

He has been a teacher in the areas of Greek, Hebrew, Bible, Speech, and English for over thirty-five years in ten schools, including one junior high, one senior high, four Bible institutes, two colleges, two universities, and one seminary. He served his country as a Navy Chaplain for five years on active duty; pastored three churches; was Chairman and Director of the Radio and Audio-Film Commission of the American Council of Christian Churches; since 1969, has been Founder, President, and Director of THE BIBLE FOR TODAY; since 1978, has been Founder and President of the DEAN BURGON SOCIETY; has produced over 700 other studies, books, cassettes, VHS's, CD's, or VCR's on various topics IN DEFENSE OF TRADITIONAL BIBLE TEXTS, on radio, shortwave, and streaming on the Internet at BibleForToday.org, 24/7/365 on the BROWN BOX.

Dr. and Mrs. Waite have been married since 1948; they have four sons, one daughter, and, at present, eight grandchildren, and fifteen great-grandchildren. Since October 4, 1998, he has been the Pastor of the Bible For Today Baptist Church in Collingswood, New Jersey. His sermons are heard both on radio and the Internet over www.BibleForToday.org on the BROWN BOX.

Order Blank (p. 1)

Name:_____
Address:_____
City & State:_____Zip:_____
Credit Card #:_____Expires:_____

Verse by Verse Preaching Books By Dr. D. A. Waite

[ ] Send 2 Peter & Jude–Preaching Verse B Verse By Pastor D. A. Waite, 215 pages ($15.00 + $8.00 @ S&H) fully indexed.

[ ] Send *1 & 2 Thessalonians–Preaching Verse By Verse* By Pastor D. A. Waite, 327 pages ($15.00 + $8.00 S&H) fully indexed.

[ ] Send *Hebrews–Preaching Verse by Verse*, By Pastor D. A. Waite, 616 pages ($30.00 +$10.00 S&H) fully indexed.

[ ] Send *Revelation–Preaching Verse by Verse*, By Pastor D. A. Waite, 1032 pages ($50.00 + $10.00 S&H) fully indexed.

[ ] Send *1 Timothy--Preaching Verse by Verse*, by Pastor D. A. Waite, 288 pages, hardback ($11+$5 S&H) fully indexed.

[ ] Send *2 Timothy--Preaching Verse by Verse*, by Pastor D. A. Waite, 250 pages, hardback ($11+$5 S&H) fully indexed.

[ ] Send *Romans--Preaching Verse by Verse* by Pastor D. A. Waite 736 pp. Hardback ($25+$8 S&H) fully indexed

[ ] Send *Colossians & Philemon--Preaching Verse by Verse* by Pastor D. A. Waite ($12+$5 S&H) hardback, 240 pages.

[ ] Send *Philippians--Preaching Verse by Verse* by Pastor D. A. Waite ($10+$5 S&H) hardback, 176 pages. fully indexed.

[ ] Send *Ephesians--Preaching Verse by Verse* by Pastor D. A. Waite ($12+$5 S&H) hardback, 224 pages. fully indexed.

[ ] Send *Galatians--Preaching Verse By Verse* by Pastor D. A. Waite ($12+$5 S&H) hardback, 216 pages. fully indexed.

[ ] Send *1 Peter–Preaching Verse By Verse* by Pastor D. A. Waite ($10.00 + $5.00 S&H) hardback, 176 pages. fully indexed.

Other Books By Dr. D. A. Waite

[ ] Send *A Critical Answer to God's Word Preserved* by Pastor D. A. Waite, 192 pp. perfect bound ($11.00+$4.00 S&H)

Send or Call Orders to:
THE BIBLE FOR TODAY
900 Park Ave., Collingswood, NJ 08108
Phone: 856-854-4452; FAX:--2464; Orders: 1-800 JOHN 10:9
E-Mail Orders: BFT@BibleForToday.org; Credit Cards OK

Order Blank (p. 2)

Name:_____
Address:_____
City & State:_____Zip:_____
Credit Card #:_____Expires:_____

Other Books By Dr. D. A. Waite (Continued)

[ ] Send *Defending the King James Bible* by DAW ($12+$5 S&H) A hardback book, indexed with study questions.
[ ] Send *BJU's Errors on Bible Preservation* by Dr. D. A. Waite, 110 pages, paperback ($8+$4 S&H) fully indexed
[ ] Send *Fundamentalist Deception on Bible Preservation* by Dr. D. A. Waite, ($8+$4 S&H), paperback, fully indexed
[ ] Send *Fundamentalist MIS-INFORMATION on Bible Versions* by Dr. Waite ($7+$4 S&H) perfect bound, 136 pages
[ ] Send *Fundamentalist Distortions on Bible Versions* by Dr. Waite ($6+$3 S&H) A perfect bound book, 80 pages
[ ] Send *Fuzzy Facts From Fundamentalists* by Dr. D. A. Waite ($8.00 + $4.00) printed booklet
[ ] Send *Foes of the King James Bible Refuted* by DAW ($10 +$4 S&H) A perfect bound book, 164 pages in length.
[ ] Send *Central Seminary Refuted on Bible Versions* by Dr. Waite ($10+$4 S&H) A perfect bound book, 184 pages
[ ] Send *The Case for the King James Bible* by DAW ($7 +$3 S&H) A perfect bound book, 112 pages in length.
[ ] Send *Theological Heresies of Westcott and Hort* by Dr. D. A. Waite, ($7+$3 S&H) A printed booklet.
[ ] Send *Westcott's Denial of Resurrection*, Dr. Waite ($4+$3)
[ ] Send *Four Reasons for Defending KJB* by DAW ($3+$3)
[ ] Send *Holes in the Holman Christian Standard Bible* by Dr. Waite ($3+$2 S&H) A printed booklet, 40 pages
[ ] Send *Contemporary Eng. Version Exposed*, DAW ($3+$2)
[ ] Send *NIV Inclusive Language Exposed* by DAW ($5+$3)
[ ] Send *26 Hours of KJB Seminar* (4 videos) by DAW($50.00)

Send or Call Orders to:
THE BIBLE FOR TODAY
900 Park Ave., Collingswood, NJ 08108
Phone: 856-854-4452; FAX:--2464; Orders: 1-800 JOHN 10:9
E-Mail Orders: BFT@BibleForToday.org; Credit Cards OK

Order Blank (p. 3)

Name:_____

Address:_____

City & State:_____Zip:_____

Credit Card #:_____Expires:_____

[ ] Send *Making Marriage Melodious* by Pastor D. A. Waite ($7+$4 S&H), perfect bound, 112 pages.

[ ] Send *Burgon's Warnings on Revision* by DAW ($7+$4 S&H) A perfect bound book, 120 pages in length.

[ ] Send *The Superior Foundation of the KJB* By Dr. D. A. Waite ($10.00 + $7.00 S&H)

Other Books By Dr. D. A. Waite (Continued)

[ ] Send *Biblical Separation–1,896 Bible Verses About It* by Dr. D. A. Waite ($14.00 + $7.00 S&H)

[ ] Send *Westcott & Hort's Greek Text & Theory Refuted by Burgon's Revision Revised--Summarized* by Dr. D. A. Waite ($7.00+$4 S&H), 120 pages, perfect bound.

[ ] Send *Dean Burgon's Confidence in KJB* by DAW ($3+$3)

[ ] Send *Vindicating Mark 16:9-20* by Dr. Waite ($3+$3 S&H)

[ ] Send *Summary of Traditional Text* by Dr. Waite ($3 +$3)

[ ] Send *Summary of Causes of Corruption*, DAW ($3+$3)

[ ] Send *Summary of Inspiration* by Dr. Waite ($3+$3 S&H)

[ ] Send *Soulwinning's Versions-Perversions* By Dr. D. A. Waite ($6.00 + $5.00 S&H)

Books By Dean John William Burgon

[ ] Send *The Revision Revised* by Dean Burgon ($25 + $5 S&H) A hardback book, 640 pages in length.

[ ] Send *The Last 12 verses of Mark* by Dean Burgon ($15+$5 S&H) A hardback book 400 pages.

[ ] Send *The Traditional Text* hardback by Burgon ($16+$5 S&H) A hardback book, 384 pages in length.

[ ] Send *Causes of Corruption* by Burgon ($15+$5 S&H) A hardback book, 360 pages in length.

Send or Call Orders to:
THE BIBLE FOR TODAY
900 Park Ave., Collingswood, NJ 08108
Phone: 856-854-4452; FAX:--2464; Orders: 1-800 JOHN 10:9
E-Mail Orders: BFT@BibleForToday.org; Credit Cards OK

Order Blank (p. 4)

Name:_____

Address:_____

City & State:_____Zip:_____

Credit Card #:_____Expires:_____

[ ] Send *Inspiration and Interpretation*, Dean Burgon ($25+$5 S&H) A hardback book, 610 pages in length.

Books By Dr. Jack Moorman

[ ] Send *Samuel P. Tregelles--The Man Who Made the Critical Text Acceptable to Bible Believers* by Dr. Moorman ($2+$1)

[ ] Send *8,000 Differences Between TR & CT* by Dr. Jack Moorman [$65 + $7.50 S&H] Over 500-large-pages of data

[ ] Send *356 Doctrinal Errors in the NIV & Other Modern Versions*, 100-large-pages, $10.00+$6 S&H.

[ ] Send *The Doctrinal Heart of the Bible--Removed from Modern Versions* by Dr. Jack Moorman, VCR, $15 +$4 S&H

[ ] Send *Modern Bibles--The Dark Secret* by Dr. Jack Moorman, $5+$3 S&H

[ ] Send *The Manuscript Digest of the N.T.* (721 pp.) By Dr. Jack Moorman, copy-machine bound ($50+$7 S&H)

[ ] *Early Manuscripts, Church Fathers, & the Authorized Version* by Dr. Jack Moorman, $18+$5 S&H. Hardback

[ ] Send *Forever Settled--Bible Doc*uments *& History Survey* by Dr. Jack Moorman, $20+$5 S&H. Hardback book.

[ ] Send *When the KJB Departs from the So-Called "Majority Text"* by Dr. Jack Moorman, $16+$5 S&H

[ ] Send *Missing in Modern Bibles--Nestle-Aland/NIV Errors* by Dr. Jack Moorman, $8+$4 S&H

Books By Miscellaneous Authors

[ ] Send *Guide to Textual Criticism* by Edward Miller ($7+$4) Hardback book

[ ] Send *Scrivener's Greek New Testament Underlying the King James Bible*, hardback, ($14+$5 S&H)

Send or Call Orders to:
THE BIBLE FOR TODAY
900 Park Ave., Collingswood, NJ 08108
Phone: 856-854-4452; FAX:--2464; Orders: 1-800 JOHN 10:9
E-Mail Orders: BFT@BibleForToday.org; Credit Cards OK

Order Blank (p. 5)

Name:_____
Address:_____
City & State:_____Zip:_____
Credit Card #:_____Expires:_____

[ ] Send *Scrivener's <u>Annotated</u> Greek New Testament*, by Dr. Frederick Scrivener: Hardback--($35+$5 S&H); Genuine Leather--($45+$5 S&H)

[ ] Send *Why Not the King James Bible?--An Answer to James White's KJVO Book* by Dr. K. D. DiVietro, $10+$5 S&H

[ ] Send Brochure #1: "*1000 Titles Defending the KJB/TR*" No Charge

[ ] Send *The LIE That Changed the Modern World* by Dr. H. D. Williams ($16+$5 S&H) Hardback book

[ ] Send *With Tears in My Heart* by Gertrude G. Sanborn. Hardback 414 pp. ($25+$5 S&H) 400 Christian Poems

[ ] Send *Dean Burgon's Defense of the Authorised Version* By Dr. David Bennett ($14.0 + 8.00 S&H)

[ ] Send *Drift in Baptist Missions, Churches & Schools* by Dr. David Bennett ($12.00 + $8.00 S&H)

More Books By Miscellaneous Authors

[ ] Send *Able To Bear It* By Gertrude Sanborn ($14.00 + $7.00 S&H

[ ] Send *Visitation In Action* By Mr. R. O. Sanborn ($10.00 + $7.00 S&H)

[ ] Send *Daily Bible Blessings From Daily Bible Readings* By Yvonne Sanborn Waite ($30.00 + $10.00 S&H)

[ ] Send *Husband-Loving Lessons* By Yvonne Sanborn Waite ($25.00 + $8.00 S&H)

[ ] Send *Gnosticism--The Doctrinal Foundation of New Bibles* by J. Moser ($20.00 + $8.00 S&H)

Send or Call Orders to:
THE BIBLE FOR TODAY
900 Park Ave., Collingswood, NJ 08108
Phone: 856-854-4452; FAX:--2464; Orders: 1-800 JOHN 10:9
E-Mail Orders: BFT@BibleForToday.org; Credit Cards OK

Order Blank (p. 6)

Name:_____
Address:_____
City & State:_____Zip:_____
Credit Card #:_____Expires:_____

[ ] Send *God's Marvelous Book* By Dr. David Bennett ($15.00 + $8.00 S&H)
[ ] Send *CCM Not The Problem–Only A Symptom* By Dr. David Bennett ($12.00 + $7.00 S&H)
[ ] Send *English Standard Bible (ESV) Deficiencies* By several authors ($7.00 + $4.00 S&H)
[ ] Send *Strong's Micro-Print Concordance* By the Sherbornes ($21.00 + $8.00 S&H)

Books by D. A. Waite, Jr.

[ ] Send *The Doctored New Testament* by D. A. Waite, Jr. ($25+$5 S&H) Greek MSS differences shown, hardback
[ ] Send *Readability of A.V. (KJB)* by D. A. Waite, Jr. ($6+$3)
[ ] Send *4,114 Definitions from the Defined King James Bible* by D. A. Waite, Jr. ($7.00+$4.00 S&H)

Question And Answer Books By Dr. D. A. Waite

[ ] Send *The First 200 Questions Answered* By Dr. D. A. Waite ($15.00 + $7.00 S&H)
[ ] Send *The Second 200 Questions Answered* By Dr. D. A. Waite ($15.00 + $7.00 S&H)
[ ] Send *The Third 200 Questions Answered* By Dr. D. A. Waite ($15.00 + $7.00 S&H)
[ ] Send *The Fourth 200 Questions Answered* By Dr. D. A. Waite ($15.00 + $7.00 S&H)
[ ] Send *The Fifth 200 Questions Answered* By Dr. D. A. Waite ($15.00 + $7.00 S&H)
[ ] Send *The Sixth 200 Questions Answered* By Dr. D. A. Waite ($15.00 + $7.00 S&H)

Send or Call Orders to:
THE BIBLE FOR TODAY
900 Park Ave., Collingswood, NJ 08108
Phone: 856-854-4452; FAX:--2464; Orders: 1-800 JOHN 10:9
E-Mail Orders: BFT@BibleForToday.org; Credit Cards OK

The Defined King James Bible

Uncommon Words Defined Accurately

I. Deluxe Genuine Leather

✦Large Print--Black or Burgundy✦

1 for $44.00+$12.00 S&H

✦Case of 12 for✦

$34.00 each+$50.00 S&H

✦Medium Print--Black or Burgundy✦

1 for $39.00+$8.00 S&H

✦Case of 12 for✦

$29.00 each+$40.00 S&H

II. Deluxe Hardback Editions

1 for $22.00+12.00 S&H (Large Print)

✦Case of 12 for✦

$17.00 each+$40.00 S&H (Large Print)

1 for $19.50+$8.00 S&H (Medium Print)

✦Case of 12 for✦

$12.50 each+$30.00 S&H (Medium Print)

Order Phone:1-800-JOHN 10:9

Pastor D. A. Waite, Th.D., Ph.D.

Earnestly Contending For The Faith
(Jude 1:3)

The Meaning Of "The Faith." Whenever the Greek Word for "Faith" (PISTIS) is used with the Greek article, it is a reference to the doctrines of the Bible. Some of these doctrines include the Deity of Christ, His virgin birth, His Blood atonement, His bodily resurrection, the verbal, plenary, inspiration and preservation of the Bible, and many other things.

Why "Contend" For The Faith? The main reason for contending for the Faith is because it has been attacked for many years and is now being attacked ferociously in our day. Formerly-sound seminaries, mission boards, denominations, and local churches have been drifting badly from their former doctrinal Faith for centuries. We must contend for the Faith now before it disappears.

Why Contend "Earnestly"? Our contention for doctrines of our Biblical Christian Faith must not be half-hearted. It must be bold. It must be earnest. Without such dedication and forceful defense of our Faith, in very few years, that Faith will be virtually extinct on our planet. May the Lord Jesus Christ raise up many more EARNEST CONTENDERS for His verbal, plenary, inspired and preserved Words.

www.BibleForToday.org

BFT 4147   ISBN #978-1-56848-108-1

www.ingramcontent.com/pod-product-compliance
Lightning Source LLC
Chambersburg PA
CBHW060506090426
42735CB00011B/2126